SCARLETT'S WOMEN

Gone With the Wind

and its Female Fans

HELEN TAYLOR

VIRAGO

1051215 2

791.
4372
TAY

Published by VIRAGO PRESS Limited 1989
20–23 Mandela Street, Camden Town, London NW1 0BQ

Copyright © 1989 Helen Taylor

*A CIP Catalogue record for this book
is available from the British Library*

Typeset by Florencetype Ltd, Kewstoke, Avon
Printed in Great Britain by
Cox & Wyman Ltd, Reading, Berkshire

0860688283

Contents

Acknowledgements

During the preparation and writing of this book I have been lucky to enjoy enthusiastic encouragement from friends, colleagues and casual acquaintances. Writing is lonely, but this has been as gregarious an experience as I could have hoped for. Many people sent information, memorabilia and anecdotes, and in other ways helped my research. Though they are too numerous to mention I would like to thank especially: Elizabeth Bird, Judy Cameron, Hazel V. Carby, Frank de Caro, Sara Davies, Madge Dresser, Kate Fullbrook, Lindy Gibbon, Nancy Homewood, Donald J. Jordan, Rosan Jordan, Merrilyn Julian, Cora Kaplan, Geraldine Kaye, Jim Pines, Darden Asbury Pyron, Louise Reverby, Diane Roberts, Marie Roberts, Pat Roberts and patients and staff of Manor Park Hospital, Bristol, Rachel Stevens, Renée Slater, Wyn Craig Wade. Bristol Polytechnic Research Committee and Department of Humanities helped with some time and travel.

While in Atlanta, I was fortunate to receive help and information from: the staffs of the Atlanta Convention and Visitors Bureau, Atlanta-Fulton Public Library and Atlanta Historical Society, Janis and Roger Caplan, Chris Colbert, Deborah James, Lynn Meyer, Bruce and Dianne Seaman, Celestine Sibley, Betty Talmadge, John Taylor. Herb Bridges was a rich source of southern hospitality, GWTW and local knowledge.

My editor Ruthie Petrie gave valuable critical encouragement. Sue Swingler, Alison Light and Derrick Price read drafts of the manuscript at all stages, and their loving advice and affection kept me going through both productive and difficult times. Derrick has shown a Rhett Butler-like nurturing concern throughout. I owe a great debt to my mother, Ida M. Taylor, for introducing me to *GWTW*, and for much else.

My deepest gratitude goes to the hundreds of people who so generously shared their ideas with me in letters and questionnaires. While I have quoted some directly, I have drawn on everyone's thoughts to construct my readings of *GWTW*, and this book could not have existed without them. Many correspondents wish to remain anonymous, but – whether named below or not – they have all made a contribution to this book, with which many of them kindly wished me luck. Those who agreed to be acknowledged by name are: Joy Adams, Roy Adams, Jessica M. Alborough, Hilary Allen, Jay Allison, Margaret Andrews, Patricia Andrews, E.H. Andrews, Gwen Ashley, Bonnie Ashurst, Eve Astley, Joanne Athay, Mrs V.R. Atkins, Winifred M. Atkinson, Mrs M.A. Audsley, Ms J.E. Baker, Nell M. Baker, Lindsay Bamfield, Vera Bancroft, Simon Barker, Margaret Barlow, Ruth Barnes, Lindsey Barnfield, Dorothy Barnish, Nicola Barton, Anne Bates, Mrs E.M. Bath, John Bean, Lee Beck, Barbara Beckford, Yvonne Bednarczyk, John B. Beam, Irene Beenham, Kathlyn V. Bell, Catherine Bennett, Hilda G. Benney, Joan Margaret Bennington, Rosette Besman, Frances Bethell, Sandra Bevan, Mrs M. Bilbrough, Jakki Billington, Catherine Bindman, Peggy Blakey, Mrs E.M. Bloomfield, Elena Bond, Sonia M. Bond, Gail Bonnington, Eve Booy, Giselle Bordelon, Margaret Bosworth, Miss P.M. Boulton, Joyce Bourne, Stephen Bourne, Mrs G.K. Boydell, Kathryn Boydell, Richard Boyett, Peggy Boyne, Elsie Bradley, Helen Winton Bramhall, Sarah Braun, Audrey M. Bream, Doris A. Brecht, John A. Brecht, Lorna Brierley, Janet Brigstock, Mrs M.A. Brinkman, Anne Broadhurst, Marjorie Broadhurst, Constance Bromley, Lesley Bromley, Marilyn Brooks, Sandra Brooks, Mrs P. Brown, Sandra

Bruno, Joyce Bryant, Philippa Bryant, Mrs P.E. Buckham, Doris Buckley, Sue Bucksey, Vera Margaret Burberry, Julie Burrell, Josephine Burrows, Annie Burton, Phyllis Bush, Adele Cabreria, Susan Caird, Neddy Campbell, Charlene H. Cappellini, Terry Cappellini, Mrs H. Carroll, Joan Carter, Madge Carter, Francesca Casci, Paula Casey, Ellane Cassagne-Héon, Diana Chapman, Tommy Cherry, Diana Churchill, Lesley Clark, Audrey Clarke, Joan Clayton, Lorna Clegg, Caroline Cobb, Elsie M. Cole, G. Michelle Collins, Mrs A.K. Cooke-Yarborough, Sandra Cooper, David Copson, Kenneth W. Cowley, Denise Cox, Elsie A. Cox, Mrs M. Cox, Mrs E. Cribb, Anne-Marie Cummins, Collette Cummins, Joan Cutts, Eithne Dallat, Julie Danton, Jean B. Darby, Gillian Darward, Gay Davidson, Nancy Davies, R.M. Dawson, Marianna Demeo, Joan Deneby, Dorothy M. Derbyshire, Leslie Dick, Barbara Dickie, Marie Dicks, Teresa Doe, Fiona Donegan, Jane Downes, Vera Downham, Patricia Drayton, Mrs E.R. Drury, Edith Dulwich, Jacquie Duvall, Pat Dymond, Phyllis Eddy, Marina Egar, Brenda Elens, Jo Eliot, Donald Elkins, Vivienne Elliott, Dick Ellis, Jane Ellison, Marie English, Doris G. Evans, Tamsin Evans, Wendy Evans, Brenda Ewens, Mrs F.M. Fenwick, Gael Ferguson, May Allison Ferguson, Jean Fernee, Paddy Ferris, Mavis Findlay, Ann Firkins, Mrs J. Fishwick, Hylda M. Fletcher, Mrs J. Fletcher, Dan Fogel, Connie M. Ford, Paul Forsey, Gwen Forshaw, Christel Förster, Kate Fowler, Louise Fowler, Lisa Fox, Tracy Francis, Dorothy Fraser, Margaret French, Cheryl Gafford, Ann Gardner, Amanda Garrett, Christine Gibbon, Elspeth Gibson, Amy Gill, Thea Gilliard, Doris Golt, Betsy Gordon, Sue Gould, Wendy A. Graham, Verna Grant, Priscilla Gray, Sarah Green, Mrs K. Greenaway, Joyce Greengrass, Angela Greenslade, Tracey Jayne Gregory, Lynn Griffin, Mrs U.B. Griffin, Christine Griffith, Roy Griffith, Jean Grimshaw, Vivian J.G. Grinbergs, Amanda Grubb, Annes Gruffydd, Mabel C. Guess,

Margaret Guyver, Herbert Haddrell, Miss J. Haines, Irene V. Hall, Pearl A. Hall, V.J. Hall, Shirley Hammerle, Joan Hammond, Joy Hancock, Alison E. Handley, Darlene M. Hantzis, Jese HärBers, Katharine M. Hardie, Peggy A. Harding, Claire Harris, Evelyn Harris, Hilary Harris, Louie C. Harris, Margaret H. Harrison, Mary G. Hart, Mrs J. Hasthorpe, Monika Häubler, Elizabeth S. Haynes, Mrs T. Head, Diana Heed-Daniel, Mrs S.J. Heffernan, Mary Hess, Peggy Hester, Dorothy Hibbard, Marjorie Hill, Jean Hillier, Susan Hillier, Joanne Hindmarch, Margaret Hirons, Mrs G.D. Hobbs, Rebecca Hogan, Elizabeth Hogg, Ann Holloway, Diana Hood-Daniel, Edith Hope, Lorna M. Hosmer, Doris D. Howard, Doreen Howells, Elizabeth Howlett, Joan Hubbold, Nancy Hucker, Mrs P. Hudson, Glenys Huntley, Joy Hyslop, Grace F. Ince, Trishy Ireland, Doris Jackson, Jane E. James, Maureen James, Dorothy Jarrett, Rosie Jeffries, Barbara Jennings, Mrs M. Johnson, William Johnson, Claire Jones, Mrs J.H. Jones, Monica Jones, Olive M. Jones, Frances Judges, Anne Karpf, Gerald Kaufman, MP, Geraldine Kaye, Jane Keber, Leontia Kehoe, Beryl Kimber, Herbert King, Sylvia King, Elsie Kingdom, Jackie Kington, Mrs R.M. Kinley, Mrs K. Kirkbright, Kacey J. Kling, Raymond A. Klune, Kitty Knight, Rachel Knight, Sara Krishna, Betty Lampert, Tricia Laurent, M. Lavelte, Hannah Layne, Joyce Lee, Estelle Lewis, Kate Lewis, Reina Lewis, Molly Lind, Mrs A.M. Lindsay, Gwenith Llewellyn, Mrs M. Lovelle, H.J. Luckwell, Mrs D.M. Lynd, Marion Lynham, Miss D. Macari, Christine Macé, John McCabe-Juhnke, Penny Macdonald, Maria Korda MacDonald, Grace McGhee, Catherine McHugh, Mrs C.M. McIntosh, Maisie McKenzie, Wendy McKenzie, Jane McLeman, Emir Mangan, Joan Marshall, Doris Marston, Tracy Martin, Gladys Mason, Enid Measures, Tracy Mellor, Claire Meyer, Suzanne Michaels, Jenny Midlen, Marlene Mifsud-Chircop, Edith Miller, Norma Miller, Gladys Millman, Elizabeth Mills, Maureen Mills,

Anne J. Mitchell, Margaret Morgan, Molly K. Morgan, SandieMorgan,MaryMorrey,KettaMorris,ShirleyMorris, GladysMosby,MelanieMoss,MelanieK.Murphy,Andrea Musher, Prue Nash, Ruth Negus, Suzanne Newell, Joan Nicholson, Molly Nicoll, Mrs B.I. Norfolk, Barry Norman, Teresa O'Brien, Cecil G. Owen, Margery H.W. Owen, Carol Pack, Gabrielle Packer, Peggy Palmer, Jennifer S. Parkhouse, Pearl Parsons, Mary Payne, Jeannie L. Peck, Angela Peckenpaugh, Molly R. Penfold, Mrs K.J. Phillips, Jane Phipps, Peggy Pilbeam, Gladys M. Poore, Matilda Popper, Christine Potter, Linda Preece, Miss V. Preston, Jane Prince, Linda Pring, John Purnell, Eileen Quaile, Mrs E. Ramsay, Yanina Ratcliffe, Ena Raw, Sheila Ray, Pat Read, Carole A. Reynolds, Mrs B. Rhoderick, Lucy Richards, Ruth Riddick, Stephanie Riegel, Pauline Riley, Norrie Roadhouse, Elma Roberts, Isabel Robertson, Jacky Robertson, Mary Robinson, Shirley F. Robinson, Anne J. Robson, Talia Rodgers, Nancy Room, Janet Rushatch, Sandi Russell, Muriel O. Ryder, Tricia Sandle, Rachel Sanger, Elizabeth Scanlon Thomas, Marion Schoenfeld, Elizabeth Scott, Shirley Scott, Ann F.M. Secretan, Dee Seilly, D. Selbeck, Denise Selleck, Penelope Shand, Ella S. Shaw, Mrs H. Sheppard, Madeline P. Sim, Marjorie Simcock, Angela Heather Sinclair, Mary Singleton, Daphne E. Smith, Deborah Smith, Derek F. Smith, Elizabeth Smith, Mrs M. Smith, Anthony W.F. Snook, Evelyn Spray, Marlene Stagg, Brenda Stirling, Greta Stoddart, Mrs E.M. Strange, Steve Strohschein, Corette Stoker, Diane Suckling, Francesca Sullivan, Mrs E.E. Sweet, Edith D. Taylor, Peta Taylor, Carl Thayer, Dilys Thomas, Helen Thomas, Joan Thompson, Kathleen I. Thompson, Olive Thompson, Miss C.M. Toal, Esme Todd, Rita Todd, Mrs K. Tooze, Sheila Tout, Brenda Townsend, Lorie Townsend, Patricia Turner, Mary Tyler, Irene Vaines, Patricia Vandenberg, Rita Vango, Joan Vaughn, Virginia Villiers, Margaret Vinall, John Vine, Elaine Wade, Kim Waghorn, Mrs E. Walker,

Jackie Wall, Mrs A. Ward, Phillis Ward, Lyn Warman, Ivy Warren, Nancy Weaver, Catherine E. Webster, Winefride Welborn, Liz Wells, Pat v.t. West, Avril Westrup, Penny Wheelwright, Mrs S. Whitchurch, D.M. White, Betty Whitehouse, Marie Whitehouse, Norma J. Whittet, Marian Widley, Mrs E.J. Wiggins, Mrs D.M. Wildgoose, Gila Wilding, Hannah Wilkins, Teresa Wilkins, Mrs J.C. Williams, Karina Williams, Barbara Williams-Jones, Helen Wilson, Jacqueline Wilson, Margaret Wiltshire, Nesta M. Wintour, Kathleen Witchell, Elaine Withey, Kathleen Witwell, Glenice Wood, Ruth Wood, June Woodford, Joyce Woodhouse, Frida Woollard, Lilly Wray, Patricia Yarnell.

1

The Phenomenal *Gone With the Wind*

Gone With the Wind seems to stand forever as great art in that timeless place where Scarlett forever runs through the fog, Elvis forever shakes his hips, Macbeth forever bewails his bloody hands ... (Hannah Wilkins)

Over the last few years, when I have told people at work, on trains or at parties that I was writing a book about *Gone With the Wind*, almost always they offered me an anecdote. A friend's mother married her father because he looked like Clark 'Rhett Butler' Gable; a student who was reluctant to leave her new kitten at home during this long film took it along to the cinema, where it slept right through. Others told me it was their grandmother's or auntie's favourite book, out of which bits were read when they felt low. A colleague who could not bear the way the book concluded read it again and again, hoping *next* time it would end differently. Someone pointed me to a house called 'Tara' near my workplace. Lots of people offered to show me their *Gone With the Wind* collector plates, tea towels and posters. No one has ever asked me, 'Gone With the ... What?'

Gone With the Wind is one of the most successful books ever published, made into one of the most popular and highly praised films to emerge from Hollywood. An instant best-seller when it was published on 30 June 1936, it sold a million copies in the first six months; twenty-five million more have sold since then. There are at least 155 editions; it has been translated into twenty-seven languages and published successfully in thirty-seven countries. It won the 1937 Pulitzer Prize. Margaret Mitchell never wrote another book, and spent the rest of her short life dealing with the publicity and fame which accompanied its phenomenal success.

The film, which had its première on 15 December 1939 in Atlanta, Georgia, has been seen by more people than the entire population of the USA. It was given its first British screening on 18 April 1940, and has been an enormous favourite ever since. The film's gross earnings are estimated at approximately $300 million. In the late 1970s MGM sold CBS the rights to twenty television screenings for a cool $35 million; 110 million people watched the first television showing. It has been sub-titled in twenty-four languages, dubbed into six. Of thirteen nominations, it was awarded eight Oscars, including the first ever to a black actor, Hattie McDaniel. It is regularly referred to as the greatest film ever made, described in movie magazines as 'the daddy of them all'.

Everyone has heard of it. *Gone with the Wind* (known as *GWTW*) is sustained in popular imagination by mani-fold references, parodies and jokes. In English-speaking countries, sayings from *GWTW* ('I'll think about that tomorrow', 'Tomorrow is another day', 'My dear, I don't give a damn' and 'Don't know nothin' 'bout birthin' babies') are recognisable catchphrases. In the year 6939 a time capsule containing the book, sealed by fans at the 1939 New York World's Fair, may be opened; Florida's 'Hall of Fame' has waxwork figures of the characters; Joni Mitchell recorded a song entitled 'Shades of Scarlet [sic] Conquering' while Merle Haggard called his 'Gone with the Wind'; Martini advertise a 'Scarlett O'Hara' cocktail — Martini Rosso, bitter lemon, grenadine and ice; Japan has produced several dramatic and musical adaptations, including an all-woman version; the Ameri-can game 'Trivial Pursuit' contains the question 'What is the last line of *Gone With the Wind*?' And so on.

Atlanta, home of Margaret Mitchell and setting for much of *GWTW*, has named a street, library reading room and elementary school after the author. The radio station's office, 'Twelve Oaks', is named after Ashley Wilkes's home; Lovejoy Plantation offers 'Magnolia Suppers' featuring Scarlett's Turnips. In 1986, fiftieth anniversary of the novel's publication, there was national and local celebration. The US Postal Service issued a one-cent commemorative stamp of Margaret Mitchell, while the Macmillan Publishing Company issued a facsimile of the first edition. During the month of June, Atlanta hosted a Rhett and Scarlett look-alike contest, an Antebellum Ball, a 'Going, Going, Gone with the Wind' auction and a display of Herb Bridges' 'world's largest' collection of *GWTW* memorabilia, as well as organising an essay contest for Georgia girls on 'Scarlett in the 1980s'. As journalist Richard Nalley wrote, '*Gone With the Wind* proved bigger than hula hoops, bigger than saddle shoes, bigger than Davy Crockett. It is a fad we never got over.'[1] 1989, fiftieth anniversary of the film, has seen another round of celebrations in Atlanta and other US cities, with yet more television specials, new publications and memorabilia production.

The press regularly features articles on *GWTW*. In 1986, two big stories hit the headlines. First was the attempt on Metro-Goldwyn-Mayer's part to produce a sequel, with screenplay by James Goldman and Burt Reynolds as Rhett Butler. The other was the rumour that director Sergio Leone was considering a remake of the 1939 film, using unknown actors as Rhett and Scarlett, with major stars in minor roles. In February 1987 the media reported the dramatic news that, after a long rearguard fight by Margaret Mitchell's executors, the right to a sequel had been won and that America's top literary agency, William Morris of New York, was now hunting for the right author to commission what one newspaper referred to sardonically (though many would agree) as 'perhaps the most serious challenge in the history of American literature'. A year later we were treated to 'the biggest publishing deal of the age', in which author Alexandra Ripley was unveiled, amid great media excitement, as the writer commissioned by Margaret Mitchell's estate to write *Gone With the Wind – 2*.

In crucial ways, *GWTW* has become an international soap opera. As book and film, the ambiguous ending (will Scarlett get Rhett back or not?) has invited speculation since 1936 that a sequel would be written, and a *GWTW–2* film be made. The lives of the book's author, Margaret Mitchell, and the film's stars – especially Vivien Leigh – became the property of the media, which dogged them for the rest of their days. From the major publicity stunt, an international two-year search for an actress to play Scarlett O'Hara, to the later struggles over a proposed sequel between MGM and the author's executor, her brother Stephens Mitchell, with Hollywood and media-induced pressure for *GWTW* clones and successors, *GWTW* has been kept in the public eye as a tantalising running story. Public interest, which is apt to flag, is stoked at regular intervals by new scandals, rumours and teases – all fuelled by publishers, film and television companies, and eagerly picked up by journalists and fans.

As soon as you look for it, *GWTW* appears to be everywhere. When I first began searching, one week in May 1984, MGM was celebrating its sixtieth anniversary by screening the film in London; a 'Scarlett' advertised for her 'Rhett' in the *New Statesman* personal column; and a Bristol pub held a 'Gone With the Wind Night' featuring 'Deep South fancy dress', bourbon and beans. I began to notice how many popular novels by women such as Danielle Steel and Judith Krantz took characters and plot lines from the original.

I spotted a still from the film (the Wilkes barbecue) being used as the basis for true-or-false questions and extended comprehension in an education textbook.[2] My attention was drawn to Joan Collins's biography, which contains no fewer than seven references to *GWTW*, while her daughter's names are Tara Cynara: the first after Scarlett's plantation home, the second a reference to the Ernest Dowson poem from which the book's title comes: 'I have forgot much, Cynara! gone with the wind, Flung roses, roses riotously with the throng.'[3] I recalled how frequently *GWTW* is alluded to in the television series 'Dynasty', in which Joan Collins plays the formidable Scarlett-like Alexis Colby. And in 1987 I enjoyed the news that the left-wing Labour Member of Parliament 'Red' Ken Livingstone, saying of his suspension from the House of Commons, 'Frankly, I don't give a damn', is now known as 'Rhett Ken'.

The 1986 television mini-series 'North and South' was compared in the press with its famous predecessor, and many viewers apart from myself must have noted several parallels, from the characterisation of Southern belles to the settings and scenes of plantation life – not to mention the startling similarity between actress Lesley-Anne Down as Madeline Fabray and Vivien Leigh as Scarlett.

Finally, as a writer myself, I am well aware that a whole academic and publishing industry has grown up around *Gone With the Wind*, and several men (though significantly few women) have made reputations out of it: men like Stephens Mitchell, guardian of Margaret Mitchell's estate and defender of her desire for no sequel; Richard Harwell, bibliographer and critic; and Herb Bridges, *GWTW* collector and author. There is an impressively large, growing body of books and articles on everything from Vivien Leigh's life, the Hollywood *GWTW* sets, detailed descriptions of the making of the film and casting of characters, to weighty collections of

scholarly articles discussing the book and film's historical veracity, literary and filmic merits, representation of
the South, women, blacks, Georgia and so on.[4] Some
titles will suggest the variety of this mounting archive:
*Scarlett Fever: The Ultimate Pictorial Treasury of Gone
With the Wind*; *Scarlett, Rhett, and a Cast of Thousands: The Filming of GWTW*; 'There Will Always be a
Tara'; 'Margaret Mitchell: *Gone With the Wind* and *War
and Peace*'; 'The Black Reaction to *GWTW* '; and 'The
Ingenious Gentleman and the Exasperating Lady: Don
Quixote de la Mancha and Scarlett O'Hara'. Best-sellers
have come out of all this: for instance, Richard Harwell's
collection of Margaret Mitchell's letters was chosen in
1976 as a Book of the Month Club Selection (as the
novel *GWTW* had been forty years earlier); the letters
have already sold over 30,000 copies. My own book
is a contribution to the insatiable market for *GWTW*
materials. The bandwagon rolls on.

One Woman's *Gone With the Wind*

I was a teenager of thirteen or fourteen when I first read
Gone With the Wind, but I can hardly recall a time when
I did not know and love it. The copy my father gave my
mother during an army leave in 1939 was one of the
few hardback books we owned, and I remember often
lingering over it. I found the opening words, 'Scarlett
O'Hara was not beautiful, but men seldom realized it',
utterly irresistible. How profoundly I identified with the
first half of the sentence, and hoped the second would
always be the case. And I vowed that when I found my
own Rhett Butler, he would bring me hats from Paris
and we would call our beautiful daughter Bonnie Blue.
    I was raised by parents who had lived through the
terrors and disruptions of the Second World War, my
father in active army service and almost killed during

the Dunkirk evacuation, my mother left alone at home to bring up a new baby (my older brother), uncertain of her husband's whereabouts but making the best of a grim war in a household shared with her sister-in-law. Both see the war as disorientating the rest of their lives; it remains an emotive subject and, as for many of their contemporaries, their most haunting memory and reference point. Wartime attitudes dominated our family life. In small ways we were extremely frugal: never threw away scraps, held on to objects till they fell apart, valued good health and made minimal fuss over minor illnesses and accidents. In larger ways, the war bred a powerful conservatism. As a family we were unshakably, solemnly nationalistic; I grew up believing that Winston Churchill won the war virtually single-handed. My parents' experience of the war confirmed for them the greatness of England and Englishness, and the importance of national stability with strong government (Conservative, of course). In the aftermath of war, what they most wanted was a strong, independent nuclear family in its self-sufficient home.

For my parents, like other men and women in the 1950s, had no desire in the postwar years to maintain that wartime community spirit and 'mucking-in-together' ideology. The communal suffering and sacrifice on the home front which were credited so much with leading to 'our boys' winning the war on the battle fronts were gratefully abandoned in favour of a privatised domesticity and the new struggle to make a good civilian life within the family. Against her wishes (she enjoyed having an only child and wanted to go out to work) my mother stayed at home with three young babies, and used her considerable intelligence and talents on domestic labour, child-care, and mopping up leaks in our rather flimsy, heavily mortgaged house. My father, a sales representative, was away much of the time and I – the only daughter – sensed and to some extent shared in my mother's anxieties over economic insecurity, family health and welfare, and our bread-winner's safety over the thousands of miles he drove on his patch. Following her around as she did the chores, I emulated her by playing with dolls and dress-ing up in high heels and rouge; and I hated leaving the warm safety of the house. The bookish child of a book-ish mother, I read my way into fictional knowledge of other societies, classes, and the world of men. Until my teens, I read few novels by women.

Gone With the Wind, which I read and then viewed in early teenage years, spoke personally to me. It depicted a world of omnipresent women and intermittently stable and dependable men; it showed a society held together – often against heavy odds – by women's energy, labour and ability to 'make do and mend'; and it presented men as objects of mystery and fantasy, creatures who seemed to offer strong shoulders for women to lean on but all too often vanished into the night, assuring women how capable they were on their own. In *GWTW* the war-time camaraderie of the women, crowded into Aunt Pittypat's parlour and gathered round the lists of war dead, echoed stories my mother had told me of the hours of waiting and watching, but also improvising and innovating, which were women's lot during 'her' war. Scarlett O'Hara's disdain for hospital work reminded me of my mother's shameful admission that she had been relieved of vital wartime nursing duties after pass-ing out during a blood transfusion. Scarlett's bewildered struggles to take on the delivery of a baby and the rebuilding of a working plantation seemed familiar to me from my mother's courageous attempts to mend the washing machine and bicycle punctures during my father's frequent absences. Most of all, the whole ethos of *GWTW* struck a chord because of its echoes in my parents' hard-working attempts to create the conditions for a respectable and comfortable middle-class lifestyle for their three children, and their confidence that we should enjoy what they did not have: good health on the National Health Service, and individual success and prosperity with new state schooling and the prospect of full employment.

Both novel and film fed easily into the philosophy of my postwar family, and also of myself as a baby-boomer, product of the late 1940s birth 'bulge'. The war had done its worst and damaged my parents' adolescent aspirations, making them thereafter highly cautious and somewhat fatalistic. But for me, the dawn of a new peacetime era (especially as it was later developed in the now legendary 1960s) offered hopes of new styles of class, generational and sexual behaviour and relationships; *GWTW* placed all the energy and life force in characters who were, by the standards of my upbringing, distinctly unorthodox. Reading and viewing it as an imaginatively restless yet rather conformist teenager, I was able to identify with a society redefined by its young rebels, and especially by a young woman who – like me – bent her head in family prayer but thought on male flesh, and believed herself destined for greater things than marriage and motherhood.

Furthermore, both book and film spoke to my strong emotional attachment to my mother. A text which helps the reader imaginatively to work through the deaths of both mother and father, it allows women reader-viewers a space in which to celebrate the mother's virtues and values, but also to challenge and disregard them. *Gone With the Wind* must have offered many a woman the opportunity vicariously to experience the consequences of not becoming like, or indeed *becoming* her own mother. So a first exposure to *GWTW* helped me to understand the kind of impact which women had on war and peacetime economies; this was of course before the women's movement had put domestic labour and women's part in both World Wars on the map. It also undoubtedly helped me to acknowledge my love for and indebtedness to my mother, with her strong conservatism and hard work both at home and in unsatisfying part-time jobs. And it enabled me to recognise that I did not need to experience for myself her frustrations and dissatisfactions, which I had always taken for granted as part of a woman's lot; nor did I need to share her philosophy or politics. *GWTW* was one of the first important texts in enabling me to resolve never to marry in haste, nor to trap myself into the restrictive and quietly desperate subordinate role of an Ellen O'Hara. Like Scarlett, I would be deviant and dangerous. I could be different from my mother, and there would probably be other women and men — like Melanie, Mammy and Rhett — who would offer me the kinds of comfort and support I felt as a child would emanate from no other source.

That said, being a gloomy adolescent drawn always to tragic texts and fates, I was spellbound by *GWTW*'s heavy air of nostalgia and regret for lost love, home, ways of life and personal values. While it spoke positively and progressively to me of my youthful yearnings and discontents, as well as desires to shape a life differently from my parents and brothers, even more did it arouse my terrors of leaving the cosy family home and breaking away from my mother's protection. Although I relished Scarlett's wilful independence of her mother, Ellen, I took the point that such a radical departure from all her mother stood for resulted in a Scarlett alone, relatively friendless and rejected finally by the best mother she ever had, Rhett Butler.

For me, as for many people, *Gone With the Wind* was the longest novel I had ever read, and the process of reading it felt and still feels like a major feat. In my teenage readings I felt I had accomplished a herculean task, managing to complete such a formidable book, being able to enter into and sympathetically identify with this grandiose treatment of human experience on a broad historical canvas. Indeed, the way the novel is organised and written persuades us readers to feel we are party to matters of weighty historical, mythic and universal significance. We refer to *GWTW* as 'epic' because of its sheer length, its formal division into five parts and two 'volumes' (mirroring both the tragic drama and the nineteenth-century novel) and its broad historical sweep and large cast of characters. Indeed, in many early reviews the book was compared with 'epic novels' such as Thackeray's *Vanity Fair* and Tolstoy's *War and Peace*.

Also – because, from school English lessons, I was familiar with Shakespearian tragedy and Victorian family sagas set amid social unrest, especially wars – I read *GWTW* as an account of the tragic disruption of noble people's lives, as a tale of chaos and disorder followed by the long haul towards restoration of white Southerners' rights and dignities. A classic story of good triumphing eventually over evil, order over disorder. The 'Lost Cause' – which, in my ignorance of Southern history, I identified simply with barbecues at plantation houses with white columns – was the tragic loss I found poignantly celebrated and idealised throughout the book, so that I felt how right it was that Scarlett should be able to return finally to her own plantation and the arms of her own Mammy, safe in the knowledge that her property and land were intact.

So I read *GWTW* in the way many readers must do, having little knowledge of the American Civil War and hazy notions of the Ku Klux Klan, Reconstruction, and so on. I accepted the historical context uncritically and found my sympathies locked unerringly into the fate of the white families of the defeated Confederacy. The way I read the book, then, meant that I focused on Scarlett O'Hara's fortunes, and those of the characters with whom she interacts most, and fitted everyone and every event into the framework of Scarlett's destiny and progress. Cheerfully skipping what I found to be boring political and social details, I concentrated hard on the central love triangle of Scarlett, Ashley and Rhett, which I found endlessly satisfying.

By my early twenties I had seen the film several times, enjoying fantasies of swapping my miniskirt for a long hooped skirt and green velvet. A product of that 1960s meritocratic generation which looked forward to full employment and political and sexual liberation, I had been raised on Hollywood images and looked to America for celluloid fantasies as well as a vision of the future. Not surprisingly, therefore, after three years as a student in London, I decided to see the States for myself, so I accepted an offer to study and teach in Louisiana. I was disgracefully ignorant of the South, to which I travelled in 1969 and where I stayed for two years – with frequent subsequent return trips. I had seen television pictures of Martin Luther King and racial battles in Alabama and Mississippi; I spent hours listening to Delta blues, jazz and rock, and watching films like *In the Heat of the Night*; I had read novels by Carson McCullers, the plays of Tennessee Williams, and the poetry of Edgar Allan Poe. I had a fairly colourful and gothic view of the region, one which was to be shaken up and toned down in the years I have spent getting to know the South and Southerners.

But as a teacher of Louisiana freshman students, I became aware that the idealised or grotesque version of Southern history and character with which I began were in some measure shared by my (mainly white) students, many of whom had been raised to be uncritical of and indifferent towards the region in which they lived. I once asked my 'Freshman Composition' class to write an essay on the period of history in which they would most like to have lived. At least three-quarters of the female students shared my own fantasy, straight from

Gone With the Wind, opting for the antebellum South, in which they saw themselves dancing in green sprigged muslin with tiny puffed sleeves, while handsome planters' sons vied for their favours. By contrast, of the small number of black students none chose this period; they preferred to stay in the present day . . .

From speaking to many Southern white women, I know the power which *Gone With the Wind* has held over their imaginations and the centrality of this novel and film to popular myths, celebrating as they do a nostalgic version of the South's glorious economic and social heyday. For the ladies who dress annually as plantation belles on Mississippi's 'Natchez Trail' and at the New Orleans 'Spring Fiesta', as well as starry-eyed Southern girls who weep their way through many a matinée showing of the film, *GWTW* is the ultimate expression of the hopes, dreams and fears of Southern womanhood. They see it as 'their' book and film and, while tolerant of my enthusiasm, felt there was no way a British woman could ever understand the essence of Scarlett O'Hara.

By the time I returned to Louisiana, a few years after my teaching experience, I was rather more informed about Southern history and culture and was preparing a book on Louisiana Civil War women writers. These women (mostly white and middle-class) had written fiction about the War and its aftermath, focusing especially on women's lives and struggles during and after the War, often making politically charged arguments about the role of women and Blacks in the late-nineteenth-century South. One afternoon, tired of reading in the library, I decided to wander down to the local cinema, which – as it seemed to do every few weeks – was showing *Gone With the Wind*. Not having seen it for some years, I was startled at its similarity, in argument, setting and characterisation, to the nineteenth-century novels and stories I was researching. Since by now I was more familiar with Civil War history and literature, I realised with a shock how historically and politically biased it was, and how passionately it was arguing its pro-Confederate case. That afternoon's viewing brought home to me the fact that *Gone With the Wind*'s vision of the Old South, the Civil War, and the subsequent violent phases before the restoration in the 1880s of white supremacy in the Southern states, was a very polemical version to which liberal and black writers would object.

Yet, offended as I too was by the political argument, I enjoyed virtually every minute of it, and felt myself swept along by its extraordinary power. The colour, music, costumes, spectacular effects – not to mention Clark Gable's devastating sexiness – moved and haunted me for days to come. In my dreams (a rerun of adolescence) I was carried upstairs by Clark-Rhett's masterful arms. Together we rode through Atlanta in flames and kissed passionately against a vivid red sunset.

The first few times I saw the film I had never seen any of the 'Southern films', depicting a romantic Old South, which were very popular in the 1930s. These films, with titles like *The Little Colonel* and *The Littlest Rebel* (1935), *Dixiana* (1930), *Dixie Days* (1928) and *The Old South* (1932), presented to Depression audiences nostalgic and idealised images of a feudal 'paradise lost' of large plantations, white-columned mansions, beautiful Southern belles and their chivalrous beaux, against a backdrop of loyal and humorous slaves. Reading film histories, I learned that *Gone With the Wind* was the last and most celebrated of this large group of Hollywood films, and that it followed the by then well-known, indeed clichéd patterns of setting, costume and characterisation – often to the extent of distorting the novel's descriptions. For example David Selznick's grand columned plantation house for Tara is very different from Margaret Mitchell's more modest whitewashed square brick house on a hill with an avenue of cedars, and Butterfly McQueen's simpering Prissy, far more of a grotesque than Mitchell's creation, uses that 'comic darky' stereotype familiar from many earlier films.

But however much I know of Hollywood's historical distortions, nevertheless I still derive great visual pleasure from this brilliant re-creation of a mythic American past with its red sunsets, white cotton bolls, and extravagant rural plantation homes and vulgar town houses. In swallowing whole this long and emotionally demanding film I also absorb an interpretation of America's real and legendary past, more vivid to me than any verbal re-creations I have read in my researches into American history and literature. Just as many Britons imagine contemporary America as one long drive-in movie or surfing party, so for me – and I am not alone – the South's agricultural past will be for ever Tara. No amount of statistics about the rarity of the large plantation as opposed to the common poor white smallholding will erase that popular myth about a harmonious South in which classes, races and sexes mingle cheerily beneath the spreading magnolias. So while I know intellectually that David Selznick's Southern plantation, built on a Hollywood studio lot thousands of both literal and metaphorical miles from the real Georgia earth, owes more to film-makers' and set-designers' fantasies than historical verisimilitude, emotionally I still revel in the luxurious, well-ordered paradise symbolised by that papier-mâché Tara.

So *Gone With the Wind* has reached and satisfied me over and over again at various levels, providing contradictory models and messages. It has helped me to resolve familial conflicts, especially with my mother, while warning me about the pitfalls of stepping out of line; encouraged and spelled out the dangers of my political and personal radicalism; and afforded me sensual pleasures – the erotic charge between the Scarlett

I identify with and the Rhett I desire, the pleasurable
spectacle of lavish costume and epic action – while
reminding me what an unpredictable and chaotic place
the world is. My life experience, years of reading about
and living in the South, have all altered my perspectives
on character and event, but a profound fascination with
GWTW remains.

*   *   *

Like many white Southern novelists before her,
Margaret Mitchell chose well the setting of her novel:
three of the most dramatic, exciting and tempestuous
periods of American Southern history – the climax of
plantation culture and the slave economy, the bloody
and tragic Civil War, and the violent Reconstruction
period leading to the eventual 'redemption' of Old
Guard white rule. The originality of the tale lies in
its ability to convey this long and complex sweep of
history from the perspective of one young woman who
begins by expressing boredom at hearing any topic discussed except herself but has to live through extreme
reversals of fortune, undergo terrible suffering and loss,
and yet survive to rebuild her old plantation and way of
life – and learn just what her role in her regional, class
and race history has been.

Scarlett O'Hara is a delicious fictional character. She
offers opportunities for reader-viewer identification at
each stage of her progress. First, as a selfish socialite
unrequitedly in love with Ashley Wilkes, the poetic
dreamer who never comes to terms with the New
South. Next, as the restless wife of three men –
Charles Hamilton (for spite because Ashley is marrying Melanie), Frank Kennedy (to pay off the plantation Tara's postwar taxes) and Rhett Butler (for sexual
pleasure, though eventual tragic separation). Most of

all, as the pragmatist who moves with the times, getting on with delivering a baby single-handedly while
the Yankees approach Atlanta, doing business with
Yankees during Reconstruction in order to pay the
bills, and then resolving to mend her broken heart by
retreating to Tara to begin again. Like all of us, she has
problems with everything and everyone: her parents,
siblings, children, her sex life, her bank balance. And
she is surrounded (rather more in the novel than in the
film) by an array of complex, vital and comic characters who flesh out a historically acute and fictionally
rich picture of the white South at its greatest crisis.
Furthermore, the action moves at a breathless but
beautifully controlled pace, shifting constantly between the rural tranquillity of Tara and the vibrancy
of Atlanta; and it presents us with a variety of character and dialogue – from Gerald's drunken Irish
schmaltz to Mammy's hectoring social commentary and
Rhett's sexy banter. And *GWTW* sustains a plangent
note of nostalgia for those powerful notions and sym-
bols of home, family, community and love.

Talking about *Gone With the Wind*

This book is concerned with the popular meanings and
associations of *Gone With the Wind* in the context of its
first fifty years of life, with that process of personal, intimate and yet also collective relationship with a book and
film which we call 'readership' or 'viewership'.[5] So I have
focused on this work not by looking critically and in isolation at the book and film, author and film producer,
or indeed just my own responses, but rather by asking
how *GWTW* lives in the imaginations, memories and
experiences of individuals and groups – that is, through
the eyes of its fans who, to judge by the statistics of book
sales, film and television viewing figures and a wealth of
memorabilia and popular references, come from many

nations, classes, races, generations and life experiences. *GWTW* is also a work which has appealed to both men and women, though from my own limited research and enquiries of friends and acquaintances, I am convinced that it is most cherished by *women*. I make no apology for focusing almost entirely on women readers and viewers. There is a story to be told about men's involvement in *GWTW* (especially men who follow war fiction and film) but that will not be the tale I tell here.

With this in view, in January 1986 I wrote a letter to dozens of newspapers and magazines, asking readers who were fans of *GWTW* to write to me about their memories, experiences and views of book and film. The letter was published in a wide range of British publications: the Women's Institute 'Home and Country', the Townswomen's Guild 'Townswoman', *Options*, *Women's Review*, *Spare Rib*, *U Magazine*, *Working Woman*, *Everywoman*, The National Housewives' Register Newsletter, *The Voice*, and two Bristol-based newspapers, *The Western Daily Press* and *Evening Post*. From these sources I received a total of 427 letters, and from these respondents and other contacts in Britain and the United States I amassed 355 completed questionnaires (only twenty-five of which came from men).[6]

Although the women who wrote to me and the few I interviewed do not amount to a representative sample of the population, they were an interesting cross-section of women of all ages, regions and backgrounds. While it is hard to generalise about the kinds of people who read particular magazines and newspapers, and people's class and income are not easy to infer from letters and questionnaires, I believe that most of my respondents are fairly middle-class women, or at least daughters of or married to men in professional or white-collar jobs. Most of them are in middle or later life, reasonably well educated, fed and housed. As far as I can tell, there was a tiny handful of replies from black women.

By eliciting letters and questionnaires from women all over Britain, and a couple of dozen from the USA, I was able to gather ideas, memories and associations which have helped me to understand the continuing appeal of *GWTW* and the place it has in people's lives – included my own. The number of responses delighted me and the articulate, witty and moving descriptions of *GWTW* were very illuminating. I have learned a great deal from the many women and a few men who took the time to write to me about their enthusiasm, and I have drawn freely on their thoughts and memories to support and question or demolish my own historical and critical readings of this controversial but passionately loved book and film. For inevitably, during the preparation and writing of this book my feelings about *GWTW* have fluctuated and changed. So as the book progresses I quote my correspondents' and interviewees' insights, and also offer my own – often contradictory – perceptions and judgements.

Reading through the letters and questionnaires has confirmed my growing suspicions about the way people think of literature and film. As a student, then teacher of English, I had become accustomed to reading in certain ways and to learning 'appropriate' critical responses to everything I read or watch. Spontaneous enthusiasm and obsessive passion for writers or works tend to lose out in this professionalised pastime. But as a teacher I had been increasingly aware that students all read very differently, with varying levels of sophistication, critical acumen and relevant response. There is a marked contrast between the solemn, dutiful way a student will demonstrate, through close reading in class, a reverential respect for D.H. Lawrence, and the emotionally charged, voluble and sardonic enthusiasm she will share with a friend in the college refectory over last night's episode of the soap opera 'Neighbours'. I know well from my own experience that a sleepy, uncritical reading of *Cosmopolitan* in bed after a long day holds as many pleasurable memories as my most keenly analytical and alert readings of Shakespeare or Doris Lessing. Everyone seems to remember with special clarity the film they saw on their first date, regardless of its aesthetic qualities, and many of us recall in considerable detail our first sexually explicit novel or television programme.

So it proved with my correspondents. Writing in this case about *GWTW*, they express passion (often secretive or slightly shamefaced) and emotional loyalty to this work, which they usually describe – in non-literary and untheoretical language – in terms of the narrative and characters, loved and loathed. For each of them, *GWTW* has a personal meaning (occasionally negative) and is recalled with careful attention to detail. It is such precise meanings this book aims to record and discuss.

The Book and Film in our Time

This does not mean that I see *Gone With the Wind* as a work which has no existence outside readers' or viewers' minds and privatised memories. *GWTW does* exist and has to be read at one level as a book which, written by a particular person at a specific historical time, was made into a film that, since its première in 1939, has broken all box-office records. And both book and film do determine, through their structure and organisation, certain kinds of interpretation which seem natural to most reader-viewers. So while I shall record the views of *GWTW*'s female fans, I shall also examine the ways in which the book was written and the film put together, as well as the kinds of critical response both have received over the years. *GWTW* commemorated and became the definitive version of a significant period of American history, so I shall draw on my correspondents' and published critics' perceptions to outline the different ways readers and viewers over fifty years have made sense of the historical, social, racial and gender issues explored in this one text.

I hope to bring together the multiple meanings and associations which *GWTW* has carried in the last half-century, and to demonstrate how such a work may both flourish in individual minds and memories, and also develop communal and social meanings which make it a particular kind of reference point across and within nations and groups. In the last fifty years *GWTW* has gone from strength to strength, but we cannot pretend that it means the same to its modern reader-viewers as it did on publication day in 1936 or at the film première in 1939. Like other popular works *GWTW* has changed with the times, carrying different meanings for subsequent generations in various countries. If we want to define its associations and resonances in 1989, we must look back over a half century of reading and viewing experiences.

2

Scarlett's Women:
Gone With the Wind in Living Memory

It's getting to the point where my husband is convinced that I think they were real people, and in a sense, to me they are. (Vivienne Elliott)

GWTW was more than just cinema for me – it was part of my growing up. (Mrs Jennifer S. Parkhouse)

As I turned over the many letters and questionnaires sent to me by *Gone With the Wind* enthusiasts, I was intrigued to catch glimpses of women's varied lives and experiences in relation to this popular phenomenon. It seems that for many women, more than any other work it has captured imaginations and made lasting connections with lives. Although many of my correspondents have read widely, and some go frequently to the cinema, they are clear about the special quality of *GWTW*. It is described repeatedly as 'unique'; using the language of the publicity handout, women refer to *GWTW* as 'immortal', 'a legend', 'the most fabulous book of all time', 'sheer magic'. Their commitment to it is less that of an impartial critic, more that of an addict: they are 'fanatics', 'hooked', 'smitten', 'spellbound' and 'obsessive'. Some may have exaggerated their enthusiasm because of the infectious impact of its very commercial success, but there is no doubt that for many women, like myself, *GWTW* has a special place in heart and mind.

A great many of the women who wrote to me about *GWTW* had read or seen it a number of times (some claiming hundreds!). Yet for the majority, the *first* experience was one of an extraordinary pleasure, which has remained a treasured memory. I received a large number of accounts of first readings and viewings, each from a woman describing the emotional power the work held over her imagination. Often this was experienced with a force which many felt to have been unusual, even unique, and therefore the memory is narrated in considerable detail.

For some correspondents, the first reading dominated daily life to the exclusion of other duties. In 1936 Janet Ruskatch borrowed it from a library and 'can still see myself bunched up on the kitchen table with a rug over my knees as it was chilly and the fire wasn't started until evening (money wasn't very plentiful). Time passed – I didn't realise how much until I heard my husband's key in the lock'; while Mrs J.E. Hancock read it in 1944 as a schoolgirl looking after her sick mother. She burned the potatoes because 'I was helping Scarlett to deliver Melanie's baby'.

The excitement and sense of occasion at this unusually long and much-heralded film's first showing testify to its dramatic impact on particular communities during the war. Sylvia King recalls an occasion in her childhood in a hamlet on the Helford River, Cornwall:

One day, ten of us children were on our way home from school – turning the corner at the top of a steep hill we bumped into our mums walking up the hill laughing and giggling.
    We were all stunned – where were our mums going – what had happened? I can still *feel* our silence! It was the biggest occasion in their lives since VE Day! They were all off to walk one mile up the road to catch the local bus to Falmouth, five miles away, to see *GWTW*, and would be coming back in a TAXI. They had saved up for several

weeks for this event and dads had come home early
from their general labouring and gardening jobs
to put us children to bed.

And Mrs A.M. Lindsay remembers similar wartime
excitement among her mother and women friends,
shipped for safety from Egypt to South Africa,
when a party of women went to Durban to see
GWTW and, because of its length, returned ecstatic
on the next morning's 'milk train'. In both cases the
film's extraordinary length required special transport
arrangements so that the women did not miss the ending;
and both describe a gregarious female experience of
pleasurable anticipation of and excitement at a popular
cultural event. Sylvia King and Mrs Lindsay point to
ways in which women in the 1940s identified certain
films as their own special treat – away from husbands and
children – and caused minor social and sexual upheavals
in their pursuit. (It cannot have been a very frequent
event for dads to come home early to see to the kids,
or for those expatriate women to stay away from home
for the night.)

GWTW's 'unique' quality means that for many
women the very ownership or borrowing of the book
or (especially for a younger generation) the video has
a special significance. In particular, copies of the book
are much cherished – especially since its cost on first
publication was prohibitively high for many people, so
a great number borrowed it from friends, colleagues,
private or public lending libraries, or bought it with
others. Hylda Fletcher writes that in 1940, receiving
for her sixteenth birthday a five-shilling book token, she
bought the cheapest edition of GWTW at four shillings
and sixpence. Her weekly wage packet at the time was
nineteen shillings and sixpence, so it is understandable
that many women had difficulty in getting hold of it at
all. Margo Cox borrowed it from a shop lending library

in 1942, paying threepence for a two-week loan, but was delighted when the following year her husband bought a copy for seven and sixpence, 'a large sum to pay for a book in those days'. Just before the war, Doris Brecht and her husband worked as assistants in the West Ham public libraries. They recall that in 1936, when the book was published, there were long reserve lists for it, and since there was only one copy at each branch library they could never take a turn between borrowers. They had to wait until the war was over before borrowing it themselves. Many correspondents record their gratitude to parents, husbands and sisters who bought them a copy for Christmas or birthday, and there seem to be a great many dog-eared, brown-paper-covered, heavily sellotaped (in one case completely re-bound!) copies. Many have dedications commemorating special events; Verna Grant has written on the flyleaf the date of each of her many rereadings. Several writers describe their distress at having lost or lent their copies, which they would dearly love to have back. For many this book is the longest they ever had or have tackled, and it seems to be one of the very few (in most cases I believe the only one) read many times over. Rereading a novel seems to be regarded by most people as a rather odd – and slightly shameful – activity. *GWTW* is their one exception.

Like reading the book, going to see the film when it first came out was an expensive and time-consuming activity. In the early 1940s cinema seats cost in London between one shilling and ten pence and eight and six, and in provincial cities from fourpence to one and six. *GWTW* often cost more than regular films because of its length. Freda Woollard recalls paying two shillings and fourpence for a seat in 1943, when earning only fifteen shillings a week as an office junior. Several women say they simply could not afford to go in the early years. For 1940s viewers this was easily the longest film they had seen, the first with an intermission (an 'interval' was something you had in the theatre, never the cinema, with its continuous programming, and many letters describe the sandwiches and flasks of tea taken to sustain the viewer) and the first for which anyone had had to book in advance or queue on the day. All of this – beside the fact that most buses had stopped running before the evening performance was over, so many had to walk a long way home – meant that actually to see *GWTW* must have seemed quite a feat, and certainly was a major event. No wonder so many women recall that first viewing in some detail!

With the advent of video-recorders, the viewing of *GWTW* has undergone a sea change. Re-viewing, which many fans like to do at regular intervals, is now possible at the touch of a switch, and many of my respondents made it one of their first purchased or recorded videos. The sense of event (and of course the epic scale) of the screened film is now lost, but the possibility of private home-based pleasure has undoubtedly increased, and the likelihood of children being introduced to *GWTW* at ever earlier ages is now strong.

Individual fans accumulate supplementary mementoes of their reading-viewing to confirm their special relationship to *GWTW*. Many of my correspondents collect press cuttings, stills, prints and so on, and discuss *GWTW* whenever they have an opportunity – the length and detail of many of their letters, as well as their expressions of pleasure in and envy of my project, testify to this 'hobby' element. Several have used their enthusiasm creatively. Penelope Wheelwright has written a play for the Mellow Dramatic Theatre Company called *Gone With The Rest*, an anti-heroin play set in a South London flat with a young female addict fantasising, as she shoots up the drug, that she is Scarlett, the heroin is her Ashley, and her moneylender 'wide boy' supplier is Rhett. David Copson has painted in oils

Vivien Leigh as Scarlett, using a still from the film. Many letters describe ways in which families use key phrases from book and film in sardonic ways, or act out scenes from both. One woman domesticated the work by writing a spoof called 'Gone with the 2.26 from Sidcup' . . .

Bringing *Gone With the Wind* Home

For fifty years *Gone With the Wind* memorabilia has been big business, catering as it does to people's desire to own a small reminder of their enthusiasm for this work. When the book was first published there was a proliferation all over America of *GWTW* dress material (Scarlett Green, Melanie Blue), mittens, hats, powder-puffs, cologne, a manicure set in the shape of the book, and wallpaper with scenes from the novel. A Pittsburgh laundry advertised with the slogan 'Gone With The Wash', and four lion cubs born at Atlanta Zoo were named – naturally – Scarlett, Melanie, Ashley and Rhett. When the film appeared there were *GWTW* dolls, children's masquerade outfits, parlour games and fountain pens.[1]

Since then, on countless shopping bags, greetings cards, jigsaw puzzles, collectors' plates, board games, books, posters and prints, the familiar faces of Vivien Leigh and Clark Gable ensure profitable sales. In the USA Grand Granite Enterprises offer a catalogue of 'GWTW and Civil War Memorabilia', including publications such as *Strange Tales of 'GWTW' or 101 Things You Probably Never Knew About 'Gone With the Wind' But Were Afraid to Ask*, the *Gone With the Wind Cookbook*, *GWTW Program* (a reprint of the première publication), and *The Pictorial History of*

Gone With the Wind. Grand Granite market posters of Rhett at poker, a lifesize Clark Gable, Rhett holding Scarlett against the backdrop of burning Atlanta – and the parody of this with Ronald Reagan holding Margaret Thatcher as nuclear war begins; as well as postcards of scenes from the film and a souvenir stamp assortment of movie stills. They also sell Rhett and Scarlett hand-fans, the *GWTW* videotape, and Civil War flags and authentic buttons, excavated from battle sites in the South. If you have $79.95 to spare you may send to 'Cinema Collectors' of Hollywood for a set of six lithographs of original *GWTW* costume designs, individually signed and numbered by the film's designer, Walter Plunkett, before his death in 1983. For a further $195 you can be the lucky owner of a fine bisque porcelain doll, 'Vivien Leigh as Scarlett O'Hara', a nineteen-inch-high Scarlett in green crepe-de-chine dress, sold by Franklin Heirloom Dolls with an MGM-approved Certificate of Authenticity. Or you could buy one of the *GWTW* series by Paul Crees, British creator of 'portraits in wax', who won a major award in the 1984 world's first Convention of Original Doll Artists for his Vivien Leigh as Scarlett the bride. The eight Edwin M. Knowles 'Gone With the Wind' collector plates have multiplied in value since they appeared in 1978. In my garden, six 'Scarlet [*sic*] O'Hara' narcissus bulbs bloom yellow with a bright red centre.

Mrs Lorie Townsend wrote to me that she and her best friend in America exchange *GWTW* birthday gifts. She sent her friend an inscribed plastic shopping bag bought in London; several people stopped her on New York streets to ask where to buy it. Among other mementoes from the States have come a *GWTW* thousand-piece jigsaw puzzle, giant pillow cover, and memo pad headed 'Tomorrow is another day'. Lorie Townsend describes her lavatory:

about twenty-five framed publicity stills of *GWTW*
. . . On the shelf are the *GWTW* books, including a Vivien Leigh colouring book featuring all
her *GWTW* costumes. The curtains are *GWTW*
large towels. On the walls are *GWTW* postcards, a
GWTW Valentine pop-up card, several *GWTW*-
related birthday cards, and a *GWTW* poster, also a
poster of Ronald Reagan holding Margaret Thatcher
in *GWTW* pose.

Hilary Harris sent me photos of her *GWTW* collection,
which includes biographies of Vivien Leigh and Clark
Gable, *GWTW* postcards in English and French, a
three-volume edition of the novel in French (*Autant en
Emporte le Vent*), and 'Vivien Leigh Paper Dolls' in full
colour. Mrs J. Fletcher, herself an avid *GWTW* plate-
collector, writes that a friend who collects prams bought
at auction the pram used by Rhett in the *GWTW* film
to push Bonnie Blue through the streets of Atlanta.

Probably the most fanatical collector of *GWTW*
memorabilia lives in Atlanta. Herb Bridges' large attic
houses a unique collection of booklets, posters, dolls,
Rhett bookends, about five hundred copies of the
book in all languages from Greek to Thai, and candies
with such titles as 'Prissy Peppermints'. It's clear that
like other memorabilia industries, especially related to
movies, the USA produces more *GWTW* mementoes
than Britain, and many of my correspondents received
theirs from American friends, or bought them on a
visit.

Another major way in which *GWTW* is appro-
priated and enjoyed by its enthusiasts is through a
choice of names from book and film for children,
pets and houses. Several women wrote to me from
'Tara', including Mrs Denise Cox, who lives in Germany:

My first home, a tiny cottage, was known as 'Tarachen', which is an affectionate use of the German language to mean 'little Tara'. We now live in our fifth home, which is still known as Tarachen amongst the close family, but it's not used as a postal address as I like to take the sign with me every time we move. One day we might live in a house as grand as Tara and will be able to do away with the 'chen' on the end!

Many women told me that their own names (Melanie, Bonnie) or their children's (Ashley, Scarlett, Vivien) were derived from their favourite book and film, though several confessed that their husbands had refused to agree to *GWTW* children's names, and one correspondent who had wanted to call a son Ashley had a daughter and 'I thought Scarlett was a bit strong!' Mrs Monica Jones read in the press that at the height of *GWTW* fever an American woman had triplets whom she dubbed 'Gone', 'With' and 'Wind'.

I suspect that the world is full of dogs and cats called Rhett, Scarlett, Pittypat, and so on. Mrs J.E. Hancock gets upset whenever *GWTW* is mentioned, as Tara was the name of her first beloved dog, though she is now looking for a cat: 'I haven't got the cat or a name yet. Suppose Scarlett is catty, isn't she?' Patricia Andrews writes:

I have always named my cats after characters from *GWTW*. This started twenty years ago, when I had a boyfriend who was an authority on the Civil War . . . I had recently met him when I was look-ing for a kitten – the first one I saw was a little grey one. My boyfriend said 'Ah – a Confeder-ate cat' and that was it! She was named Belle after Belle Watling (we had heard her mother was rather promiscuous). Belle turned out to be the shy retiring type so was rather misnamed, poor thing.

This naming practice is described, as the few examples from many offered illustrate, in a light-hearted and humorous manner (especially in relation to pets' names). There is a combination of self-conscious embarrassment and nervous pleasure at sharing these private references with an unknown correspondent. But from the letters it is clear that for some women such references add to the intensity of their memories, associated as they are with their specific joys and obsessions. For women used to subordinating or being secretive about their reading of romantic and historical fiction, this incorporation of names into their most intimate relationships represents a small act of personal power and assertiveness.

Shared Experiences and Special Times

But the enjoyment of *GWTW* is not simply individual and private, confined to the solitary reader and film-goer. For a number of women this is a pleasure they have shared with other women, one which has become a bond between mothers, daughters and friends. It is not unusual for a woman to describe her first reading or viewing as inspired or directed by a female relative or colleague. Like me, a large number of respondents were introduced to the work by their mothers, and those women with daughters say that they too have communicated their enthusiasm to the next genera-tion (though a few note a shared love with husbands or fathers). Pauline Riley is not untypical:

I first read *GWTW* aged fourteen years in 1945, by which time all my female relatives . . . had read

and reread it; it became not only a family favourite
but an obsession. Everyone quoted Scarlett O'Hara,
particularly 'I'll think about that tomorrow', a
phrase I have continually used for forty years; I
actually have the saying in my kitchen on a plaque
which I bought in America . . . I passed my love of
the book on to my two daughters, now grown
up, and any friends they had who hadn't read it
were bullied into doing so. How I envied their first
discovery. I now have a six-year-old granddaughter
and will give her a while before she too will
be introduced to Scarlett O'Hara.

Shirley Robinson recalls fighting with her late mother
and sisters for possession of the book, as none of them
could bear to put it down; the very dilapidated 1940ish
copy is now in her possession. With her mother, Reina
Lewis has 'a raging controversy going over whether
Scarlett gets him back or not'. Many women with
growing daughters (but few with sons) say they can
hardly wait to introduce them to *GWTW*, and a few
who were apprehensive have been rewarded with a new
generation of fanatics. For a handful of correspondents,
GWTW provided a kind of neutral territory on which
a mother and daughter could safely meet. For example,
Elizabeth Haynes writes: 'I went with my mother the
first time I saw the film and it was one thing we could
talk about during those difficult teenage years.'

One cannot generalise as to how mothers and daughters share such an enthusiasm, though its rarity is
commented on by one or two correspondents. Lorie
Townsend wrote: 'Normally anything you as a parent
like and approve of, your children are bound to hold in
a greater or lesser degree of contempt', and it appears
that several women resisted falling for *GWTW* precisely
because their mothers recommended it (often coming
later in life to love it, by independent choice). One

woman was so tired of hearing her mother rave about
it that she read *GWTW* for the first time only when, at
fourteen, she went to stay with cousins in Canada. Joan
Cutts had endured through childhood her mother and
aunts discussing *GWTW* and queuing to see the film,
which she found 'overlong and very boring' – on first
viewing, presumably under duress. Her life experience
meant that in adulthood she returned to it and is now
a firm admirer. Lorie Townsend's mother was strongly
critical of the work, disapproving strongly of her daughter's obsession and even more of her granddaughters'
enthusiasm. By contrast, Wendy Evans describes the
film as representing 'the essential differences/problem
between me and my mother. She vaunted it through
my childhood as a great love story, and is still not open
to any acknowledgement of any other issues in the film.'
A significant number of mothers, daughters and sisters
engage in long exchanges of *GWTW* dialogue.

GWTW has also been a bond between friends. Several
respondents describe reading it with a friend or work
colleague, often participating in lively discussions about
who should play the leading roles in the film. Part of this
sharing stems from economic factors – especially during
the war, when book and film came out: the book and
cinema seats were relatively expensive or available only
to those in towns. Elizabeth Mills was delighted to be
given a copy of the book as the war started:

> The book had already been going the rounds in
> the laboratory where I worked and it seemed that it
> would never be my turn to read it. Of course
> it wasn't a 'group' book, but we were all hard up
> and buying a book was out of the question so
> books were lent out – and I was well down the
> pecking order!

Edith Hope describes working in a factory during the
war:

> A girl I worked with on the night shift had seen
> the film and each night while we worked at the
> machine she told me the story in instalments.
> I looked forward each night to hearing the next
> episode.

And Jean Darby lent her copy, bought in 1943, to
a friend who was killed by the second V-2 rocket
dropped on London; the film therefore always brings
back memories of her 'dear friend Olive'.

Later generations of women have shared, if not the
same copy, at least the same enthusiasm. Marion
Schoenfeld describes an experience I imagine is fairly
common:

> I first read GWTW together with a friend when
> we were eleven years old − I say together, because
> it was a joint obsession − we memorised sections,
> quoted passages to each other, and virtually took it
> as a guidebook to life for some time.

And Christine Gibbon watched the video over and over
again with a group of friends during the 1985 Christmas
holiday, all of them adopting it as their film of the year,
and thus 1986 as their 'year for getting' − following
Scarlett's example in the life, college and job changes
which were to come.

Christine Gibbon and friends are not alone in using
GWTW as an inspirational text for life changes, and
many of the letters and questionnaires I received describe
it as a source of comfort, strength and support in key
moments and periods of women's lives. So strongly associated is GWTW with special relationships and times
that it is frequently referred to as an 'old friend'. Two
letters illustrate this well. Margaret Andrews, working
away from home for the first time at nineteen, became
very homesick: 'However, I saw that GWTW was showing, and rushed off to see all my old friends. This seemed

to cure my homesickness.' Gillian Darward wrote lyrically of her copy of *GWTW*, received on her eighteenth birthday:

> I still have that copy — now well thumbed, tear-stained, tea-stained, beer-stained, tomato-sauce-stained, as it saw me through my student days at teacher training college in Aberdeen. It was here that my close friends and I became firm devotees. The memories! — of gin-sodden readings of the book, afternoon viewings at the fleapit, when we should have been at education lectures . . . With the advent of the video, *GWTW* afternoons are sheer delight. Food, sherry, hankies in the middle of the floor, silence only broken by eating and crying noises.

For a great many of my respondents *GWTW* has a life of its own, and is held in their affections with a passionate loyalty. Like a good friend (and more reliable than most) it has seen many through sleepless nights, times of trouble and loneliness, sexual and emotional frustration and longing, as well as national and personal turmoil.

For some readers, the memory of their first encounter with *GWTW* gives it a treasured place in their personal histories. It is most closely associated with erotically charged moments or decisive/key points in sexual and family relationships; the film is often recalled fondly because it was seen on a first date with a special girl- or boyfriend and/or wife/husband-to-be. Jennifer Parkhouse is not unusual in saying that the film 'clarified the idea of the man I would want to seek as a partner' (though several suggest it was hard for *any* man to measure up to Rhett Butler . . .), while another respondent writes that after her first viewing she asked her current lover to marry her: 'He turned me down, but at least I asked!' Mrs K.I. Thompson received the book in September 1938 and was still trying to finish it on the morning of her wedding, since it was too heavy to take on honeymoon; she does not specify what effect it had on her early days of married life.

From my correspondence it is clear that *GWTW* has also helped many a baby into the world, especially in the 1940s and 50s when women were kept in hospital for as long as two weeks after the birth, with plenty of time to read. Kate Fowler, who read it during labour, describes it as a 'wonderful antidote to childbirth', though the very vivid scene in which Melanie gives birth is the reason Rosette Besman's mother did not want her to see the film, in case it made her afraid to have children. By contrast, Pearl Parsons introduces a humorous note in her description of a hospital stay while recovering from a hysterectomy:

> I was thrilled [with *GWTW*] until the groans from other like sufferers to myself caused me to cover the title up when I was reading it, for wind is one of the worst after-effects of this particular operation.

For younger women, especially those reading the book or seeing the film in the 1930s or 40s, its risqué and sexually charged elements are most cherished, particularly when the work was forbidden by adults. It seems *GWTW* was a brown-paper-cover text in some homes and schools. Joan Hubbold's mother was horrified to find her reading such a 'disgusting' book, while two other correspondents describe choosing *GWTW* – one with a book token present, the other as a school prize – along with a sober Christian text to appease disapproving adults. When the film first came out the Catholic Church granted it a 'B' rating, indicating that it was 'morally objectionable in part for all' because of 'the low moral character, principles and behaviour of the main figures as depicted in the film'. (By 1968 the Church had considerably tempered its view, describing *GWTW* as 'morally unobjectionable for adults and adolescents'.)[2] It is not surprising, therefore, that Matilda Popper was lectured at her convent school about the film's 'immoral nature', while a rota of prefects was drawn up to prevent any girl slipping off to the local cinema. Matilda writes that this proscription 'made [the film's] name stick in my mind and it represented for me the choicest of forbidden fruit, so I determined to see it at the first possibility'.

By contrast, however, a few women of the same generation see *GWTW* as a restrained and decorous work, especially in the light of sexually explicit material in current literature, film and television. Enid Measures speaks for several when she writes that her enjoyment of the film stems from the fact that 'it is a family type and causes no uncomfortable feelings when watching with members of the family . . . Very few films of this type are made nowadays.' Shirley Robinson, deploring the 'present trash' on our screens, praises its erotic suggestiveness. Describing Scarlett sitting up in bed the morning after Rhett's violent but satisfying lovemaking, she says she is 'smiling like the cat who has been at the cream, and that smile says far more about the preceding night than all the "explicit" scenes in today's films.'

Several women admit to having modelled themselves on or identified strongly with Scarlett O'Hara, to such an extent that families joke about the obsession. One young woman gets birthday cards addressed to 'Katie Scarlett' and looks forward to marrying in a Scarlett dress, while another (fourteen years old) astonished her mother by sobbing uncontrollably throughout the film, sharing in Scarlett's unrequited love. Other women have clearly been strengthened through identification with Scarlett. Many echo the words of Francesca

Sullivan: 'I think as a girl I held up Scarlett as a kind of model for myself, especially in regard to her "never give up" sentiments', and of Annes Gruffydd:

> I have reread the book on numerous occasions and seen the film as often as possible. I have the record of the film music which I play constantly. I find all three very therapeutic activities . . . Scarlett's 'I'll think about it tomorrow' and 'Tomorrow is another day' I have found useful maxims during the last twenty years.

In two different but complementary accounts we can see the impact of *GWTW* on a woman's determination and decision-making. In both cases, a close identification with Scarlett gave the viewer a strong sense of her own power. Mrs Edith D. Taylor first saw the film in the early 1940s while she was training at Newcastle General Hospital: 'I did see in Scarlett part of myself. In my case, a grim determination to obtain my nursing examinations and "get somewhere".' By contrast, Pat v.t. West was training at The Hospital for Sick Children, Great Ormond Street, London:

> I was trying to impress both sides of the family by following in the two most admired aunts' footsteps by taking up nursing. I couldn't abide wearing the uniform . . . and couldn't abide the lack of understanding generally extended to hospitalised children. Also, I was terrified of the responsibility most of the time and intimidated by ferocious ward sisters.
>
> I saw Scarlett O'Hara enter that barn, take one look at the wounded men – and walk out! That was a real turning point in my life. I realised in an instant that you could walk away from illness and from what everyone expected of you. I guess it was my first real anarchist moment. I promptly threw

in the towel and left after two and a half years of misery.

Changing Perspectives

Comforting, strengthening, erotically stimulating, liberating ... *GWTW* has been all these and more for different women in various situations and moments, but we also need to recognise that such impressions or feelings are not static and may alter over time. In women's intellectual and emotional growth there is often a shift over years in perceptions of *GWTW*, or perhaps a set of personal or family tensions which prevent unalloyed enthusiasm. For some women life experience enhances their appreciation, perhaps especially after the deaths of close family members (in particular a mother or daughter, making resonant the deaths of Ellen and Bonnie Blue) and the subtlety ('true-to-life' quality often described) of the ending – often resented in adolescence – is appreciated fully in adult life. For some, age diminishes enthusiasm. A few older women express irritation at the immature, headstrong Scarlett with whom they had identified so closely when young, and some women have to maintain an enthusiasm often against considerable hostility or derision from family and friends. Suzanne Newell's obsession is treated as a joke by her nearest and dearest, so she never admits to rereading the novel and watches the video when no one is around (something shared by Margaret French, who can enjoy it only if she can watch without the presence of 'a cynical husband and teenage son who think it is awful').

For several women a change of heart towards *GWTW* has come from altered perspectives on issues of race: more than one woman claimed to have shifted her views on the black characters and treatment of slavery over the

years in which she had been a fan. For younger, anti-
racist feminists, conflicts arise over mingled responses to
the work itself. Reina Lewis describes the 'palm-tingling
kick' she gets out of book and film, and the hours she
spends theorising over why so many feminists secretly
read what she calls reactionary heterosexual romance.
Lise Fox speaks for several correspondents:

> It is racist, sexist and twee. The slavery, links with
> 'the Klan', the treatment of Blacks and women
> (especially the black women) go against all of my
> political beliefs, and I wince inwardly. But – my
> love of the cinema in general will not let me forget
> that technically it's brilliant and a great achieve-
> ment in cinema history. It is a good piece of work
> . . . I will still defend it wholeheartedly. I regard it
> as a private vice almost, because I am active in so-
> called 'left-wing' activities such as CND [Campaign
> for Nuclear Disarmament] etc; and have always
> regarded myself as a feminist.

Pat Read finds shameful GWTW's 'apologia for the
activities of the KKK' (not named in the film, as she
points out). She reflects, though, that

> it is probably a historically correct, though not
> honestly slanted, record of the attitudes of those
> times and . . . those attitudes were as much
> a part of the period as Scarlett's 16½-inch waist
> and pantalettes. God knows, the world still suffers
> because of racism, but to make it sound so
> attractive, so honourable, so reasonable is very
> sinister.

But racism-awareness is not the main reason my
correspondents gave for a change of mind toward
GWTW. Most often, women record a disappointment
at the film re-viewed on television – an understandable
sense of the diminished nature of a work they had

recalled as monumental, impressive, sweepingly epic, and so on. Of course, the experience of *GWTW* in 35mm on a large cinema screen in the dark is by definition a much more awe-inspiring experience than *GWTW* on a twenty-inch television screen in a well-lit, busy family living-room. It is hard to blame the film itself for that reduced sense of grandeur (though it is an interesting reflection on the new video generation and the problems of watching films designed for large cinema screens on a small domestic television set). There is also the problem of communal home viewing: the intense *private* pleasure of a woman's memory of the film is often spoiled by family television viewing, which not only prevents total individual absorption in the screen but also often colours her response. Irene Beenham describes this well. After detailing her passionate involvement in the *film*, she tells of sitting her daughters in front of the television:

> But as it unfolded, it seemed to have shrunk in stature to fit the screen. The dialogue seemed corny, the colour wasn't bright, the sounds were 'tinny'. The family started to fidget, make jokes about it, and before long I had to reach forward and turn off what had been a small but very bright and emotive part of my growing up.

The poignancy of that sense of loss is echoed by several respondents, while for those who still feel as they once did about *GWTW*, the knowledge of its being there as an 'old friend' is crucial.

*   *   *

In these days of mass marketing and video outlets for film distribution other books have sold more copies, and other films have grossed greater profits with larger audiences. But fairly consistently over a half-century, *Gone*

With the Wind has established what looks like being a permanent place in popular imagination and memory. And through various commercial and private means, it has acquired a host of public and individual meanings and associations which ensure its longevity.

It is time, then, to examine this phenomenon in closer detail. As we have seen from these vignettes and brief quotations, *GWTW* offers many different identification points and sources of pleasure to women of a variety of ages, class and educational backgrounds. In the following pages I shall focus on aspects of book and film in order to explain its enormous impact on the female reader and film-goer. The issues I have selected are those to which my correspondents returned most frequently, and on which they have the strongest views. So there are chapters on that most fascinating figure, Scarlett O'Hara; on the problematic and compulsive nature of the hero and the inconclusive ending; and on the black characters and racial issues which are deeply controversial and for many reader-viewers disturbing. Finally, I shall explore women's general attitudes to historical novels and films, and our specific response to *GWTW*'s angle on the past – with a sideways glance at the tourism and heritage industry's exploitation of Margaret Mitchell and her book.

First, however, I want to discuss the woman at the heart of this fascinating phenomenon. Margaret Mitchell has been the subject of many biographies, articles, and television and radio programmes; two volumes of her letters (though alas, no autobiography) are in print. In my discussion of Mitchell, I hope to explain why such a woman, writing in the late 1920s and 30s, could produce a text of such power for so many women readers. I shall discuss her in the context of her times, city, class, religion and race, and analyse the ways in which her own preoccupations, fears and perspectives to some extent determine women readers' responses.

Of the enormous body of critical writing about Mitchell and *GWTW*, most has been written by men unconcerned with feminist issues and unfamiliar with the women writers who influenced her and on whom she drew. My discussion of Mitchell will emphasise her connections with earlier women writers and with women's issues and problems. For it was no coincidence that Margaret Mitchell wrote so meaningfully to other women. She had good precedents for – and quite a lot of practice in – doing so.

3

The Woman Who Started it All: 'Margaret Mitchell of Atlanta'

I am Margaret Mitchell of Atlanta, author of 'Gone With the Wind'.

Long ago, I gave up thinking of 'Gone With the Wind' as my book; it's Atlanta's, in the view of Atlantians; the movie is Atlanta's film. (Margaret Mitchell, *Letters*)

As soon as it was published, *Gone With the Wind* was a huge critical and popular success. Its author, a modest ex-journalist housewife, was treated like a film star, besieged at her door by photographers, reporters and fans alike. 'Alas, where has my quiet peaceful life gone?' she cried, horrified at the loss of privacy and all the impertinent questions posed by her callers. For there was general curiosity about this woman – unprepossessing in appearance and dress, standing less than five feet tall, never before having published a novel – who had produced a monumental epic that was taking the world by storm. From the time of its first publication thousands of people have tried to establish who this one-book writer was and just how she came to write a blockbuster best-seller. And because of her desire to protect herself and family, and her reluctance to indulge in self-disclosure, Margaret Mitchell succeeded in tantalising readers, critics and friends until her death in 1949, and ever since has puzzled her biographers.[1]

Margaret Mitchell claimed to hate all the intrusions and trappings of fame, yet she never hired an agent to handle enquiries and visitors and for ten years after the book appeared did not get an unlisted phone number. As numerous accounts suggest, Margaret Mitchell felt both humble and self-effacing, and also extremely proud and possessive about her creation: on the one hand, refusing to allow interviews or biographical articles and denying co-operation with the film's producer; on the other, writing long, angry letters to people who commented on her and her book, and taking a keen and quite manipulative interest in the progress of the film, casting of stars and accuracy of accent and setting.

While she wrote no autobiography, at college Mitchell wrote a series of revealing letters to a friend, Allen Edee, and from the time *Gone With the Wind* came out to her death thirteen years later she sent approximately 20,000 letters to fans, critics, friends and strangers. Several of the letters begin with the sentence 'I am Margaret Mitchell of Atlanta, author of "Gone With the Wind" ' and, as both her biographers suggest, in many ways the story of *GWTW* 's genesis and success is the story of Mitchell's own life. This is especially true since she was the product of a staunchly patriotic upper-middle-class white Atlanta family and apparently recorded the sufferings and triumphs of her own class, to which she had listened for hours on Atlanta porches, and even more so since she never wrote another work of fiction but spent her life – as she put it – 'cleaning up after *GWTW* '.[2] The biographers see her life as leading towards and, in many ways, culminating in the publication of a book she worked on over ten years. Anne Edwards, her most recent biographer, argues that at this point Mitchell ceased to grow, intellectually and emotionally, so the logic of her life was simply to respond to and deal with *GWTW* 's correspondents, foreign rights deals, and hangers-on.

Peggy Mitchell and Pansy O'Hara

Margaret Mitchell's life was one of considerable contrasts and crises, heavily punctuated by the illnesses and vulnerability of herself and her family, and from 1936 to 1949 – when she died (as she had predicted) in a road accident – one dominated by the book and film. Born in 1900, she had grown up in a lawyer's family, prosperous and proud of its Confederate ancestors and long residence in Atlanta. Her maternal grandparents had refused to flee the city in the Civil War; their house had been used as an army hospital. Her great-aunts, who lived in a farm near Jonesboro, Clayton County (the setting for Tara), were great raconteurs of Georgia's history and recent past. As a child she was taken to parades commemorating Atlanta's Confederate dead, taught Civil War songs and details of battles, and forced to listen for hours to discussions of battle wounds, gangrene smells, the burning of Atlanta by the notorious General Sherman, and the sufferings of the postwar 'Reconstruction' period. As she said in a radio broadcast, 'I heard everything in the world except that the Confederates lost the war'.[3] This pride in the South, the state of Georgia, and the family's home city, Atlanta, remained with Margaret Mitchell all her life and gave personal and political motivation for the writing of GWTW. In many other ways too, 'Peggy' (as she was called by the family) was a loyal daughter of the Old South, who learned well the lessons of Southern belle-ism and who, in the second half of her life, settled down to a conventional Southern lady's lot – devoted daughter, non-working wife and charitable tender of the sick and needy (though her many illnesses tell their own tale of how difficult such accommodation was . . .).

But if she became in later years an uneasy version of Melanie Wilkes, she certainly lived through experiences characteristic of Scarlett O'Hara. Raised by her conservative parents to become a debutante and dilettante who would live, even after marriage, in the parental home, Peggy rebelled in both small and – in the case of her first marriage – major ways. She grew up to share her family's enthusiasm for local history and affairs, and after a brief period away at Smith College in Northampton, Massachusetts, lived in Atlanta near her family all her life. Her mother died when she was in her freshman year at Smith, so she returned to become housekeeper to father Eugene and brother Stephens. For the next couple of years she was both dutiful daughter and also debutante and small-time flapper, hosting parties and causing a stir with her considerable capacity for alcohol, tobacco, flirting and wild dancing. After an Apache dance for which she dressed in a slit satin shirt and black stockings she was snubbed by the ladies of an important social club, the Junior League (and got her own back years later by snubbing them at the *GWTW* première).

Among the many men circulating around her were two flatmates who were both to marry Peggy Mitchell: Red Upshaw, dashing and sexually vibrant bootlegger, and John Marsh, worthy, bookish and puritanical journalist and later publicist. Red and Peggy married on 2 September 1922, but a few months later the marriage was over; it seems that Red's alcoholism led him to abuse his wife, and there were disputes over a previous relationship and Peggy's insistence that they live with her father. With the collapse of their marriage and Red's departure, Peggy's interest in insecure and exciting affairs seemed to die – especially when, after a few months, Red returned to Atlanta and assaulted (or probably raped) Peggy in her own bedroom. Although she was traumatised, she was shaken into taking herself in hand and abandoning her somewhat dilettantish way of life. She persuaded the male-dominated *Atlanta Journal* to hire her as a cub reporter; from December

1922 until May 1926 she worked there full-time, with considerable success. For a while she continued to work after her marriage, in 1925, to the man who had been best man at her first wedding, John Marsh – by contrast with the shiftless Red, he worked in the public relations department of Georgia Power and Light Company. But it seems clear from the biographies and Mitchell's letters that both partners agreed John should work to support them and Peggy should quit her job. Even though she enjoyed its stimulation and the local recognition she received, Mitchell managed to twist an ankle so that continuing to work became too painful. For the rest of her life she blamed her own illnesses and accidents, as well as those of her family and friends, for her inability first to work outside the home, then – after the success of *GWTW* – to write anything else.

Biographers point to the obvious connections between Peggy Mitchell's own life and elements of *GWTW*. There is the similarity between the two main characters' names to Peggy and Red: Pansy (Scarlett's original name) and Rhett. Red Upshaw seems a clear model for Rhett Butler in terms of his unpredictable, passionate and violent behaviour and his ability to survive through lucrative illegal activities – bootlegging and blockade-running. His sexual abuse towards her is mirrored in Rhett's use of force in the marital bed – though the novel reports Scarlett's pleasure, very different from the trauma which biographer Anne Edwards describes. Pansy/Scarlett was, like Peggy Mitchell, torn between very different definitions of Southern womanhood, and felt herself uncomfortable with the attitudes of her time to femininity. Melanie is modelled on many of Peggy's contemporaries in Atlanta, while Ellen is a transparent tribute to her dead mother, Maybelle. Gerald O'Hara's distraught near-madness, witnessed by Scarlett returning to Tara from Atlanta, parallels the state in which Peggy found her father, Eugene, after returning from Smith to her mother's funeral. After Maybelle's death Peggy had to pick up the pieces of the family household and her own life, just as Scarlett has to do . . . and so on.

There are many such personal parallels to delight a biographer, and of course there are the local and national parallels beloved by critics. Although the novel was written in the 1920s and published in the 1930s, many felt that Mitchell was writing an inspirational novel for the Depression, to assure those who had endured the Wall Street Crash of 1929 and its aftermath that they would survive to face 'another day'. Others applauded *GWTW* for its warning against rising communism and its adherence to the old values and bourgeois morality. The radical press saw ominous signals in terms of the revival of the Ku Klux Klan in Atlanta, and the publication of this book (like the national showings of the pro-Klan film *The Birth of a Nation*) as a revived incitement to racial hatred. One might equally see the novel as a response to and reaction against women's new rights and the emergence of the 'new woman' in the 1920s. With women gaining the vote for the first time after World War I, Scarlett seems both to celebrate those liberated desires and powers and also to sound a cautionary note against the hardened flapper who thought she could have her cake and eat it too.

Disruption, Crisis and Survival

In a revealing letter written – but never mailed – to a young man who wrote to Margaret Mitchell to complain of the lack of security his generation could enjoy, the author of *GWTW* replied in ringing Margaret Thatcher-like tones. Scolding her correspondent for wishing for a state she felt was appropriate only for 'the old and the tired', she generalises at length about the history of the United States, her ancestors, her generation as well as the young man's. Risk-taking, insecurity, hazard were all that the early pioneers, 'the youngsters who went out with Washington', those in the '49 Gold Rush, even 'the girls who came from sheltered homes' of her youth, expected and wanted. Speaking, as she often does, in personal terms, she describes her ancestors in the Revolutionary War, the 1812 War, the Seminole Indian troubles, the Civil War, and so on as 'a tough and hard-bitten lot', risk-takers who never sought security. Her own mother is cited as one who 'would have laughed' at the idea of security in youth, as she married in the mid-1890s panic, lived through the panics of 1907 and 1914, and – with Mitchell's generation – experienced a war which led them to see 'the Victorian Age crash about our feet'. She then writes bitterly of her correspondent's generation, who – through Franklin D. Roosevelt's New Deal – have come to expect that the world owes them a good living, and have lost the 'courage and daring' she feels appropriate to the young.

The obsessive tone and defensive length of this letter suggest to me that Mitchell is haranguing herself for the opting out she chose as her security net. Her 'safe' marriage, leaving a job which was posing challenges she failed to meet, and her resolutely domestic and family-centred lifestyle, represent kinds of cowardice which she obviously despised. And that lack of generosity to and impatience with youth also betray her conservatism and the pomposity of a mature adult who resented the privileges she saw younger people enjoying – especially when she felt her own youth to have been rudely curtailed through deaths of loved ones, a World War, Prohibition, the Crash and Depression, not to mention the failure of a violent marriage and the settling for a comfortable, if dull partnership. This was also a woman who, out of fear of her first husband, kept a loaded pistol by her bed each night until his death by suicide and who, in her journalist days, was struck by 'the sad things and the horrible things that go on in the world'.[4]

On the surface, it seems that Margaret Mitchell wrote *GWTW* from an assurance – even arrogance – about her own class, race and sex. The novel recounts the sufferings, defeats and triumphs of a white upper-middle-class elite who are seen as the main targets of a vengeful Northern government and army, but rise again and reassert themselves. Mitchell's ancestors were among those people, and it is easy to read *GWTW* as a kind of celebratory autobiographical family and class chronicle. But the book, unlike the film, makes an argument which it develops throughout, and which becomes more strident towards the end – an argument about the nature and value of 'the old days' and the ways Southerners should cope with them; and especially how Scarlett, embodiment of female survival, should now live. The book has a defensive air which indicates Mitchell's lack of security and need to work out questions and dilemmas specific to her, and special to her class and race.

A clue to this is given in a letter Mitchell wrote shortly after the book was published. Writing to the critic Henry Steele Commager (who had praised *GWTW* in print), she commends him for selecting as significant Rhett's words about Ashley's 'breed' being useless and valueless 'in an upside-down world like ours'.[5] She says that these words, which she put into Rhett's mouth and which go on to discuss the way worlds turn upside down and people have to begin again with their own resources (of which Ashley has none), were spoken to her originally by her mother. When she was six years old, she claims, Maybelle drove her down the road ('the road to Tara') past ruined houses, telling her that the secure world in which families had lived there had exploded beneath them: 'And she told me that my own world was going to explode under me,

some day, and God help me if I didn't have some
weapon to meet the new world.' Maybelle's lecture
(at least in her daughter's version) was typically spiked
with feminist fervour, urging Peggy to get an education
so that she could always cope with life. With typical
self-deprecation, Mitchell writes that she was impressed
enough by those words to learn enough rhetoric to get
a newspaper job.

In the following paragraph she credits Commager
with observing that Scarlett wanted to be her mother's
daughter but was not. In many ways Mitchell was
haunted by the fact that she was not Maybelle's dutiful
daughter, and she seems to have felt judged, if only
by her mother's memory. She was conscious of the
ways in which she differed from her strict, feminist
Catholic mother (her truncated, undistinguished college
education, marriage to a non-Catholic alcoholic, her
frowned-on divorce and her traditional second marriage
in which, without children, she seemed to become a
cipher of others' problems, something her mother's
deathbed letter warned her against). But Mitchell had
listened well to her mother and internalised Maybelle's
lessons about femininity, even if she did not act on them
all. At one level, *GWTW* seems to me an exploration
of her mother's profound sense of the insecurity of
Southern white female middle-class existence, and how
it had to be sustained by the unreliable status and
economic power of white men in a city notorious for
its rapid growth and unstable social and racial identity.

Maybelle came from a Catholic family which had
endured religious prejudice in Protestant Clayton
County where they settled, and whose parents had
stayed put in the Atlanta Sherman was burning to
the ground. Family stories, told endlessly on porches,
were all about dramatic turns of event and fortune
in a state and city which had experienced massive
recent disruptions. And Maybelle Mitchell had learned

of hardship not merely from her parents' dramatic wartime exploits. Shortly after marrying Eugene, who seemed an economically promising choice of husband, she watched him lose a great deal of money in the 1893 depression; Eugene's lack of commercial resourcefulness and daring was a source of constant irritation. After her death, during the 1920s, Eugene got into further troubles because the boll weevil devastated Georgia's fields, drastically cutting cotton production and causing a severe agricultural depression. As a result, financial institutions were badly hit and his speciality of real-estate contracts was not in great demand.

In 1917, the year the USA finally declared war on Germany, Atlanta experienced an ominous rerun of 1864. A major fire swept through the city, and although it claimed only one life it destroyed the Mitchell family's old house and eleven houses owned by Maybelle's mother. According to biographer Anne Edwards, the family suffered perhaps greater financial losses than any other, and Margaret played an active role at the refuge centre set up to reunite families and treat the injured. In 1918 her fiancé, Clifford Henry, with whom she had enjoyed a brief romantic affair, was killed by a German bomb, and in early 1919 Maybelle died of flu as Peggy made her way home from Smith to her bedside.

By the age of nineteen, as her mother had predicted, Margaret Mitchell had experienced her world exploding beneath her. She was thrust into the position of being virtual head of a household, organising the ailing family finances because her father was distraught and enfeebled by his wife's death. This followed two important deaths in six months (she had been present at neither, so grieving was delayed), the uncertainties and problems of a war – albeit on a smaller scale and on different soil from the Civil War – and failure to make much of her educational opportunities at Smith College. Difficulties with her father and the friction (and brief breakdown of relations) between Margaret and her imperious grandmother, Annie, were a constant reminder of the fragility of family harmony and the need for vigilance in close relationships. 'Survival', managing to 'turn in a good performance' and caring for yourself before (but not without regard for) family obligations were the lessons Maybelle wanted her daughter to learn. She warned the young Margaret: 'You are seeing the end of an era', and urged her to enjoy it to the utmost. This fatalistic and stoical philosophy was one Margaret Mitchell relied on for the rest of her life and used to chronicle the fortunes of her Southern women ancestors in *GWTW*.

Margaret Mitchell and the Klan

But there were other explosions and threats to survival in the young adult Mitchell's life, and these provided an important focus for the racial subtext of *GWTW*. Many commentators have pointed out the fact that *GWTW* takes a line on the causes of the Civil War (1861–65), the nature of the slave-turned-freedman, and the development of the Ku Klux Klan. Like other Southerners of her generation, Margaret Mitchell subscribed to the views of a number of turn-of-the-century historians (including Woodrow Wilson, John Ford Rhodes and William A. Dunning) who had described that period of 'Radical Reconstruction' after the War in terms of vicious Northern Carpetbaggers and scalawags, insolent, violent Blacks, and heroic Ku Klux Klansmen who saved white womanhood and Southern honour from despoliation.[6] Despite the publication of many revisionary and opposing accounts, this line on the War became received wisdom for the first sixty years of the twentieth century, undermined authoritatively only by the work of 1950s and 60s historians, especially C.

Vann Woodward. Woodward and others demonstrated
that the years following the Civil War and emancipation
of slaves saw the victory of aggressive Southern Whites
determined to prevent racial equality – economic, social
and educational – through the use of illegal and violent
measures to ensure the restoration of white power.
Mitchell, like many others, swallowed the Wilson-
Rhodes-Dunning line and used it polemically in her
novel. The film, significantly, is far less politically
strident than the novel, since David Selznick – a liberal
Jew – was sensitive to criticisms from black and radical
groups that a film glorifying the Klan was inappropriate
in the late 1930s.

In only one published letter does Margaret Mitchell
venture her own views about the Ku Klux Klan.[7] In
response to a letter asking whether the Klan's sole purpose was to protect Southern women she referred to
the many histories of the Klan, saying that it began
by protecting women and children, then was used to
keep Negroes from multiple voting at elections. But
she argues that it was 'used equally against the Carpetbaggers who had the same bad habit where voting was
concerned' – a stand against 'unscrupulous or ignorant
people' who might seek office in the South. Giving
the example of South Carolina as a state that suffered
from 'corrupt and ignorant officials', she endorses the
Klan's intervention to prevent Negro judges or gover-
nors. Although this is Mitchell's only direct reference
to the rights and wrongs of the Ku Klux Klan, in a
later letter she says revealingly: 'As I had not written anything about the Klan which is not common
knowledge to every Southerner, I had done no research
upon it.'[8] Since she researched and cross-checked every
other historical detail with some care, this confidence
in her knowledge is startling. It does, however, bear
out my point that Mitchell, like her contemporaries,
had accepted as gospel the Wilson-Rhodes-Dunning

version of Reconstruction and the Klan's development, and drew deeply on that accepted, 'common-sense' version of Southern racial history.

But I would suggest that Mitchell's unconscious attitude to the Klan, as revealed in *GWTW*, is more complex and problematic. The Ku Klux Klan of the Reconstruction period was a movement directed primarily and specifically at the *Negro*, though motivated, as Mitchell says, by a bitter resentment towards the North's white as well as black 'Carpetbagger' intervention in Southern political and social life. It was an underground guerrilla movement of white men who attempted to intimidate black voters and workers by night rides and home visits, flaunting robes and hoods to stir up black fears, burning churches and homes, and engaging in rapes, assaults and lynchings. The Klan's popularity was mainly spent by the turn of the century, especially after the restoration of white domination and the withdrawal of Northern legislators and imposed black judges, politicians and so on.

But in 1915, the Klan – originally a rural movement – moved into cities as far apart as Dallas and Detroit. Its revival was spearheaded in Margaret Mitchell's home city, Atlanta. Atlanta – a city which has boasted in recent years that it is 'too busy to hate' – was the scene of a very serious week-long race riot in 1906, when Peggy Mitchell was six years old. This followed an election for governor in which racial prejudice was stirred up by the candidates, as well as the recent sensational reporting by some local newspapers of black men's assaults on white women. In the riot, twelve people (ten of them black) were killed, while seventy (ten white) were injured.[9] This was both a reminder of the rumbling racial frictions which existed in the city, and also an ominous early taste of the city's later racial violence.

Although the Klan had not originated in Georgia, its

second and third phases, in 1915 and 1946, began in
Atlanta. In 1915 'Colonel' William J. Simmons rededicated the Klan on Stone Mountain, just outside Atlanta
– a large granite mass on which, a year later, the United
Daughters of the Confederacy commissioned a carving
of a Confederate memorial (a site to which Margaret
Mitchell proudly took her editor, Harold Latham, on
his first visit to the city). Atlanta became 'the imperial
city of the Invisible Empire',[10] setting up a national
office on Peachtree, the street where the Mitchells
lived, a few doors away from the *Atlanta Journal* offices
where Margaret worked and where she sited the house
Rhett Butler built for his bride, Scarlett O'Hara.

While it was a predominantly blue-collar, lower-
middle-class movement which alienated professionals
such as Eugene Mitchell, nevertheless the highly
successful Klan encountered little public opposition
in Atlanta. The Klan contributed a fair amount to
the city's economy, employing many workers at its
headquarters, printing works and robe factory, and its
frequent conventions brought in welcome revenue. It
first went public in 1919, marching behind Civil War
veterans in a Confederate parade, the kind of parade
the young Peggy Mitchell had often attended with
her patriotic family. In 1922, while her marriage
was breaking up and she was considering a career as
journalist, the Klan held two Klonventions, attracting
thousands of Klanmen to parades, pilgrimages and
barbecues at Stone Mountain. That year the Klan
approached the height of its power and influence,
claiming millions of members. Throughout the 1920s
it was said to enjoy as much support in the USA as
organised labour, and it was a major force in securing
passage of the 1924 Immigration Restriction Act. In
1923 Atlanta had a mayor, governor, senator and
Supreme Court judge who were 'Kluxters'; its city
government and police department were thoroughly

infiltrated. It was in the Atlanta of 1921 that reporter
Rowland Thomas began his investigations into the Klan's
national influence, and his newspaper *The World* began
its campaign against the Klan which resulted in an
abortive congressional investigation and massive new
recruitment of Kluxters.[11] And all this coincided with
the 'Forward Atlanta' campaign, which boasted of the
city's relatively harmonious race relations.

Margaret Mitchell had no need to read histories
of the Klan because from childhood she had been
steeped in Southern versions of the Klan's foundation.
The girl who had learned to sing Confederate songs
like 'I'm a Good Old Rebel and That's What I Am'
had also dramatised the novel *The Traitor*, written by
Thomas Dixon, one of the most blatantly racist of the
Southern white apologists. Dixon's novels, including
The Traitor, celebrated the white South and focused
on the rise of the Ku Klux Klan. The subtitles of his
three most famous novels (*The Leopard's Spots*, 1903;
The Clansman, 1905; and *The Traitor*, 1907) reveal
his obsession: *A Romance of the White Man's Burden
– 1865–1900*, *An Historical Romance of the Ku Klux
Klan*, and *A Story of the Fall of the Invisible Empire*.
The Clansman is dedicated to his uncle, 'Grand Titan
of the Invisible Empire Ku Klux Klan'. Dixon's novels
glorifying the white-dominated South came out at a
time when racial feelings were running high (as the
Atlanta riots testify) and were among a group of public
lectures and books which were stirring up Southern
white racism. Blacks were portrayed as degraded and
bestial, in works with titles such as 'The Negro a Beast'
and *The Negro, A Menace to American Civilization*.
The educator Thomas Pearce Bailey drew up a 'racial
creed of the Southern people' which included white
domination, Teutonic race purity, and the right of the
South to settle the Negro question in its own way.
There was much nostalgia around for the period of

'Redemption', the last years of the nineteenth century in which a white Democrat South got its own back on the Northern Carpetbag government.[12]

The year before Atlanta's race riots, a dramatic version of Dixon's *The Clansman* was a huge hit in the city. Ten years later the silent film version by D.W. Griffith – originally called *The Clansman*, then resonantly renamed *The Birth of a Nation* – was screened there to huge cheering audiences. This film, seen to date by over fifty million people, had an instant and continuing success in the South of the 1920s and 30s, and helped to justify and glorify the activities of the newly rededicated Klan. This was not surprising, as the book and film argued that – contrary to historical facts about Whites' intimidation and violence towards largely impoverished and demoralised freed Blacks (though consistent with the versions circulating in his time) – Reconstruction Whites were at the mercy of violent Blacks. Griffith's freed Black, if loyal to his or her former master, is gentle and enduring, but if fleeing from him he appears sinister, ruthless, greedy and insolent. As state legislators impose on the South, ignorant Blacks eat and drink with their feet on the desk, while impoverished Whites are 'helpless'. The Freedmen's Bureau, set up by Congress to help Blacks adjust in the transitional period between slavery and freedom – in labour relations, medical, legal and educational matters – is 'the charity of a generous North misused to delude the ignorant'. Most significantly, the black man is always potentially, and sometimes actually, a rapist of white women. In *The Birth of a Nation* such a rape results in the young girl's suicide, with the Ku Klux Klan then processing with dignity in hoods and white robes as the only organisation fit to save the South from black-inspired anarchy.

Like thousands of her contemporaries, Margaret Mitchell was a great fan of this film. A report published in 1933 argued that it had had a major influence on children; it had been screened repeatedly across the country to enthusiastic audiences. With its vast epic and heroic scale, it almost certainly inspired Mitchell to write her own version of the War and its effects on Southern women in an epic and romantic-historical mode. And the line which *GWTW* takes on the Klan is remarkably similar to that in *The Birth of a Nation*. *GWTW* excited Thomas Dixon who, by the time of its publication, was writing novels in the same vein as his earlier work, but now with little success. He wrote to Margaret Mitchell praising her book and saying he wished to write a study of it (a project he never completed). She promptly replied with thanks for such enthusiasm, assuring him that she was 'practically raised on' his novels, which she loved very much. Mitchell was comfortable with justifications of the formation of the original Klan, and happy to continue in her own novel that conservative fictionalised version which Dixon, Griffith and others had already made familiar. It is no coincidence that she never wrote of the *second* phase of the Klan, with its close-to-home attacks not primarily on Blacks but precisely on people like her.

In what ways, then, was the second Klan a threat to Margaret and the Mitchell family? In the only oblique reference to the events of this period, Finis Farr quotes Stephens Mitchell saying that their father Eugene was not afraid to 'place-himself in danger of violence, at a time when Atlanta had dangerous mobs, and when riotings and lynchings were common'.[13] Anne Edwards describes the ascendancy of the Klan in the early 1920s as the 'self-styled vigilantes set fire to [Blacks'] churches, farms, and small businesses' and the family servant Cammie refused to go out after 7 p.m. or to walk near the Klan headquarters. Edwards describes the Klan's rebirth as creating 'a wave of anti-black, anti-Jewish, and anti-alien demonstrations'[14] — all of which is true. But what she does not mention is that the fierce 'anti-alien' (that is, new immigrant) feeling was largely anti-Catholicism.[15]

Unlike the first phase of the Klan, this second Atlanta-based movement was violently WASP (White Anglo-Saxon Protestant), more concerned to attack those groups – Jews, and especially Catholics – who were felt to be taking over 'American' society. Referring to that well-worn 'melting-pot' concept of a multiracial USA as a 'mess of sentimental pottage',[16] the mainly urban 'Klaverns' argued that a Romanist political uprising – led by 'a Dago Pope in Rome'[17] – was a possibility, and the Klan newspaper The Searchlight regularly attacked Catholic teachings. It even pointed to the 90 per cent of executed criminals it claimed had received the Last Sacrament as evidence of the dangers of a papist nation, and alleged that the men who had shot Presidents Lincoln, McKinley and Roosevelt were all Catholic. Along with this obsession it gained the support of American men, and especially women, by arguing not only for 'the tenets of the Protestant Christian religion' but also for 'pure womanhood': temperance, moral rigour, as opposed to 'modernism' – liquor, bootlegging, short skirts, dancing, petting in cars, and so on. As Kenneth Jackson put it, the Klan 'provided a focus for the fears of alienated native Americans whose world was being disrupted'.[18]

I have pointed out that Margaret Mitchell was living and working along the road from the national Klan headquarters, at the height of its success in the early 1920s, and that she had been raised a strict Catholic who had spurned the faith in order to enjoy a Jazz Age flapper-like social life of dance, illegal drinking and flirtation, culminating in a civil marriage to a violent, sexually experienced bootlegger. Both biographers describe the ways in which Mitchell's social and sexual wildness broke family taboos, especially upsetting her

Catholic grandmother and relatives (the wedding at home, presided over by an Episcopalian minister, was a family disgrace).

But neither biographer Finis Farr nor Anne Edwards explores the effect on her of Atlanta's rising Klan-dominated anti-Catholicism and moral panic. The Junior League snubbed her by not inviting her to join its exclusive women's social club – an unexpected blow, apparently because of Mitchell's ostentatious and flighty behaviour. Margaret's brother later claimed that this rejection, combined with her Catholic heritage, 'detracted from her marriageability'.[19] It seems that the Atlanta old guard, together with the new forces of reaction ushered in by Prohibition and the Klan, combined to intimidate the motherless socialite in ways which, along with her father's disapproval, profoundly affected her. In *GWTW* we can perhaps see more evidence of marginalisation, rebellion and repression than critics allow. In Scarlett O'Hara, Mitchell created a 'bad' Catholic girl and young woman in a predominantly WASP culture who breaks rules and taboos in order to survive. Is it not significant that at a period of intense Klan activity – directed as it was predominantly at her own people rather than Blacks – Mitchell should have returned to that much-fictionalised period of the Reconstruction South to justify the ways of the first-phase Klan to her fellows and to the South's detractors? By placing *racial* tension between black and white firmly back on the agenda, emphasising its tragic part in the South's history, Mitchell was in some ways fending off the immediate challenges which her own family – and, indeed, her own fragile marriageability – were facing in 1920s Atlanta. The book could be seen as a warning that white solidarity, regardless of religious or national origin, must be upheld in her racially tense region, state and city.

'Margaret Mitchell of Atlanta'

There seems little doubt about where Margaret
Mitchell's conscious – or at least public – intention
lay in writing her novel. In letter after letter she
refers to herself as 'Margaret Mitchell of Atlanta', a
'Southern author', 'Georgia author'; she makes it clear
that the praise she won from Southerners gave her most
pleasure. 'You see,' she wrote, 'this section has taken the
book to its heart and that is something which makes me
prouder than anything else.'[20] Indeed, Mitchell became
convinced that over the years *GWTW* not only took on a
life of its own but increasingly spoke for the South, which
guarded it jealously. In a letter to her Georgia friend
Susan Myrick (who was advising David Selznick on
Georgia dress, accents, and so on for the film) she joked
that it was only Susan's presence, and that of Georgia
Civil War expert Wilbur Kurtz in Hollywood, that was
preventing 'a violent Southern revolt'. She warned that
Selznick (who, not being Southern, 'knows nothing of
our psychology') had better not send the Kurtzes home
before they ensured absolute accuracy and authenticity
of Southern backgrounds:

> It sometimes seems to me that 'Gone With the
> Wind' is not my book any longer; it is something
> about which the citizens are sensitive and sore at
> real and fancied slights and discriminations and are
> ready to fight at the drop of a hairpin.[21]

The language of warfare, threats (however frivolous)
of the War between the States beginning all over again,
recur throughout the letters; Mitchell saw herself as
Southern spokesperson and as guardian of a Southern
legend which she felt was absolutely true to the historical
detail and spirit of the South's recent past. Writers all
remark on the extraordinary number of Mitchell's letters

to even casual correspondents, and to every favourable reviewer (usually before they wrote to her). As she kept carbon copies of most of these, you begin to understand how seriously she took her book and its contribution to general – not just Southern – knowledge about the War and the South's sufferings. She clearly saw her role as representative of that 'much-maligned Southland' which needed to be heard and understood by those outside – of whom she often spoke as if they were from a different planet.

This places her in a direct line with many nineteenth- and early-twentieth-century Southern women writers who also saw their role as representing the South, speaking for it to the world.[22] This not only dignified their fiction-writing with a solemn purpose (so they could justify taking it seriously) but also gave them a sense of having a role in their section, state and city – one which gained them considerable significance in the eyes of their peers. It also enabled them to escape from the label of sentimentalist or romance-writer, which would trivialise their reputation, and – if their work was received virtually as historical document – allowed them to attain that status of quasi-historian which is usually accorded to men. There is also a scent of battle fever in the air. *GWTW*, like other novels by largely forgotten Southern women writers, fought the Civil War all over again, but this time on the terms and through the eyes of a woman who could redefine the battle sites and the nature of physical and emotional sufferings involved. Note, for instance, Mitchell's pleasure at the critic Herschel Brickell's noticing the parallel between Scarlett O'Hara and Atlanta; she intended her embattled heroine and city to complement each other.

In terms of her own responses, as the first rush of success hit Margaret Mitchell shortly after publication, she dramatised in several letters her flight from Atlanta, bearing – she claimed – 'a typewriter, four murder novels, and five dollars' (an exaggeration; she also had at least a chequebook . . .). Driving around looking for somewhere quiet where she knew no one and could find some rest, alone, she enacted an exhilarating dash reminiscent of Scarlett's fleeing the city in flames. Also, by tapping out a series of letters describing this, she could see herself as a kind of battle reporter. It is tempting to see Margaret Mitchell's whole post-publication strategy in terms of war: she feels herself besieged (but stays put in her small apartment, answers the door, telephone and mail personally) and digs in, determined to continue to live and behave normally as if nothing had happened, just like those brave ladies of war-torn Atlanta. Her refusal to hand over matters of film, foreign and translation rights to an experienced agent, burdening her husband and herself with details they were often incompetent to handle, is a further example of the way Mitchell saw her role in historically significant terms.

It is easy to dismiss as personal greed her careful correspondence over foreign deals, but she claims to be fighting these for *all* writers, especially as she felt herself to be at the centre of a renaissance of Georgia writers for whom, in letters, she began to speak. The publication of *GWTW* came to be seen as a riposte to other kinds of popular representation (or misrepresentation) of the South available at the time. In a speech given at the Writers' Club, Macon, Georgia, she quoted a conversation with Harold Latham of Macmillan. When she told him she did not like Erskine Caldwell's *Tobacco Road* (1932), he said: 'If Southerners felt that they were maligned by such books as "Tobacco Road" why didn't they write books to show themselves as they truly were?' In the same speech, she asserted: 'We must tell the truth, we writers of the South, we must give a true interpretation of our section, and so set our

Southland right with the world.'[23] Besides, she wrote
most warmly and at greatest length to Southerners
– often in exile in the North – whom she called
'homefolks', upon whose opinions and sympathies she
felt she could count. The journalist Herschel Brickell,
and Clifford Dowdey and his wife Helen, received a
great many letters in which Mitchell unburdened her
feelings about fame, the reception of *GWTW*, and the
way non-Southerners were reading and criticising it.

Margaret Mitchell always assumed from these people
political agreement over the radical ('pinko') reviews of
book and film, and she had good reason to do so. The
Southern novelist Stark Young sent her – with a comment showing that he disagreed profoundly – Malcolm
Cowley's highly critical review in the radical magazine
New Republic, September 9, 1936. She replied that
when her Atlanta friends read Cowley's comments on
the book's celebration of the legend of the Old South
(a legend he called 'false in part and silly in part and
vicious in its general effect on Southern life today') they
would 'throw themselves on the sofa and laugh till they
cried'.[24] She also went on to say that she would be 'upset and mortified' if the left-wingers liked the book; the
reason she gave, significantly, was that had they done so,
'I'd have to do so much explaining to family and friends.'
Although this may have been intended as ironic, I think
it betrays yet again Mitchell's fiercely insular loyalty to
her region and Southern people. Those of different political or intellectual convictions could be dismissed and
laughed at because obviously they could not understand
the South and its concerns: 'Everything about the book
and the mind are abhorrent to all they believe in.' In
such ways we see how polemically Mitchell saw her
own work, and how defensive she was throughout her
life about the white South's version of its own history.

A Stickler for Detail

And she could never let go. Mitchell was obsessively anxious to be acknowledged as historically accurate in every detail of the book. Her husband John Marsh drew up a seventeen-page glossary of terms to ensure consistency of dialect, while she claimed that she could cite at least four published authorities for each non-fictional statement in the novel. She answered correspondents in response to such points as: a query about her reference to Federal desecration of Southern cemeteries (Mr K.T. Lowe, August 29, 1936); a criticism that she used a Mr Harry Slattery's surname for her poor white family (Mr Harry Slattery, October 3, 1936); a correction to her suggestion that iodine could be used as an antiseptic (Mr John Macleay, November 23, 1936). Seeing a student's paper alleging that Scarlett would not have known of the Confederate defeat at Jonesboro before leaving Atlanta, she triumphantly produced the record of a telegrapher, showing the exact time when the news reached the city . . .

Far from ignoring trivial or spiteful criticisms, Mitchell wrote long replies, often quoting pedantic chunks from her own published sources, which she had extensively checked in the months between manuscript acceptance and publication. She was obviously nettled at any suggestion that she had inadequately researched the tiniest detail and took great delight in sending stern, carefully illustrated letters by the dozen. Although she was unwilling to oversee script-writing or production details of the film it was she who suggested that Selznick should hire Susan Myrick and Wilbur Kurtz to ensure no gaffes were committed, and she took a certain malicious delight in commenting on the casting and on historical inaccuracies and flaws which appeared on the screen (such as the inappropriate columns of Tara, and the choice – unpopular with her and Southern friends – of

Clark Gable as Rhett). It seems that Mitchell was more delighted at the recognition she received for her accuracy of small detail (especially from those she respected, usually Southerners) than for her acute characterisation, plotting, and so on.

Margaret Mitchell is not unusual in this respect. Historical novelists of the South and Civil War have all been defensive about the accuracy of their research and the correctness of their minutest detail. Harriet Beecher Stowe, accused of inventing information about Southern states and plantation life for her 1852 novel *Uncle Tom's Cabin*, three years later published *A Key to Uncle Tom's Cabin*, in which she documented all her sources. Half a century later, Thomas Dixon offered to pay a thousand dollars to anyone who spotted an error of detail in his *The Clansman*. Alex Haley called his *Roots* (1976) 'faction', arguing its *spiritual* accuracy, but he – like Stowe – promised to publish a book which would authenticate his disputed and discredited historical sources. John Jakes's *North and South* (1982) contains an 'Afterword' in which Jakes defends his own 'accurate reflection' of the historical period and pre-empts criticism by admitting to 'minor alterations of the record in a few places' (and gives two specific examples, supplemented later in the 'Afterword' to his second volume, *Love and War*). William Styron, who in 1968 turned an already published pamphlet, 'The Confessions of Nat Turner', into a novel of the same title, attempted (very unsuccessfully) to avoid criticism over detail by arguing that his work was 'less an "historical novel" in conventional terms than a meditation on history'.[25]

In Margaret Mitchell, as with these other writers, there was a strong desire to control the way in which *GWTW* was read, received and translated into film. She cared deeply that she should be recognised as a serious historical researcher and writer, not as someone interested in making a fast buck out of sensationalist Southern fiction (like Caldwell). But it is curious that this focused so strongly on historical *detail*. Maybe it stemmed partly from a fear of not being taken seriously by her journalist peers, the literary critical establishment, and friends and acquaintances. Ironically, it is the last concern of any of the readers with whom I have corresponded. Historical accuracy may worry scholars, but for most women the book's satisfactions and problems are of a very different order.

Indeed, obsession with detail is something of more importance to the writer him/herself, the critic and scholar, than to the general reader. Like BBC producers assuring us that the lace used on a dress in a Jane Austen production is genuinely early 1800s, authenticity becomes a matter of professional pride and obsession rather than of popular importance. Many of my correspondents noted that the film excluded two of Scarlett's three children, but not, I feel sure, because that detail is of importance in itself: it is crucial to the characterisation of Scarlett throughout. Getting historical detail right – and proving it! – is no way of disarming criticism or directing a reader's response in the way you want. The historical, intellectual and emotional integrity and significance of a work go beyond the single detail and in many cases excuse considerable trivial inaccuracies. Moreover, history is not just 'there' to be written into fiction. But writers use the question of historical truth as a way of trying to control the impact of their novel or novel-made-film, and many who have fictionalised Southern themes – from Harriet Beecher Stowe to Grace King, Ellen Glasgow, Thomas Dixon and Margaret Mitchell – have had clear political intentions in doing so and have therefore been anxious to stake their claim to a serious hearing. (I will return to questions of historical accuracy and interpretation in chapter 8.)

Femininity and a Female Literary Tradition

Historical details may not concern my correspondents but issues of gender, sexuality, and especially femininity certainly do. And if we read closely Margaret Mitchell's biographies and letters, the conflicts and ambivalences within the writer herself are at the heart of her creation of a series of vividly imagined women characters, all of whom embody the various expectations and problems of the female condition, especially at a time of social and political crisis and change.

Mitchell was always happy in the company of boys and men, and her early training in listening to Civil War exploits made her good company for male family friends, colleagues on the *Atlanta Journal*, and social contacts. The daughter of an active feminist who took her to a woman's suffrage rally addressed by the renowned Carrie Chapman Catt, president of the National American Woman Suffrage Association, Peggy was raised both to behave decorously and fit into the social role of a Southern belle, and also to question male dominance and female subordination. Although she never discusses feminism in her (published) letters, and it seems to have been a subject she shied away from publicly, women's rights must have been on the agenda among her working women friends and the sophisticated social world of Atlanta in which she moved. Anne Edwards repeatedly describes Peggy's tendency to wear childlike or incongruous clothes and ugly orthopaedic shoes while protesting, after the success of *GWTW*, that she had no time to buy anything pretty. Add to this her liking for keeping up with men's heavy drinking; her pleasure in the male-dominated atmosphere of the *Atlanta Journal*; her writing of *GWTW* while dressed in eyeshades and men's trousers; and her dislike for traditional Southern female traits, those domestic skills of cooking and home decoration; her decision – apparently rational, because of John Marsh's epilepsy – not to have children . . . all these indicate that Margaret Mitchell was more her mother's daughter than she would openly admit. And although her letters never discuss her conflicts in terms of gender confusion, they do describe an irritable, exasperated, often desperate sense of being out of control of her own life ('a dynamo going to waste') – often expressed in terms of worries about the illnesses and physical ailments to which she and her loved ones seemed peculiarly prone.

More like a Victorian than a flapper, Mitchell spoke her dissatisfaction and confusion over her life and relationships in physiological terms and in ways which seem to have blocked any closer sharing or examination of the distress and sorrow which success and financial security brought her. Reminiscent of earlier Southern women writers, Mitchell expressed panic at the way she felt forced to go public: all her training as a Southern lady (despite Maybelle's suffragist speeches) had led her to seek self-effacement and privacy, a quietly supportive role as wife to a prominent professional man. As she wrote to Mrs Julia Collier Harris, the 'old-fashioned Southern way' dictated 'a lady's name appears in print only when she's born and buried'.[26]

Fame, and the extraordinary degree of visibility and public prominence this forced upon her, made Mitchell both complain and claim a loathing of the whole publicity machine, but also ensured that her intentions in writing *GWTW*, her views on its critics and fans and on its film interpretation, were heard indirectly or by stealth. Through those thousands of letters, many repeating the same points, Mitchell established a public persona – historically concerned, proud of her region and city, quiet, industrious, teetotal, devoted

daughter, wife and friend, and humble aspirant to
the ranks of great writer and celebrity. Unless more
personally revealing letters remain in the vaults of
the University of Georgia Margaret Mitchell Papers,
it seems that 'Margaret Mitchell of Atlanta' was a
persona well preserved. Rumours of divorce, plagiarism,
an acting role in the film were quickly scotched; it
appears that Mitchell tried hard to live the dull life
she described to correspondents, constantly aware of
the imminence of catastrophes, small or large, usually
in the form of accident or illness. Just as *GWTW*
itself ends inconclusively, and Mitchell firmly refused
to answer the question 'Does Scarlett get Rhett back?'
or to write a sequel, so Mitchell's own life seemed to
be held in suspension until death. Her new wealth and
the freedoms it could have afforded seemed to bring
the Marsh couple nothing but anxiety and they devoted
their time not to relaxing into it, or indeed to further
writing, but rather to damage limitation – fussing over
foreign rights and royalties and fighting off enquiries,
imposters, a plagiarism suit, and so on.

GWTW took Margaret Mitchell many years to
complete. If her resentful letters are to be believed, the
endless, insistent demands on her time by others made
the writing of the novel tough going. There are scores of
complaints by women writers of very different periods,
recorded, often in diaries, journals or letters, that the
duties and tasks expected of them as women, whether
daughters, wives, mothers or friends, have made writing
at best an intermittent, often an impossible task. The
strong and determined – and healthy! – have persisted;
the less assertive and physically or psychically fragile
have become silent, or broken down in various ways.
In an echo of complaints by women as disparate as
Elizabeth Gaskell, Alice James, Virginia Woolf and Tillie
Olsen, Margaret Mitchell expressed these sentiments in
letter after histrionic letter. For instance:

> When I look back on these last years of struggling
> to find time to write between deaths in the
> family, illness in the family and among friends . . .,
> childbirths (not my own!), divorces and neuroses
> among friends, my own ill health and four fine
> auto accidents . . . it all seems like a nightmare.
> I wouldn't tackle it again for anything.[27]

Although she pays little lip service to them and in her correspondence tends to encourage the idea of herself as a unique phenomenon, the Southern woman writer who explained the South to the world, nevertheless Margaret Mitchell owes a considerable debt to earlier and contemporary Southern writers. Many male critics assume that *GWTW* was heavily influenced by *Vanity Fair* and *War and Peace*; Margaret Mitchell assured many correspondents that she had never read either. More usefully, critic Kathryn Lee Seidel traces *GWTW* back to nineteenth-century male 'plantation fiction', locating Scarlett's origins in such figures as Bel Tracy, heroine of John Pendleton Kennedy's *Swallow Barn* (1832) and Virginia Beaufort in John W. DeForest's *The Bloody Chasm* (1881).[28] And like dozens of women writers who wrote fiction which both mourned the loss of antebellum Southern society and celebrated the role of white women after the Civil War in the restoration of the white South, Mitchell relied on the autobiographical and fictional writing of other women for inspiration and challenge. Her letters are scattered with brief references to such women: Mary Johnston, Georgia author of *The Long Roll* (1911) and *Cease Firing* (1912), whose novels her mother read to her, weeping all the while; Augusta Evans Wilson, whose *St Elmo* (1867) provided an early model for Rhett Butler; Ellen Glasgow and Caroline Miller, whose fiction about the Southern states made a great impression on her; and many Civil War diarists, published and unpublished – such as the Georgian

Eliza Frances Andrews.[29] Again, following in other Southerners' footsteps, she began her fiction-writing by experimenting in a well-worn genre. Her novella 'Ropa Carmagin', about a white girl in love with a former slave mulatto man, has the tragic ending of most of its kind: the mulatto lover is killed and Europa is forced to leave her ancestral home.

Mitchell was also clear from which women writers she wished to dissociate herself. Like conservative Southern white women before her, she denounced the book which President Lincoln cited as the cause of the Civil War, *Uncle Tom's Cabin*. Replying to a Mr Alexander L. May who wrote to her from Berlin in 1938, she claimed to be 'very happy to know that "Gone With the Wind" is helping refute the impression of the South which people abroad gained from Mrs Stowe's work', a book she claimed 'had a good deal to do with the bitterness of the Abolition movement'.[30] And of the Grimké sisters, who left the slave state South Carolina to go north and became distinguished figures in the Abolition and women's rights movements of the 1830s, Mitchell told an anecdote about family friends. According to her the Grimkés were distant family ancestors, but these friends were deeply embarrassed about it (being 'most unreconstructedest of Rebels imaginable') and claimed that the sisters were 'mentally unbalanced'.[31] Mitchell enjoyed the joke on these women who were seen, outside liberal circles, as traitors to the white South.

Besides dissociating herself from certain women writers, to many of her correspondents Mitchell was anxious to deny any didactic intention in writing the novel. In one of the few letters that admit to a conscious purpose, she claims she was tired of Jazz Age fiction and wanted to write something which did not use the term 'son of a bitch' and in which 'no one was seduced and there wouldn't be a single sadist or degenerate'.[32] In this letter she is anxious to assure Mrs Harris that it was not prissiness or shock at Jazz Age fiction, and she had no desire to write 'a sweet, sentimental novel of the Thomas Nelson Page type'. Page was the classic writer of moonlight-and-magnolia romances which celebrated the white-dominated South and by the 1920s were regarded as presenting an outdated version of the region. What Mitchell wanted to do in her novel was to create a central female character (as well as some minor characters) who 'does practically everything that a lady of the old school should not do'.

This letter indicates that Mitchell's conscious purpose in writing *GWTW* was partly to celebrate the extraordinary mixture in Southern women of strength and gentleness. Repeatedly, she talks of the women who survived the war and Reconstruction period as 'remarkably tough, hard, resistant, strong', 'not lavender and old lace ladies'. However, always conscious of the paradox of Southern womanhood and the need for these women not to appear 'unfeminine', Mitchell celebrates them as 'tough and fearless and outspoken – and very gentle', and claims that her heroine is Melanie, an example of the 'gentle ladies who could fight wild cats, if the necessity arose'.[33] And in an important departure from her mother's suffragist philosophy, Mitchell admires these figures for scorning *collective* organisation in terms of votes for women in favour of *individual* action: being able to get civic improvements by reducing a mayor and city council to jelly with 'a few well chosen words concerning male shilly-shallying and inefficiency'.

It is interesting that Mitchell celebrated the strength and moral fibre of her great-grandmother and grandmother rather than her mother. As for many Southern women writers before and contemporary with her, the individual female struggle in a pre-suffragist period half a century earlier proved easier to fictionalise than the more fraught and personally threatening challenge of her own apparently more emancipated times. Margaret Mitchell found herself more comfortable with the female rebellion of 'the stout-hearted Atlanta matrons who defied the shells and took care of the wounded and defied poverty'[34] than with those women who had secured the vote for her generation. She might have been speaking of herself when she wrote to a fan about Scarlett: 'She was able to appreciate what was beautiful in her mother, even if she could not emulate her.'[35]

But Mitchell found, both in *GWTW* and in her earlier writing, that to portray these 'stout-hearted matrons' was far from straightforward, and that the strength and self-reliance she tried to demonstrate were often read as 'wickedness'. As a journalist on the *Atlanta Journal* she had had a taste of the disapproval she received from some quarters with *GWTW*. Anne Edwards describes Mitchell's approach to her editor Angus Perkerson, asking that she be allowed to write rather more meaty articles than the light society pieces required (for instance, 'Football Players Make the Best Husbands'). Her idea, clearly one which later found voice in her novel, was for a series on women in Georgia's history, to which Perkerson reluctantly agreed. The first piece appeared, scrupulously researched and enthusiastically written, about four Georgia women: the first woman senator; a woman who dressed like her husband and enlisted in the Civil War with him; a native American of the Creek Nation; and a woman who in the Revolutionary War killed a Tory and captured a troop of Redcoats in her kitchen.[36]

There was a postbag of protests at her article, accusing her of everything from defaming the womanhood of Georgia to falsifying history; Perkerson cancelled the rest of the series and refused to allow her to publish a piece proving that her research was authentic. It is not clear from her biographers or letters how she responded to this, but I think it is safe to assume that she took to heart a few clear warnings for future work. First, it taught Mitchell about the mercilessness of critics who challenged material they disliked on the grounds of historical accuracy; so with *GWTW* she researched each last detail and responded personally to her critics. Secondly, it must have indicated that ideals of Southern womanhood were rigidly and passionately adhered to, especially among Southerners, and that any fictional woman she devised would be scrutinised closely within the South, and judged according to fairly stringent moral and social codes.

It is perhaps not surprising that Scarlett dislikes sex and is allowed no sexual pleasure outside the marital bed, nor that she – seen by many as a 'bad woman' (a view Mitchell herself shared) – is carefully juxtaposed to and contrasted with a number of the 'wonderful women of the Old South' (as she puts it) who are apparently intended to provide Scarlett with an appropriate ethical framework. Rather unconvincingly, Mitchell writes to the Very Reverend Monsignor Murphy that although Scarlett has been attacked as a 'bad woman', the figures of Ellen, Melanie and Mammy stand as her conscience, able to distinguish right from wrong.[37] But she also admits to shock that children are reading the book, even though a Sister Mary Loyola had assured her that it was 'a basically moral book' suitable for young girls. (This is interesting in the light of the responses of the Catholic Church and the parents and teachers of some of my correspondents – see chapter 2.) Much more convincing is Mitchell's pleasure in the frequent response she received from readers in which, far from admiring those 'stout-hearted matrons who knew right from wrong', they expressed a pleasure in and personal identification with the amoral determination, courage and 'gumption' of Scarlett O'Hara.

4

Scarlett Woman:
the Undisputed Heroine

And who can not sympathise with Scarlett, who is better
than she means to be, who never understands herself or her
best interests, who longs to be as she is not and can never
appreciate her own virtues – who hasn't, in some minor way,
been in the same position as Scarlett, realising too late what
she really wants and needs? (Lorie Townsend)

Shades of Scarlet [*sic*] conquering
She says 'A woman must have everything' (Joni Mitchell, *The Hissing of Summer Lawns*)

In a 1957 survey of an American high school class, when
girls were asked if they 'identified with' Scarlett O'Hara
or Melanie Wilkes, all but one chose Melanie, a choice
which would have pleased Margaret Mitchell, who saw
Melanie as 'my heroine'.[1] The experiment was repeated
in a similar class in 1970; this time three-quarters of
the girls named Scarlett. Of my questionnaire group,
asked in the mid 1980s to name their favourite character in book and film, the vast majority said 'Scarlett'.
Scarlett O'Hara is a household name. Hers is one of
the largest and most celebrated roles in fiction and
film. She dominates each page of the book and in
Selznick's film appears in an astonishing nine out of
ten of 680 master scenes. And while other women
characters offer important contrasts to her, measures
against which she is judged, and supports for her activity
and wrong-footedness, nevertheless Scarlett dominates
book and film. It is she who is the hub of *Gone With the Wind*.

The Name 'Scarlett'

It usually amuses people to learn that 'Scarlett' O'Hara began life as 'Pansy'. Her author was urged to change it by the publishers because, they argued, the word 'pansy' was associated with homosexual men. Mitchell's revised name, which now seems the only one possible, was straight out of Irish class struggle: 'the Scarletts who had fought with the Irish Volunteers for a free Ireland and been hanged for their pains' (while the surname came from the O'Haras who 'died at the Boyne, battling to the end for what was theirs').[2] So her creator gave Scarlett a name which signified righteous struggle and martyrdom of a collective kind: Scarlett as symbol of a nation, a class, a family which saw its fight over land as historically and symbolically crucial. A more stirring choice than the floral Pansy . . .

But for most reader-viewers, 'Scarlett' does not signify Irish struggles. Scarlet is the colour of blood, passion, anger, sexuality, madness – the name conjures images more appropriate to a heroine who fights, rails against her lot, has to face without cracking up the grim realities of war, childbirth and death, and prostitutes herself in order to keep her ties with the red earth of Tara. If we see the book and film as demonstrating the full spectrum of femininities and female roles, with sexless madonna Melanie at one extreme and warm, inviting madame Belle at the other, Scarlett's story shifts within that range of possibilities.

Selznick's film visualises this well. The reds of sky, earth and wounded men point to the intensity and passion of this period of history, and the O'Haras' role within it. And the film makes an interesting

visual comment on Scarlett's sexuality. Belle Watling, dressed in pink and carmine, with her artificially
red hair and lips, never flouts her 'scarletness'. As
in the book, she is a shadowy figure – seen in her
own rooms, inside or emerging from a carriage. She
knows her place both within society and in Rhett's
life; even her (and probably Rhett's) son is sent away
so as not to see his mother's disgrace. And the only
other 'scarlet woman', Mammy, who secretly wears
the red petticoat Rhett bought her, also conceals that
evidence of her sensuality. But these figures of sexual knowledge and knowingness (the opposite of the
idealised Southern belle) are upstaged dramatically in
one of the film's most memorable images. At Ashley's
surprise party, the Scarlett woman steps over Melly's
threshold wearing a stunning and unashamedly red
dress (a Selznick innovation, since Margaret Mitchell's
Scarlett wears jade green). This motif is continued
into the dark red dressing-gown Scarlett dons before
descending the crimson-carpeted staircase to get a drink,
and encountering Rhett, who then (as he acknowledges
the following morning by apologising and leaving) treats
her like the scarlet woman she has become in the eyes
of the world.

So a variety of sexual and temperamental meanings
of redness are suggested in the book, and underlined
with vivid Technicolor photography, dramatic lighting
and costume design within the film. And always there
is the red earth of Georgia – intended unequivocally
in book and film to suggest that womblike security of
hearth and home, the loss and restoration of Tara itself
which are at the heart of GWTW. But it is perhaps salu-
tary to note the racial meanings of Mitchell/Selznick's
welcoming red earth. I am thinking of the black writer
James Baldwin's view of the 'rust-red earth of Georgia'.
He describes his thoughts as he looks out of a plane
window:

I could not suppress the thought that this earth
had acquired its color from the blood that dripped
down from these trees. My mind was filled with
the image of a Black man . . . hanging from a tree,
while white men watched him and cut his sex from
him with a knife.[3]

A resonant name, then, whether you associate 'Scarlett'
with Irish nationalist struggle, the redness of the female
body and its passions, or with Baldwin's blood-soaked
soil of lynchings. However you read it, Scarlett's name
is a suggestive pointer to the variety of meanings this
single character carries within *GWTW*.

Scarlett and Vivien

Of course, it is almost impossible to think about the
figure of Scarlett O'Hara without conjuring up the
actress whose name has been associated with hers for
fifty years. Ever since the film came out, the name
of Scarlett O'Hara has been for many people synony-
mous with that of Vivien Leigh. The actress herself
was rewarded and dogged all her life by the identification of the two. When her daughter Suzanne gave
birth, the headlines read 'Scarlett O'Hara Now Granny';
when she collapsed with tuberculosis at fifty-three, the
papers announced: 'Scarlett O'Hara is dead.' In all the
accounts of Vivien Leigh's life, and of the filming, writers emphasise the similarities between character and
star, and the appropriateness of Leigh's (at the time
unexpected) casting as Scarlett. Her latest biographer,
Alexander Walker, finds it 'difficult not to believe the
novelist had had Vivien in mind' while Gavin Lambert

(in *GWTW: The Making of Gone With the Wind*) saw the British actress in Scarlett's image: her 'mixture of exquisite control and passionate excess' were 'very close to the way Margaret Mitchell described her heroine', with that combination of 'beauty [NOT Mitchell's term for Scarlett – H.T.], grace, manners, charm', and underneath 'something neurotic and driven'.[4] This seems to have been confirmed by Margaret Mitchell herself, who was pleased with Leigh and is quoted often as having said 'She is *my* Scarlett'.

So generally accepted is this identification between the two (and downplaying of Leigh's craft as an interpretative actress) that Leigh's many biographers dwell at length on the ways in which her personality mirrored Scarlett's, implying to film-buff and *GWTW* fan alike that Vivien was destined for the role, which was the perfect climax to an uneven career and a tempestuous personal life. And her interpretation and appearance are used as models for the Southern belle in subsequent films.

Vivien Leigh won the longest and most prestigious female role in Hollywood's most ambitious epic film at the climax of its 'golden age' when the star system was most fully developed and films were financed, promoted and celebrated on individual star names. Stars were seen by the studios as a form of capital and were used as 'marketing devices',[5] promoted by publicity hype months or even years before the film was actually screened. The casting of key roles in Hollywood films was of crucial importance; and the charismatic appeal of particular stars was exploited by producer and director alike. Stars also wielded considerable power, to the extent of influencing studio arrangements for distribution and sales.

A frequent publicity device used by the studios was the concoction of a 'discovery'; indeed, *GWTW*'s producer, David Selznick, had already used this when seeking to cast the leads of his films *David Copperfield* (1934) and *The Adventures of Tom Sawyer* (1938). By the time the film of *GWTW* came out – December 1939 in the USA, April 1940 in Britain – enormous public excitement about it had been generated in news-papers, in magazines and on the radio. For Selznick had spent several years bringing it to production, getting the script he wanted from seventeen script-writers, and the 'authentic' costumes, sets and cast necessary to make this his greatest personal monument and the most memorable film of Hollywood's heyday. Most sig-nificant of all, he had spent over two years selecting the actress to play Scarlett O'Hara, and making the heavily publicised 'discovery' of Vivien Leigh.

Vivien Leigh was chosen after a two-year, interna-tionally publicised and carefully orchestrated 'Search for Scarlett O'Hara'. It was conducted 'like a parody of a Presidential election' and became 'the most famous talent search in history'. It was used satirically in Clare Boothe's anti-fascist play *Kiss the Boys Good-bye* (1939), featuring the search for an actress to play a certain Vel-vet O'Toole, and melodramatically in Garson Kanin's television film *The Scarlett O'Hara War* (1980).[6] Each account of this celebrated search describes the number of talent scouts sent across the United States; the Tallulah-for-Scarlett Campaign run by the aunt of the Alabama actress Tallulah Bankhead; the greater space given in the New Orleans *Times-Picayune* to talent scout Kay Brown's arrival in town than to the sensational news of Edward VIII's abdication to marry American divorcée Wallis Simpson; and so on. It is a much-documented story, the struggle by thousands of unknown actresses, as well as Hollywood's biggest female stars, to win the plum part in a film which everyone suspected would be as huge a success as Margaret Mitchell's best-selling novel. Fourteen hundred women were interviewed and ninety tested for the part, while women turned up at

Selznick's door in droves, even delivering themselves in packing cases. The search, with advertisements, personnel and other expenses, cost Selznick $92,000 – a bargain, since he and his film were internationally famous before a single scene had been shot.

Kanin's *The Scarlett O'Hara War* concludes with the familiar romantic version of the choice of Vivien Leigh – one repeated in all the biographical accounts. David Selznick, still agonising over his choice for Scarlett, was under financial pressure to begin shooting the film, so he used the opportunity to burn old sets cluttering up his studio lot (*King Kong*'s among them) to shoot the burning of Atlanta sequence, using stand-ins for the major characters. Legend has it that Selznick's brother Myron, agent to Vivien Leigh, and her lover – later her husband – Laurence Olivier, brought Vivien to the lot; David Selznick turned and saw her greenish eyes reflecting the orange flames, while Myron said: 'I want you to meet Scarlett O'Hara.'[7]

The real story is more complex and rather less romantic. Vivien Leigh had made several approaches to Selznick, and he had seen her in a couple of films early in the 'search'. Gerald Gardner and Harriet Modell Gardner speak of the 'Cinderella Hoax'[8] with its perfect fairy-tale ending. Selznick himself, however, was delighted to see this magical story circulate. In fact, after his death, among his effects were found a print of an early film featuring Leigh, and memos concerning her and her love life.[9] Vivien Leigh, who had decided as soon as she read the novel that she would have the main part, was not the easiest choice. She was finally selected from an eminent shortlist – the others were Paulette Goddard, Joan Bennett, Jean Arthur – only after considerable thought, and an inspired gamble on Selznick's part. Leigh was first of all *English* (actually of Catholic French-Irish ancestry, just like Scarlett, but undoubtedly seen in Hollywood as a classic English rose). By

1939 there was an isolationist cultural ethos in the United States and considerable anger about the number of 'foreign' actors taking Hollywood's best parts, not to mention directing and producing films there. As Selznick predicted, the formidable Hollywood gossip columnist Hedda Hopper was furious at this insult to American actresses, and the United Daughters of the Confederacy made protests. Margaret Mitchell, however, felt there was much to recommend an English actress. She wrote to Selznick: 'Southern voices and English voices are frequently similar, and often more similar than the voices of Southerners and those of people in other sections of the United States.'[10]

Besides, Hollywood stars were then judged severely in both political and moral terms; it was crucial that no damaging scandal emerged to taint their godlike images among the public, especially with the gossip-mongers. It is widely recorded that Paulette Goddard, long Selznick's favourite, failed to secure the role of Scarlett because of her suspected non-married relationship with Charles Chaplin, and his rumoured communist sympathies. At the time of her casting as Scarlett, Vivien Leigh was a married woman conducting a passionate affair with the (also married) matinée idol Laurence Olivier. Both had abandoned spouses and very young children in order to live together. Had this affair become common knowledge, or been leaked to a newspaper, magazine or radio programme, Vivien Leigh too would be a mere footnote in the famous search. But the lovers were advised to be discreet; the studios, exerting their power over the columnists, ensured a veil of silence until divorces came through; and Selznick's press release announced that 'Mrs Leigh Holman, the wife of a London barrister', had got the part of Scarlett. At this stage, not only her adulterous liaison but also her Englishness were played down — though surprisingly this latter aspect was to prove an asset. For there had been strong feeling in the American South that no *Northerner* was fit to play the part. The casting of Vivien eventually delighted the Daughters of the Confederacy and other Southern belles – she may not have been an American, but at least she was not a damned Yankee. (They might not have been quite so triumphant had they heard the story of Leigh's arrival for the film's première in Atlanta; to the band's playing the Southern anthem 'Dixie' she exclaimed: 'They're playing the song from the picture.'[11])

But in another way I think Vivien Leigh was an inspired choice. If he was going to choose an unknown actress, Selznick needed his Scarlett to bring a special dimension to the part. And Leigh's particular contribution was a kind of English 'class', derived both from her own background and also from the aristocratic, quasi-royal associations of herself and Olivier. Known to be the upper-middle-class daughter of an English officer in the Indian cavalry and a strict Catholic French-Irish mother, Vivien had been presented as a debutante at the court of King George V. She was later to marry that 'heir apparent to the crown of the English theatre', 'prince among players' who was knighted Sir Laurence Olivier, youngest ever actor to win that honour. This 'golden couple', 'uncrowned royalty', lived until their divorce in the magnificent thirteenth-century Notley Abbey, endowed by Henry V.[12] These connections and the couple's regal aura became important both in her initial casting as Selznick's Southern aristocrat (he gave Scarlett a grander class origin than did Margaret Mitchell) and in the subsequent promotion and adulation of her as star of the film.

Thus in 1939 *GWTW* acquired a classic tone from its English female lead, and as the years have gone by, with Leigh's death in 1967 followed by the rise to international superstardom and grand reputation of Olivier,

popular interest in this glamorous couple and their relationship to the *Gone With the Wind* phenomenon has
never waned. There is a large body of published works
devoted to each star – and if my Bristol public libraries
are anything to go by, long lists of borrowers waiting to
consume them. In British Film Year, 1985, Vivien was
the only woman of a distinguished group of five actors
and directors to be commemorated by postage stamp.
Angus McBean's dramatic photographs of the star (one
of which was used for the stamp) are much reproduced.
For a British audience especially, that affection felt for
GWTW, supported as it is by popular biography, television movie, stamp, postcard, and so on, may partly stem
from a chauvinistic pleasure in the choice of an English
actress to play what became possibly the best-known
and most celebrated female role in a Hollywood film.

For Vivien herself, however, the film's great success
became a millstone round her neck. She had secured the
part while visiting Olivier in Hollywood for the filming
of *Wuthering Heights*, and everywhere they later went
together they were dubbed 'Heathcliff and Scarlett',
hailed by the press (with curious disregard for their
British origins) as 'America's most famous lovers'.[13]
Although initially the adulation accorded the couple
helped both careers and their relationship, ultimately it
grew oppressive, and Vivien Leigh became most reluctantly identified with two roles only – both Southern.
As Scarlett she was celebrated for strength, versatility,
beauty and guts, while as Blanche DuBois in *A Streetcar Named Desire* (1951) she was seen as hysterical,
nymphomaniacal and depressive. The fact that Vivien
herself became prey to severe fits of manic-depressive
behaviour, compounded by an attack of tuberculosis
and nurtured by heavy drinking and smoking, as well
as her frequent insomnia and her sexual indiscretions,
seemed to lock her firmly into an unstable Southern
belle persona. From *GWTW* onwards this rewarded her

materially but also limited her growth, causing the end of her marriage to Olivier and a considerable degree of isolation and despair.

In these two famous roles, Vivien Leigh embodied the two sides of Southern womanhood most familiar in fiction and film. Victoria O'Donnell, in a discussion of the way film frequently represents Southern women (especially in the 1940s and 50s with film versions of Tennessee Williams and William Faulkner novels) sees Leigh as an icon of the belle, and *GWTW* as the film which contains the four most frequent female types: the vain, proud, uppity Feminine Woman (Scarlett), the capable, loyal, wise Female Woman (Mammy), the pure, genteel Real Lady (Melanie), and the trapped-in-the-past Fallen Woman (Blanche and Belle Watling).[14] The fallen woman, best represented by Blanche, is certainly a more familiar female protagonist than Scarlett. That hysterical, unstable and sexually desperate figure is a common feature in the Deep South melodrama (such as *Walk on the Wild Side*, 1962; and *Hurry Sundown*, 1967) as well as those films which allow her more earthly and carnal experience such as *Cat on a Hot Tin Roof* (1958) and *The Last Picture Show* (1971). In fact, Vivien Leigh as Scarlett comes closer to the strong, independent 1930s and 40s star roles in the 'woman's picture' played by Bette Davis, Katharine Hepburn and Joan Crawford (all considered for the Scarlett part) than to the more self-destructive and dependent figures of the 'Southern film', whether of the 1930s 'happy plantation' type or the dark melodramas of the 1940s onwards.

Scarlett and Jezebel

In any discussion of the Hollywood Southern belle role, it is interesting to compare Vivien Leigh as Scarlett with her immediate rival, Bette Davis as Jezebel. Bette Davis had wanted the *GWTW* part as badly as Leigh, and was Americans' favourite actress to play it. However, because of a dispute over loan-out by Jack Warner, to whom Davis was contracted, Selznick ruled out this popular and eminently suitable actress, so in order to pre-empt Selznick's success Warner provided and rushed out a competitive vehicle for Davis's talents. Completed in just eight weeks, *Jezebel* (1938) is the story of an unorthodox Southern belle living in the New Orleans of 1852, during a yellow fever epidemic. Bette Davis plays Miss Julie (an interesting parallel, perhaps, with August Strindberg's rebellious heroine of the same name) who defies conventional sexual mores and sartorial rules. Taunting her wimpish fiancé Preston (Henry Fonda), she appears defiantly at her own party in riding clothes and at the Olympus Hall in a red dress – when all other unmarried girls wear white. Her fiancé, unable to cope with this outlandishness, jilts her and marries a meek Northern woman. At the family plantation, Halcyon, Preston and bride take refuge from the 'Yellow Jack' epidemic, and witness the wanton Julie causing a duel. To atone, Julie insists on accompanying the sick Preston, suffering from fever, to the leper colony island where she can assist him by using her local knowledge to speak creole dialect and fight for his life. The film ends, to the swelling notes of *GWTW* composer Max Steiner's triumphal music, with Julie and Preston processing through New Orleans, past purgatorial lamp-flames and flickering furnaces.

In many thematic and formal ways *Jezebel* anticipated *GWTW*. Its central figure is also a feisty Southern belle who breaks codes of femininity and flaunts a shocking red dress; there is an Ashley-like male protagonist who provokes the anti-belle figure into rebellion; and Max Steiner wrote emotive scores for both films. David Selznick was so incensed by the similarity of some scenes in *Jezebel* to his own proposed film that he demanded at least one cut, and was alarmed at its box-office and critical success. He should, however, have been grateful for what it achieved: a revival of interest in the Old South as the subject of film – with all those trappings of grand plantations, chivalrous officers, loyal family slaves, and so on. As Roland Flamini records, 'The Civil War was no longer box-office poison.'[15] So the film put the War on the map again, and paved the way for *Gone With the Wind*.

But it also offered a version of the Southern belle which looks in retrospect like a fascinating preview of Scarlett and Blanche. Julie's excessive rebellion, waywardness and independent action have tragic results. Buck Cantrell is killed in the duel she provokes; she loses the man she loves to another woman – and to yellow fever; and so she is seen as hysterical, irresponsible and punishable. Her excesses are primarily sexual, too – a restless desire to be mastered and saved from her own autonomy is epitomised by her mesmeric gaze at the hickory stick which Preston (more Ashley Wilkes than Rhett Butler) refuses to use on her. The only way she can redeem herself is to take a course of action which becomes familiar in the 1940s 'woman's film': love-and-sacrifice. Because of her love, and her unfeminine demands, she must sacrifice herself to the dying Preston, in a final ride through New Orleans which is redemptive but also self-abnegating. Four years later, in an even more sacrificial role, Bette Davis played a viciously grasping Southern belle-gone-to-the-bad in the Warner Brothers adaptation of a work by Southern novelist Ellen Glasgow. *In This Our Life* (1942). After a series of execrable deeds, the androgynously named protagonist Stanley – Bette Davis (cast against Olivia de Havilland, repeating the good Southern lady role she played in *GWTW*) – is killed in a car crash.

So a year after *Jezebel*, Vivien Leigh's Scarlett O'Hara embodied much of Jezebel/Julie's sexual restlessness and restrained power, and her fate may be seen as similarly self-destructive; she does, after all, undervalue, neglect and lose almost everyone who has loved her and whom she also loves. But the punishment and curbing of Bette Davis's Julie (and her later Stanley) are not emulated. Scarlett is seen to be wrong: in her actions, judgements, loves and desires. But her punishment is not absolute, and the open ending – with its hope for new beginning and a new triumph – avoids a restoration of woman to her 'proper place'. In the classic Hollywood narrative woman is usually returned to an appropriate position or sphere, either by accepting her proper 'role' or by being punished for her transgressions through exclusion, outlawry or death.[16] In *Jezebel*, as in so many films of the period, Bette Davis is indeed punished by social exclusion (her red dress loses her social approval and fiancé) and outlawry and death (her fate in the leper colony). To Scarlett, neither of those normal narrative conclusions applies. There is still hope that Rhett – who 'loves you so', as Melanie tells her – will be won back after she has planned a new 'campaign'. And even if he is not, there is always the earth of Tara against the scarlet sky. In one way Scarlett may be restored to her proper place, but the open ending does not batten down all the hatches as *Jezebel*, *In This Our Life* and so many other woman-centred Hollywood films did. Jezebel becomes the tabooed scarlet woman, and receives her 'just' deserts. Scarlett O'Hara's fate is more vital and hopeful and in this, as in other ways, she has lived on to be admired and reinterpreted. *Jezebel*, once a successful and much-praised film, has sunk without trace.

Scarlett's Women

The story of Vivien Leigh's casting as Scarlett and the way it subsequently affected her life are the stuff of both romantic legend and the tragedy of doomed stardom. For a 1930s and 40s film-goer, the love affair of two beautiful young British rising stars; their joint successes in theatre and film, followed by a knight- and lady-hood; and the boost to British chauvinist pride that they captured some of the best Hollywood roles and awards at a time of such hot competition and American cinematic dominance . . . all contributed to an involvement in and commitment to the success of *GWTW* long before it was premièred in London in the early years of the war. Since then, the darkly romantic story of Vivien Leigh (who, like all legends, died too early) has been told and retold in many versions, so that the association of Scarlett O'Hara with Britain's most renowned actor's dead wife is endlessly reiterated and recirculated. (Indeed, it remains one of the key problems for any sequel-maker: how to overcome popular memory of Vivien Leigh as the only possible Scarlett.)

In the 1980s it is rare among my correspondents that any disjunction is recorded between the actress and her role. Marjorie Simcock was unusual in calling Leigh 'a washout' because she and all her friends wanted Bette Davis to get the part; far more common is the response of David Copson, who has gone so far as to paint in oils the actress as Scarlett. He says:

> The first and most lasting thing that struck me was
> Vivien Leigh. Until I went to see *GWTW* Vivien
> Leigh was just another film star, but by the end
> of the performance her beautiful face was indelibly
> stamped on my mind's eye.

Since the vast majority of my respondents had read the book, it seems significant how few of them comment on Leigh's performance; it is as if most reader-viewers accept her interpretation of the role as naturally right. That this affects and in some ways closes off other readings of Scarlett, and other ideas about how she might look, speak, behave, apparently does not concern them. Few of my respondents, I suspect, would agree with Angela Carter's denunciation of

> Vivien Leigh's anorexic, over-dressed Scarlett O'Hara . . . one of the least credible of Hollywood *femmes fatales*, most of whose petulant squeaks are, to boot, audible only to bats.[17]

My own feeling about Vivien Leigh is that, while she plays remarkably well the various stages through which Scarlett passes, she does not express that sense of being uncomfortable in her own body and with her sexuality which the novel's Scarlett does. When I read the book, I find pleasurable opportunities to identify with a woman who is always fighting the constraints of a strictly coded femininity, even after the War in which those codes have apparently been rendered irrelevant. Grandma Fontaine says shrewdly that Scarlett has 'a man's way of being smart' because she knows how to make money, while she lacks 'a woman's way' because she is not 'a speck smart about folks', and I feel that for a woman reader it is the androgynous quality in Scarlett which allows imaginative free play – just as Rhett, on the page, can be imagined as lover *and* mother, masterful man of action *and* feminine confidante and fashion adviser . . . Maybe this creative play can occur only in reading; in film, character is too firmly fixed by the casting, and especially by associations and charisma of particular stars. Clark Gable's much-celebrated masculinity (elaborately reinforced by publicity photos and materials), beside Vivien Leigh's petite and somewhat fragile-looking beauty and femininity, creates superbly a sexual tension between complementary figures of sharply contrasted sexual difference. But for me, if not for my correspondents, only rarely do they explode difference and explore sexual ambivalence.

For many women readers and film fans, Scarlett is recalled as a 'first', a new kind of heroine. Hardly any of my respondents was familiar with the long tradition of 'Southern Belle' American fiction, from the early nineteenth century to the present day – a tradition which Margaret Mitchell herself knew well, and consciously alluded to and departed from in GWTW.[18] Nor is the Southern film of the 1930s known to the majority – a handful of women reported having seen the odd film, including Jezebel, but GWTW was the only one to have remained in their memories and affections. One respondent called Scarlett 'perhaps my first "flawed heroine" ', while another identified her as 'the first heroine I had read about who was ruthless, scheming and selfish'. A third wrote that GWTW was

the first book I ever read in which a woman is not just the 'heroine' but the prime mover of the story, using all available means to be mistress of her own fate. The idea was a revelation and an inspiration to me, raised on Hollywood films of the 50s in which women were prizes to be fought over and in which they did little but wave misty-eyed farewells to departing warriors.

Again and again, women described to me their identification with and admiration of the strong, resourceful Scarlett, getting what she wants out of life – something many of them have obviously failed to do! They point to the way she creates order out

of the chaos of a ruined world and also experiences
the horrors of unrequited love, motherless isolation,
and loss of parent, child, friend and husband. A large
number comment on their identification with Scarlett
as she realises her feelings when it is just to late, and
with the irony of misunderstandings, crossed wires
and false perceptions within male/female relationships.
'True to life' is a term used often, and it is used with
resignation or cynicism. Scarlett does not offer women
cosy reassurances and sentimental comfort. Where she
does help is in demonstrating female grit, in proposing
a homespun philosophy which it seems many women
have carried through their lives to counter despair,
depression and inertia: 'I'll think about that tomorrow.
Tomorrow is another day.'

Many women express ambivalence towards Scarlett,
either because they think they ought to despise her
for her outrageous behaviour or because she expresses
herself in a way they are reluctant to acknowledge as
valid for themselves. 'She's such a con — but also a very
clever woman', says one, and another: 'You can't help
admiring her gumption in spite of her faults.' Adjec-
tives with negative connotations, like 'ruthless', 'greedy',
'go-getting', 'flighty' and 'strong-willed', are juxtaposed
with positive attributes such as 'strong', 'powerful',
'courageous' and 'having zest'. Scarlett is understood
as a figure who embodies powerful desires and yearnings which are almost all disappointed or denied. A
great many who had read or seen GWTW as young
girls describe its inducing 'sexual longing' in them,
and associated desires for impossible states of joy and
satisfaction. Though all the characters are part of
this pattern of loss and desire, Scarlett especially
embodies for women a state of yearning and frustration
which has no consciously identifiable object.

Some correspondents express total identification with
Scarlett and all she does. Several are secretly thrilled to

be compared with her by boyfriends and mothers, and others acknowledge complete sympathy: 'I *am* her'; 'I sympathise with Scarlett O'Hara's mistakes and blindness, her immaturity, and her greed and zest'; 'Scarlett always seems to be chasing the unattainable – like me!'; 'I think Scarlett is in all women, she is the personification of so many characteristics we all have.' For others – usually those who read the book or saw the film when they were close in age to Scarlett – she is a prototype of female action or attitudes: 'I think as a girl I held up Scarlett as a kind of model for myself, especially in regard to her "never give up" sentiments'; 'The fact that Scarlett rises to the occasion and, being unburdened with conscience, copes so well and becomes mistress of her life and fate was very encouraging to an adolescent girl – despite the final discouragement of forever-thwarted love'; 'Such a strong character – spoilt, beautiful, bitchy – as we would all like to be'. She is admired for being a 'solver of problems'.

Furthermore, her kind of beauty (seventeen-inch waist, black hair, green eyes – the latter very unusual in the 'Southern belle' novel) is the object of envy for a certain number, as is her rebelliousness, which many women found her most exciting characteristic. Gabrielle Parker says she was 'always glad when Scarlett danced when she should have been in mourning', and a respondent who signed herself 'a seventy-year-old baby-sitting granny' wrote of her feelings: 'An office girl – the Depression only just receding and a war advancing. What I would have given to be able to kick the traces.' The writer Molly Haskell, an American Southerner, says that for her generation (growing up in the 1940s and 50s), 'Those of us who were ambitious would use our femininity like Scarlett O'Hara used hers: would flirt, tease, withhold sex, to get what we wanted.'[19] A model, yes, but also a warning, and an example of how *not* to negotiate femininity. Jean Grimshaw saw her 'partly as an object lesson in how to get it wrong and lose your man', while Jane Ellison felt uncomfortably, 'Identifying with Scarlett gave me a depressing feeling that maybe the world would never be ready for truly tough women.'

One common pattern of response to Scarlett appears to be a quasi-maternal disapproval or indulgence. I wonder if this points to a way in which women use fictional figures, considering and evaluating the actions and words of characters who are surrogate children, less immediate and thus problematic than our real ones. Certainly the language used by several respondents was that of a concerned, indulgent or critical parent: 'I cried for Scarlett. I ached to smack her at times – I laughed at her'; 'One wanted to shake her for her infatuation with Ashley Wilkes'; and

> When I was young I felt as Scarlett did, but now
> I want to tell her not to be foolish – but at that age
> how can one know that sexual desire is not love
> . . . I know how deeply she is going to be hurt and
> want to be able to stop her.

One woman, identifying with the saintly Ellen O'Hara, found Scarlett's moral outlook 'dreadful', and said: 'I always felt how upset her mother would have been at her behaviour.' Throughout *GWTW*, Ellen's memory is invoked as a reminder of how far Scarlett has departed from the rules and expectations of her mother's upbringing, and she therefore offers the maternal reader a point of identification. We too can become the disapproving eye, and enjoy the piquancy of shock at and disapproval of our surrogate daughter.

For many of us, Scarlett's novelty as a heroine lies in the daunting variety of situations she has to face, setbacks and tragedies she must overcome, and defeats which knock her back: emotional, domestic, regional and community. Each major crisis, it seems, must be faced alone, or at least with Scarlett *in loco parentis* or as reference point for everyone else – be it on the road to Tara, standing alone at Ashley's party in public disgrace, or at Rhett's final departure. Whether comforting her deranged father after Ellen's death, delivering Melanie's baby, killing a Yankee soldier, or facing the accidental death of daughter Bonnie Blue, Scarlett is required to find superhuman resources of courage and self-reliance in order to cope. And it is not every heroine who can come up from under a decade of deaths of family and friends, the loss of a magnificent home and social world, unrequited love, three unsatisfactory marriages, war, childbirth, near-rape, miscarriage, social and sexual chaos . . . and still decide she can get what she wants by thinking about it tomorrow. When my correspondents talk repeatedly of Scarlett as a 'survivor', this is obviously what they mean.

This notion of 'survival' is a common enough theme in women's historical writing of various periods, and in the 1980s has taken on a new vigour with female saga-writers such as Jackie Collins and Barbara Taylor Bradford. Margaret Mitchell, writing the novel in the 1920s, saw Scarlett and Rhett as 'survivors' who endured suffering, defeat and humiliation but knew how to make the best of a bad job and look after Number One. Rhett's speech to Scarlett in Atlanta, after Ashley's return from the war, was acknowledged by its author as the book's key words. Rhett expresses contempt for Ashley's 'breed', saying it is 'a natural law' that such people, who cannot adapt to change and upheaval, should go under: 'They just aren't smart, Scarlett, and only the smart deserve to survive' (p. 756).

Grandma Fontaine echoes this Social Darwinist theme when she too lectures Scarlett on types of survivor. She sees the secret of the South's survival as its ability to adapt and play along with 'lesser folks' who can be used and then kicked and climbed over 'when we're strong enough' (pp. 701–02). This invokes that well-worn Confederate sentiment of revival which you can still find on Southern T-shirts: 'Our folks get flattened out but they rise up again' (ibid.). Despite all this careful explanation, Scarlett – the most dramatic example of one who 'rises again' – is characteristically ignorant of this philosophy: she complains to Ashley of Rhett harping on about 'the survival of the fitting [*sic*]'.

Like my respondents, most critics see Scarlett's fate as that of a survivor (with the refreshing exception of Louis D. Rubin, Jr, who argues that the war liberates Scarlett, who never wanted to be a lady. She is shown to grow not in spite of but *because of* social cataclysm.[20]) It is clear why the critics, readers and film-goers of the 1930s and 40s would see 'survival' as a powerful theme in *GWTW*, and would select that recurrent motif as appropriate to Scarlett's progress. Published in 1936, as the Depression had taken a severe toll on the United States and Britain, Mitchell's novel promised hope of an end to struggle, hunger, poverty and a life on the breadline with no frills. The film, released in 1939 as both nations emerged from the Depression but were plunged into a world war, promised that although war might end 'civilisation' or society as it was known, nevertheless new possibilities and regenerative projects would ensure the continuity of particular classes and groups. Scarlett's final return to a reconstituted Tara – once again the working plantation of 'the old days', with Mammy still there behind the fluttering white curtains – was undoubtedly an image of hope and inspiration for those Americans and Britons whose homes were under nightly threat of bombing, and whose families had been torn apart by conscription of soldiers, war casualties and evacuation of children from the cities to the country.

Indeed, the 'survival' theme has since spoken powerfully to one woman whose parents almost did not survive the war. Anne Karpf wrote:

My parents are survivors of the Holocaust, and
I've often fantasised as to how I would have coped,
or somehow tried to ready myself for a recurrence.
For me, *GWTW* was a story about loss – the loss
of the family, family home and land – with which
I could profoundly identify. Scarlett found herself
in the position which I've imagined myself occupying – struggling somehow to survive. And the way
in which her life was so sharply divided into two
mirrors my parents' lives, pre-war and post-war.
The loss of Scarlett's privileged life and home,
the rupture of the family – these are the *GWTW*
stories that really spoke to me.

Scarlett as a symbol of collective, class, social survival:
this is how she has been described in many accounts
by women who lived through – and recalled reading
or seeing *GWTW* during – the war. And Anne
Karpf's words are a reminder of the ways in which
later generations also made resonant connections with
Scarlett as a figure of symbolic regeneration and
endurance. The fact that the collectivity for which
Scarlett stands extends only to the white middle-class
plantation-owning family is something on which few of
the wartime reader-viewers comment. If my respondents are typical, it seems that only later generations grasp
fully the race and class implications. For those women
who read or saw *GWTW* in the 1950s and 60s, women
who did not remember the war but were busy reacting
against their war-scarred, security-minded parents,
Scarlett's 'survival' is seen in more personal, individualist
terms: 'She was a bit before her time in some ways – but
she certainly always did her own thing!'; 'She was a
rebel who beat the establishment.' Scarlett's rebellion
and outrageousness are models for my baby-boomer
generation who benefited from a welfare-state society
which accorded them particular value, promising them

a good standard of living and an apparently stable and secure society. The allowances which women of a previous generation made for Scarlett's selfishness and single-mindedness because 'she worked and schemed the whole time to keep Tara not just for herself but for her family' are unnecessary for later generations, who tend to see Scarlett as an example of gutsy individualism or feminist self-determination

*   *   *

For a 1980s generation, Scarlett is understandable in terms of Thatcherite/Reaganite models of career feminism and yuppie success. It is easy to imagine a modern-dress version of *GWTW* with Scarlett doing very nicely on the Stock Exchange, comfortably ensconced in London's fashionable Docklands or New York's Upper East Side, with or without live-in lover Rhett . . . Scarlett's fate, however – to be left alone with only her work – may also offer a timely spur to those upwardly mobile childless career women (like the character played by Diane Keaton in the film *Baby Boom*, 1987) who are reputedly considering quitting the rat race in favour of bare feet in the kitchen. Furthermore, for a 1980s woman interested in the new popular feminist psychotherapy, *GWTW* seems a perfect illustration of the thesis of Luise Eichenbaum and Susie Orbach, in *What Do Women Want?* .[21] Rather than women being the dependent, cared-for sex, it is boys and men who receive nurturance throughout their lives from women, and women learn early on that they will be the source of this care. Thus in sexual and family relationships women are the emotional, if not economic providers; they will receive precious little nurturance for themselves. So, however Scarlett is cherished by Rhett, and from time to time helped along by other characters, her lone pilgrimage from poverty to new prosperity is largely accomplished alone, and with her own resources. Her early upbringing, promising the possibility of life-long dependence on a man, comes to seem extremely hollow.

The survival which draws on female endurance and adaptability, rather than Rhett's 'survival of the fittest' Social Darwinism, is a feature of book and film much cited by my correspondents. They often note the distance Scarlett has to travel between her pampered childhood and the adversities of young adult life: 'She showed strength and fortitude when circumstances forced her out of her traditional role as a flighty tempt-ress'; 'I admire the rather silly girl, developing into a resourceful woman, who could stand on her own feet.' And that famous philosophy, expressed in mottoes, has been picked up by women of all generations – for them it is a key to their own survival. One writer described the determination to think about it tomorrow as 'doing a Scarlett O'Hara', and 'a Scarlett O'Hara' is something women do with different effects. While for one it helped 'living in the day and not getting bogged down in things one cannot control anyway', for another it was the perfect recipe for procrastination. Either way, women understand Scarlett's repeated homilies as pragmatic guides to everyday living. What appears in *GWTW* to be superhuman courage and strength which we might find intimidating and alienating is cleverly domesticated and brought to a level with which most of us can iden-tify. Scarlett may face more in five years than most of us hope (or fear) to in a lifetime, but she handles it all largely by living a day at a time and by delaying major problems and anxieties when reality gets too much.

Is Scarlett a Feminist?

Scarlett is often seen as a progressive figure and model for women because of her refusal of all that simpering

Southern belle-ery involves. Many women saw her as an early feminist – 'a premature women's libber', as one put it. This is expressed in different ways, and often by women over the age of fifty in terms of bravery and 'guts'. One woman commented on the 'egalitarian nature' of Scarlett's relationship with Rhett, and her 'ability to succeed in a man's world' – both elements other women observe with approval. A great many note with considerable awe and envy the fact that Scarlett knows what she wants, and then goes ahead and gets it: 'In her own way she affirms women as individuals', as one writer said. Lee Beck, however, wittily sent up the idea of Scarlett as a self-determining New Woman: 'You have to admire a woman who can rifle a dead man's pockets, steal her spinster sister's fiancé, and still look down her nose at Belle.'

In her study of women in the movies, Molly Haskell describes Scarlett as the 1930s antebellum version of the 1920s 'flapper', defying all conventions except sexual ones. Haskell sees her as a forerunner of the modern career woman, obsessed with work (Tara), possessing business acumen and energy from sexual repression – since sex was something she used to get what she wanted, but did not need or enjoy. Certainly Scarlett is excessively grasping. She intends (or so she says) to be a 'great lady' like her mother; in fact, her aspirations are closer to Rhett's, her models more traditionally masculine than feminine. She wants too much, and she wants it regardless of what is involved in getting it. In leaps and bounds, from her first dance in widow's weeds at the Confederate auction to her offering, then selling, her body for Tara's taxes and insisting on a lone business trip which indirectly causes her second husband's death . . . in a multitude of minor and major ways, Scarlett flouts all codes of her family and community, and disregards the morality of her sex and class as taught by her mother, in order not just to survive but also to flourish.

On her pilgrimage from poverty to wealth, from old stable Tara to raw restless Atlanta, and back again, Scarlett comes into conflict with each member of her family; walks off with her sister's beau; tries to abduct her best friend's husband; kills a man; marries twice for the most dubious reasons; indulges in ruthless business practices, including the hire and mistreatment of convict labour; and shows virtually no interest in her three children (not to mention her three husbands). You might imagine it would be difficult to care for or identify with such a character. Surprisingly, it is not. Although some respondents express censoriousness, seeing her as 'spoiled', 'scheming', 'silly', 'A Study in Selfishness', more often than not this is mingled with admiration: 'She is not a very "nice" person but she has so much gumption.'

As with figures like Alexis Colby ('Dynasty') and Emma Harte (*A Woman of Substance*), excessive behaviour is accepted remarkably uncritically by reader-viewers. That intense self-absorption and self-righteousness which all three women share, which are so trying in real people and so hateful in community life, nevertheless express an intensity which opens for us a sense of utopian possibilities in our own lives. Although we may judge adversely characters' behaviour and speech (and in the book Scarlett is less sympathetic and more amoral than the always charming and sparkling Vivien Leigh, who is given only *one* child to neglect), the pleasure of this text perhaps lies beyond morality and bourgeois norms of courtesy, family responsibility, and so on. Through a figure of excess like Scarlett, our own timid conformity and careful adherence to codes we value and honour are mocked as the luxurious values of the untried and untested. Identified with a brand-new city (Atlanta), new people (the Carpetbaggers and scalawags) and new money (an industrial rather than settled agricultural economy), Scarlett O'Hara becomes the very symbol of the New Woman, recognised as such by 1940s wartime women workers and mothers, 1960s liberationists and careerists, and 1980s 'Me'-generation post-feminists.

A Bevy of 'Scarletts'

My research has shown that various generations, nationalities and individuals have discovered different 'Scarletts', and that those who have never seen Vivien Leigh in the film version recall her with different memories from those who switch on their video whenever they feel like a good cry. I know from reading letters and questionnaires by white and black American and British *GWTW* fans that Scarlett bears a host of associations for women – some derived from interpretations of the character in book and film, some bearing the weight of autobiographical associations and memories. For a 'Georgia peach' who has been raised to emulate and recognise all the subtleties of the idealised Southern Belle, Scarlett's inconsistencies are understood with a profundity impossible for a British reader-viewer whose knowledge of the American South comes almost entirely from *GWTW* itself. Scarlett undoubtedly has special meanings for a woman who has lost loved ones in war, seen a child die, or unrequitedly loved someone else's husband.

As a model and measure of femininity Scarlett seems to me an interesting failure, and my respondents' maternal, moralising or mixed feelings about her appear to bear this out. As in many historical novels and films before and since *GWTW*, the codes and rules applying to femininity and female sexuality are more rigid than contemporary ones (in most social and racial groups in America and Western Europe, at least). There is a great *frisson* of reader-viewer pleasure in observing Scarlett

straining against the corsetry and social and sexual constraints of her age. Think of that much-reproduced film
still of Hattie McDaniel's Mammy lacing Vivien Leigh's
Scarlett into her barbecue dress, pulling hard to pinch
in the seventeen-inch-waist so that free movement is
impossible, while a girl's figure is shown off to advantage
to the voyeuristic spectator, who must not touch . . . an
image which, like the red dress, suggests a classic porno-
graphic figure under restraint who will be punished for
her sexuality but endlessly goaded and teased to display
and unleash it. Scarlett's problem with sexual feeling
and expression are at times comic or simply titillating,
at others erotically profoundly charged. And as in much
pornography and many 'romantic' novels which place
considerable obstacles in the way of sexual fulfilment
between two predestined lovers, it is the *difficulties*
which give pleasure and arousal, both of which are
heightened by the eventual shattering of strong taboos
within a culture that strongly represses female sexuality.
Hence the power of the famous Rhett-carrying-Scarlett-
upstairs-to-ravish-her scene.

Like her practical and financial struggles, Scarlett's
sexual and emotional trials are far from straightforward.
She is, after all, a spectacular emotional failure: although
she is a splendid businesswoman she is a 'bad' daughter,
sister, wife, mother, friend and lover. She fails to understand all the key people in her life. As the critic Elizabeth
Fox-Genovese points out, Scarlet spends much of the
book working through a sense of loss of her mother by
yearning for Ashley, a man in many ways very similar
to Ellen. Because she fails to understand her needs and
desires, Scarlett longs to be a man and cannot find
adequate objects for their desire: 'In the end, Scarlett
has only herself.'[22] All her relationships demonstrate
the difficulties Scarlett has with her own identity, and
especially femininity. She loves an image of a man who,
she ultimately realises, has relied on her like a pathetic

child; she grasps the importance of her love for Melanie and Rhett far too late. She resents having babies, and takes little interest in her children. And her decision to 'think about it tomorrow' is too often an excuse to delay confronting those uncomfortable realities and repressed feelings which urgently need to be faced.

Paradoxically, it is her failures which are so magnetic. For most of my respondents, the centre of her appeal seems to be that restlessness and vitality which characterise her uneven and often wrong-footed or catastrophic relations with others. Watching the film recently, I was struck by how many times Scarlett hits people (Ashley, Prissy, Suellen and Jonas Wilkerson once each, Rhett three times) and how well that rather childish gesture expresses all her emotional violence towards a world she sees as endlessly frustrating her. And although other women characters suffer distress, anguish and heartbreak of a similar kind, Scarlett's observer is drawn to her consistent refusal to accept her lot, and her insistence that she deserves better of life. Grandma Fontaine's philosophising, Melanie's silent endurance and Mammy's practical adaptability are all very well, but not the stuff of excitement or female heroism. In small ways *GWTW* demonstrates the cost to women of social and emotional accommodation, of the kind which Scarlett refuses (albeit with near-tragic results). Her own mother dies whispering, not for husband Gerald or even Scarlett herself, but for her dead cousin Philippe, the man she loved and for whom her husband was a poor substitute. Melanie, conceiving a second time against her doctor's advice, dies in childbirth. Belle does her bit for the Confederate cause, and saves Ashley's life – but she gets her beloved Rhett only at times when Scarlett discards him. Scarlett alone is described as having 'found the road to ladyhood hard', but for which of them – indeed, any of us – can it be said to be easy?

I am reluctant to generalise about the impact of Scarlett O'Hara on the millions of women (and a sizeable number of men) who have been fascinated and moved by her. As I have discussed, her appeal to and power over women come from many sources of private and collective history and fantasy. Women reader-viewers respond to her with admiration, scolding, recognition, disapproval . . . What she seems to offer, as a fictional and filmic character, is a range of identification possibilities. Scarlett's life story is that of Everywoman – from innocent untested virgin to wife, mother, widow, career woman, prostitute; her personal story is also one of any nation and any class (if not race) within the last century, going from prosperity to destitution, from peace to war, class and race stability to chaos and conflict – and back. The reversals of national, racial, class and gender history are embodied in Scarlett as both representative of and rebel against her specific historical, social and personal position. For many women reader-viewers, the epic heroism demanded of Scarlett at a historical moment when all certainties and fixed social relations are dramatically disturbed, and thus called into question, not only gives weight and dignity to one woman's experience but also affords us opportunities of seeing our own lives as part of a wider class, race and generational historical struggle.

5

The King and the Wimp:
The *Gone With the Wind* Men

The man I married heard me discussing *GWTW*. No doubt inspired by this, one evening when we were both a little tipsy, he decided to carry me upstairs for a night of grand passion. The effect was slightly marred by the fact that, unlike Clark Gable, he had to pause several times for breath on the way up – and totally ruined by the fact that he cracked my head on the landing wall. We were divorced in 1980. (Pat Read)

In conclusion, I would like to say . . . if Scarlett did not want Rhett, I would have him like a shot. (Mrs S.J. Heffernan)

Scarlett is at the heart of *Gone With the Wind*, and everyone else in some way complements and contrasts with her. But what of the two men she claims to love? How do we women think and feel about Ashley Wilkes and Rhett Butler? As I leafed through correspondents' letters and questionnaires, I was extremely curious to see how women judged the two central male characters. Sympathetically treated as they both are in book and film, I expected mixed responses and some ambivalence – especially since I was aware that Leslie Howard, who played Ashley, was a major star in the 1930s and immediate postwar decades, and was thus regarded as the heart-throb appropriate to play a man considerably his junior. I certainly anticipated an enthusiastic response to his role from women who had been avid film fans during his heyday.

Wilkes the Wimp

I was not prepared for the extraordinarily one-sided nature of reactions. Hardly a word was said against Rhett Butler and Clark Gable, who played him; Rhett was voted 'most favourite' character almost as much as the favourite, Scarlett. But in response to the item on my questionnaire which asked for 'least favourite character', though names like Jonas Wilkerson, India Wilkes and Prissy were mentioned, one was the overwhelming choice: Ashley Wilkes. The reasons given amounted to a remarkably homogeneous verdict on Ashley/Leslie Howard: over and over, the character (in book and film) was described as wet, weak, wimpish, wishy-washy, spineless, insipid, boring, a ninny, indecisive, a failure, a moral coward, too good, ineffectual, timid, dishonest, pathetic, defeatist, a sop. 'He hid behind the ladies' hoops', went one reply, while another dismissed him with a withering list: 'no charm, selfish, bland, dully dutiful, namby-pamby, niminy piminy'. Reader-viewers by the dozen felt that Ashley was not straight with Scarlett, and thus contributed to 'ruining her life'; by implicit contrast with Rhett Butler, they accused him of acting without clarity and honesty, of 'lacking balls'. Ashley's idealism is seen as contemptible, not complex, and his tormented desire for Scarlett, in conflict with love for Melanie, merely as a sign of weakness and escapism.

It is hard to know whether Ashley's critics are so severe because of Leslie Howard's performance (and certainly many writers referred to this). In all accounts of the making and critical reception of *GWTW*, Howard's infelicitous performance is singled out for censure. Margaret Mitchell's husband wrote to friends that he and Margaret felt Howard was 'wretched beyond compare',[1] and Richard Harwell notes Mitchell's 'greatest disappointment' in the portrayal, which created 'a much weaker character than she had written.'[2] Howard himself had resisted taking the part. By that time much celebrated in Hollywood for parts such as Philip Carey in *Of Human Bondage* (1934), Romeo (1936) and Professor Henry Higgins in *Pygmalion* (1938), this blond, blue-eyed Englishman had acquired a considerable screen reputation as 'the troubled man of thought'. Howard was tired of such typecasting, and saw Ashley as 'one more in the long line of watery weaklings' he had been forced to play.[3] He also felt – probably correctly – that at forty-five he was too old for the part. Agreeing to the role only on the understanding that he could co-produce *Intermezzo*, he failed to learn a Southern accent and arrived late on set; acted with reluctance; and generally gave the lacklustre performance which many critics and most of my correspondents condemn.

In terms of the film, however, Leslie Howard's lukewarm acting is not the only problem. Despite Max Steiner's musical score emphasising throughout the Ashley–Scarlett relationship, the screenplay and Victor Fleming's direction tended to favour scenes that focus on Scarlett O'Hara's relationship with Rhett Butler rather than romantic intellectual Ashley (though readers imagine that Ashley plays a more prominent role in the novel than he actually does; physically absent and thus silent for much of the time, he is so very present in Scarlett's thoughts and fantasies). In a quick scene count, I reckon Rhett and Scarlett appear alone together in three times as many scenes as Ashley and Scarlett, and there is far more frequent use of medium close-up, close-up and big close-up camera shots to emphasise the sexual tension between them. Leslie Howard's Ashley tends to be hunched, seated or moving evasively away from Scarlett; Rhett is usually fixing her with a sardonic, engaged or piercing gaze, and most scenes bring the two, by stages, physically close together. Clark Gable's Rhett demonstrates a physical confidence with himself and with Scarlett that leads him to touch, embrace, kiss and handle her roughly. He also has the advantage of making many a dramatic appearance – at the foot of the staircase, as hero of the Confederate bazaar, at Scarlett's front door after Melanie's baby comes – always immaculately dressed, usually by powerful contrast with the rags and homespun of his peers. Gable's Rhett had more costume changes than any male star in cinema history to date; he had his own tailor for the film. As I will shortly show, his star appeal and sexual charisma were already legendary. No wonder poor Leslie emerges so feebly against such stiff competition.

But in thinking of both book and film, there are structural reasons for Ashley's contemptuous reception. In terms of the quartet of central characters, Melanie and Ashley seem to function largely to offset the central drama between Scarlett and Rhett. Both of them represent the lost causes around which the narrative circles – patriotism, honour, gallantry, Southern belle-ism, duty and fidelity. All these qualities are the subject of sceptical questioning throughout *GWTW*, even if the ending suggests a new perspective on them. So the childhood sweethearts who remain true products of their anachronistic region and its ideologies are gently satirised and rendered ineffectual. Melanie's modesty at removing her nightdress to wrap round the dead soldier, and her insistence on a second, fatal pregnancy; Ashley's ineffectual helplessness at Tara after the War, and his inability – in Rhett's words – to be 'faithful to his wife with his mind or unfaithful with his body' (p. 914) . . . these contrast markedly and unfavourably with Rhett's supercilious, decisive self-interest and flair, and Scarlett's no-nonsense ability to roll up her sleeves and survive. Idealism and complexity of thought come out badly in *GWTW*, and Ashley, most of all the characters, embodies the worst elements of both. Pragmatism and enlightened selfishness are the keys to staying alive and economically and emotionally viable in a changing world. Of all the characters, the one to show most genius at adaptation and coming up smelling of roses is Rhett Butler.

Rhett the Rogue

I make no apology for dwelling at length on the figure of Rhett Butler and his film interpretation by Clark Gable. He so clearly overshadows Ashley/Howard in popular imagination that, like my correspondents, I make short shrift of the lesser figure in order to focus on the central male protagonist.

Margaret Mitchell's Rhett is an original who has influenced the creation of many subsequent romantic heroes, but in other ways he is a carbon copy, even a parody, of earlier fictional figures. He comes at the end of a long line of fictional men with an enigmatic, shady past history, a reputation for sexual excess and scandal, exquisite taste and perfect self-control, a proud and determined ability to keep his distance and appear cruel to the woman he eventually overwhelms with passion. The stock romantic hero of Victorian melodrama, this reformed rake or misunderstood idealist is well known to fiction readers from the pages of the eighteenth- and nineteenth-century novel and poem – among many others, Lovelace in Samuel Richardson's *Clarissa*, Byron's Don Juan, Madame de Staël's Lord Nelville (*Corinne*), Jane Austen's Mr Darcy (*Pride and Prejudice*), Charlotte Brontë's Mr Rochester (*Jane Eyre*), Heathcliff (Emily Brontë's *Wuthering Heights*), Rawdon Crawley and Lord Steyne of *Vanity Fair*, and Augusta Evans's St Elmo.

Like Shakespeare's Hamlet and the decadent cynics of Edgar Allan Poe, Rhett dresses in black and has a discursive, abstract turn of mind (though unlike them he can, and does, act to his own and others' advantage). As fantastic as Scott Fitzgerald's Great Gatsby, he has a mythic past composed of disinheritance, world-roaming, a part in the Gold Rush, gunrunning, professional gambling and something vague in South America and Cuba. Drawing on earlier literary models, Mitchell emphasises his lack of reputation, outsider status, association with all things wicked and proscribed, and his intellectual strength – after all, he predicts the South's defeat and is shrewder than anyone at feathering his own nest out of a war disastrous for most of his class and race. In classic fictional fashion, while we know where our heroine is throughout, we have no clear idea what happens to Rhett Butler for much of the time: is he in New Orleans, Charleston, at sea, in a brothel or gambling house? He turns up with romantic, dashing *élan* as the bearer of an expensive bonnet, the leader of a mad dash from a burning city, the favoured prisoner in an Atlanta jail; he disappears without warning and goes no one knows where. Rhett's characteristics both concentrated the most desirable qualities of fictional precedents, and also revitalised them for later romantic epic novelists. His name, a forceful mono-syllabic 'Rhett' followed by a down-to-earth surname, has set a pattern for the Bruce Carlton, Ralph Culver, Hayes Banister, and so on, of subsequent romantic fiction.

Rhett's attraction lies in his mystery, self-assurance, humour, canniness and association with evil, crime, piracy and all that is thrilling (in fantasy, anyway). Most of all, Rhett is almost tangibly physical – none of the intellectual dreamer or spiritual prince here. He is described obsessively in terms of his shape, size and the space his body occupies. Poor Melanie, for instance, is overcome at seeing him after Scarlett's miscarriage: 'He was so very large and male, and excessively male creatures always discomposed her'(p. 945). His very first appearance in the hall at Twelve Oaks emphasises how discomposing he was: 'powerfully built', 'such wide shoulders, so heavy with muscles, almost too heavy for gentility' (p. 97); his entrance at the bazaar makes this ungenteel point even more explicit: 'a body that was powerful and latently dangerous in its lazy grace . . . a man of lusty and unashamed appetites' (p. 177). Not only does he look sexy, but he seems to revel in it. He has exquisite taste in clothes that fit beautifully; and of course − unlike many of the other men − he remains *whole* throughout the novel. (While tending the wounded in Atlanta, Scarlett admits to herself a pleasure in seeing this healthy dandy around.) And his clothes show off a body that positively betrays its desires and appetites; it is described in terms of muscles swelling and rippling, with predatory bestial qualities ('animal-white teeth', 'thin hawk nose' [p. 97], 'lazy as a panther stretching in the sun, alert as a panther to spring and strike' [p. 296]).[4]

Moreover, Rhett is associated with the forces of evil, mystery and male sexuality, with his black eyes, hair, face and clothes, and his wild stallion. His darkness allies him also with other legendary and fictional figures, from the pirate and villain of melodrama to the swarthy Victorian hero and the gangster.[5] Attractive but sinister, sexually irresistible but possibly morally repulsive − all these are connotations of the dark and inscrutable Rhett Butler. In Selznick's film, Rhett is often associated with a staircase: his famous first appearance, at the foot of the Twelve Oaks stairs; his proposal of marriage to Scarlett, after watching her come unsteadily down Aunt Pittypat's stairs after generous helpings of brandy; his bearing Scarlett up the stairs of the Atlanta mansion for a night of passion; his arrival home and provocation of Scarlett into falling down those same stairs, leading to her miscarriage; and his dramatic final exit down them, telling Scarlett he is leaving for good. This association of Rhett with that transitional passageway in a house – between the social and private rooms, the mundane downstairs and the delicious nocturnal, the pleasantries of reception rooms and the passion of the bedroom ... the stairway is a good symbol for Rhett's mysterious mobility, versatility and sexual vibrancy.

There are hints of a troubled emotional past, one which has possibly yielded him an illegitimate son (whom he visits in New Orleans as his 'ward') and first-hand experience of a lover's abortion. But as with all tall, dark and handsome heroes, this disturbed past has made him what he so unashamedly is: cautious, wary, sardonic, pragmatic, and wise beyond compare. And possibly his greatest attribute for the female reader-viewer is that capacity to sympathise with, guide, comfort and especially understand women. He not only knows about the latest fashions (even – oh so naughty – in underwear) and is attuned to his daughter's every whim and minor problem – as well as being ready to push her buggy down the street[6] – but also, literally and metaphorically, he *sees through* women. From his first appearance in the hall, when Scarlett exclaims that he seems to know what she looks like without her shimmy, Rhett demonstrates his extraordinary insight into feminine psychology as well as the workings of the female body (he knows a lot about kissing, orgasm and pregnancy). This at first troubles Scarlett, who views his 'habit of seeing through her' as 'disconcerting' (p. 860); it is seen to be the source of Rhett's great power over her, and eventually is the quality which makes her love him. Just before he drunkenly bears her upstairs for the violent sex which gives her a first taste of real pleasure, 'He read her like a book. He had always read her and he was the one man in the world from whom she would like to hide her real thoughts' (p. 912).

Scarlett has read nothing much since leaving the Fayetteville Academy, and understands little about others (both Ashley and Rhett call her 'so literal'); Ashley reads books, yet he can neither interpret his own feelings nor understand how to act in a changing world; but to Rhett, who has read a great many tomes and women, all is an open book – and there is no lying to or dallying with him. That, of course, is why he is such a perfect confidant and friend, this man with whom (unlike husband Frank and beloved Ashley) Scarlett 'never ran out of things to say' (p. 662), whose company has 'the feeling of ease and comfort afforded by a pair of old slippers after dancing in a pair too tight' (p. 611).

That is probably because he is not really so 'very male' as Melanie feels; this swarthy dark stranger with the rippling muscles who smells, like Gerald, of brandy, tobacco and horses, has a mouth 'clear-cut as a woman's' (p. 296), small waist and feet, manicured hands and an attention to details of dress which might be regarded as effeminate in another. And, like *Ellen* O'Hara, he can address a woman about intimate details of sex and confinement; comfort her in tears with a voice 'so gentle, so quiet', arms 'so tender, so infinitely soothing', not to mention a clean handkerchief. While he is more fearless and ruthless than Ashley, he can weep over his wife and dead daughter and inspire the admiration and love of women as diverse as Melanie, Mammy and Belle. As journalist Lesley Garner put it:

> He is as handsome as a pirate, as dangerous as a crocodile. He is dashing and brave and devil-may-care but, and this is where Margaret Mitchell was so clever, he is also thoughtful and sensitive and tender and loving. He is just clever enough to hide his soft centre from Scarlett behind a diamond breastplate of mockery and wit.[7]

He must surely be the twentieth-century prototype of the hero of postwar mass-produced romance fiction, he who combines a restrained violence with gentle nurturant loving, and who remains (until the end) a sexually magnetic enigma.[8]

More than any other male character in *GWTW*, Rhett understands women well because he genuinely likes them and enjoys their company and conversation. But it is also true that he is especially drawn to women who resemble men, or have difficulty with their femininity. He worships the saintly and ultra-feminine Melanie, but has difficulty relating to her besides paying unctuous respect to her madonna qualities and sobbing childishly into her skirts. For fun, he chooses Scarlett and Belle, the businesswomen, tough cookies who shock and are censured by their society, and use their sexuality to survive and prosper. For Rhett can relate to all that without the inconvenience and boredom of conventional Southern belle qualities and timidities; indeed, he encourages Scarlett to do as he does and ignore public opinion and proprieties. He urges on her a life like his own – that of male outsider, wanderer, rogue; he shows little sensitivity to the dangers that path offers for a *woman*. To be an outcast belle is a far more serious fate; there is no way a Scarlett doing just as she wishes, with whom, could ever again be received in the homes of Atlanta and Charleston (as Rhett can). No, to follow his path is to become what Belle Watling is, and for any woman reader-viewer the constant equation of the two women adds a *frisson* of pleasure and terror to the figure of Rhett. For of course, Rhett says 'Do what you want and I'll be there', giving him enormous power over Scarlett.

Rhett is usually described by my correspondents as a rebel, a 'dark horse' who is the servant of no ideology or constricting loyalty. I suspect this is the *film*'s influence; in the novel, his eventual capitulation to the strictest rules of society is spelled out and becomes a major contentious issue between him and Scarlett. While initially an outsider, cynic and critic of the South's values and mores, after going to fight in the War – and especially after becoming a father – Rhett is won round to all that his region and class hold most dear. Telling Scarlett's son Wade Hampton that he will go to Harvard and become a lawyer, and reproving Scarlett for allowing Bonnie Blue to associate with Republican 'riffraff' (p. 880), he reproves her for not ensuring years ago a place for the children 'in the social scheme' (p. 881). Though Scarlett scoffs (it is, after all, only a short time since he urged her to forgo reputation, and scorn the Confederate 'lost cause' mentality in others), Rhett buckles down to winning back for his family a solid Southern white Democrat respectability – and it is for *that* he leaves Scarlett at the novel's end. In a fit of mid-life crisis, he tells Scarlett that she too may understand when she is forty-five; but meanwhile he is off to regain those things he had scorned, 'the clannishness of families, honour and security, roots that go deep' (p. 1008).

This change of heart can be seen as laughable, as in critic Floyd C. Watkins's witty condemnation: 'Rhett is a tough guy who could get along well with the roughest of Hemingway's characters, but when he softens he is a blithering patriotic old sentimentalist, for all his rough ways with women.'[9] On the other hand, it is interpreted more seriously by critic Anne Jones, who sees the novel (she does not discuss the film) as confirming the Southern social order and a traditional view of the nature and roles of the sexes. Pointing out that those who rebel most against their society, as well as gender roles, in the end turn back, she suggests: 'If there is a winner in *GWTW*, it is the "old days".'[10] And one of my correspondents, Claire Meyer, suggests an interesting position which clarifies some of our ambivalent feelings towards Rhett as turncoat. She suggests that by being too typically a romantic hero, Rhett undercuts gender stereotyping and thus parodies the genre of romantic fiction. Of his much-discussed cynicism, she says he 'recognises the worth of the things he exposes; is cynical in order to make people think, not merely to destroy.' She goes on to argue that Rhett will not allow others to get away with moral inconsistencies, so while not conforming himself, he is not irresponsible but serves to clarify the hypocrisies of others. I believe this is what many other respondents meant when they described Rhett as 'the most honest' of the characters.

'Dear Mr Gable – You Made Me Love You.'
(Judy Garland, *Broadway Melody of 1938*)

In a witty short film made in 1985, *The Woman Who Married Clark Gable*, a late-1930s Dublin setting provides the context for the drama of a childless working-class couple. A factory worker grows a Clark Gable-style moustache to please his wife, who is a dedicated home-maker and Gable fan. She goes to see Gable in the film *San Francisco* – first with her husband, then alone in the afternoon a couple of times – and reads movie magazine articles about her idol's love affairs. Fantasising that her (bewildered) husband *is* Gable, she speaks in film dialogue to him, with comic inappropriateness ('You're so rough' she whispers in bed to this gentle, timid man) and confesses to her priest – who calls him 'Mark Cable' – that she identifies the two men. After an angry bout of drinking alone, the husband shaves off his moustache and the unhappily childless couple go together to see Gable-free *Bringing Up Baby*; back home, she acknowledges that she 'feels better now'.[11]

The film is a nostalgic reflection on the nature of Hollywood stardom, 1930s gender relations and female fantasy, all commented on from an affectionate 1980s perspective. And it is significant that the focus of fantasy by this woman, whose tentative attempts to translate icon into flesh comically fail, is the star Clark Gable. For, as Joan Mellon says, 'the thirties belonged to Gable'[12] and his major successes belong to that single decade: from *A Free Soul*, with Norma Shearer; *Susan Lenox*, with Greta Garbo; and *Possessed*, with Joan Crawford – all in 1931 – to his most enduring hit, *GWTW* (1939). In 1938, after a national poll conducted through Ed Sullivan's syndicated newspaper column, twenty million voters elected him and Myrna Loy 'King and Queen of Hollywood'; with Gable, the title stuck. Several of my correspondents refer enthusiastically to 'the King'.

* * *

Clark Gable (1901–60) was one of MGM's great triumphs although, ironically, his two most successful roles – in *It Happened One Night* (1934) and *GWTW* – were achieved on loan-out to other studios. Like other stars in the years when Hollywood's studio and star system was most developed and profitable, Gable was controlled and moulded carefully by his boss, Louis B. Mayer, and hence by publicity staff. After his initial successes in 1931, his image was cultivated. He achieved unexpected popular success with *A Free Soul*, during which he tamed a spoiled rich girl by picking her up and throwing her into a chair; thousands of letters arrived at MGM about 'the guy who slapped Norma Shearer'.[13] Although he had not 'slapped' Shearer, MGM capitalised on this enthusiasm by making Gable hit Barbara Stanwyck in *Night Nurse*, produced later that year.

This broke with a tradition of genteel and gently

romantic heroes, producing a star who – if his woman resisted his charms – 'either booted her in the fanny or carried' her over his shoulder to the cave she'd never leave'.[14] Gable was publicised as a 'real' man: lover of guns, hunting, fishing, riding horses and fast cars, an all-American athlete who was sexuality in motion. Carefully concealed by MGM were his real German name, Goebel(s); his two rather mercenary marriages to women considerably older and less glamorous than himself (the studio discreetly arranged his second divorce as GWTW went into production); and the false teeth he had fitted (in around 1933). The only wife allowed much photographic exposure was his third and most glamorous, Carole Lombard.[15] His athletic-looking body – actually *not* the product of all the activities boasted – was much celebrated, and his part in *Test Pilot* (1938) suggested a man who liked physical danger in the heroic Hemingway mould. Unlike Leslie Howard, portrayed in public shots with an avuncular pipe in his mouth, Gable was portrayed surrounded by cigar or cigarette smoke, a masculine mannerism later adopted by Clint Eastwood.[16]

Notably lacking from most of the extraordinary media hype and articles published about Clark Gable is detailed reference to his acting ability. Despite the considerable training he was given by his first wife, Josephine Dillon, and his years of experience in the MGM stable (and the Academy Award he won for the Columbia Frank Capra film *It Happened One Night*), few critics dwell on his technical skill. What all emphasise is Gable's charisma, star quality and sexual magnetism (on and off screen). His latest biographer, Jane Ellen Wayne, blatantly entitles her book *Gable's Women*; she justifies this because 'To understand Clark Gable is to understand the many interesting women in his life'.[17] In Roland Flamini's book about the making of GWTW, Gable's image is described as 'one of aggressive sexuality – a man for the stormy season of the post-Depression, who coped with women and adversity with the same confident, cocky assurance of knowing what he is and where he is bound for.'[18]

His 'balls' are the subject of many a quote, including Sam Goldwyn's famous words about Gable: 'When a person like Robert Montgomery comes on the screen you know he's got balls. When Clark Gable comes on you can hear them clacking together.'[19] Gerald Gardner and Harriet Modell Gardner's *Pictorial History of Gone With the Wind* features more chapters on Gable than any other star or subject, and in a chapter called brazenly 'Gable and Sex' (illustrated by film stills of the star embracing eight different actresses) it argues that Gable 'symbolized sexual potency and the cocksure male' (p. 30). Susan Myrick, consultant on the *GWTW* film, fell for him like most of the women on set, and described him as 'fairly bursting open with IT'.[20] Jane Ellen Wayne dubs him 'a symbolic blend of man and beast' who replaced the gentle, rather fey Rudolph Valentino of the 1920s with a 'rough-diamond image . . . raw, crude, and hardened'. With lascivious enthusiasm, she describes her subject as the archetypal 'all-American guy . . . a devil, a man's man, a woman's Lancelot, a movie fan's dream, Scarlett's Rhett, a King of Kindness and integrity who just happened to like the bedroom more than applause'.[21] Wayne provides all the information any hungry fan might wish for about the women Gable bedded, married, betrayed and divorced. This was a logical biography to satisfy a public appetite for details about this walking set of genitals (who, paradoxically, is much quoted as being 'a lousy lay').

Judging by my correspondents, who write rather more discreetly about Rhett's sexual attractiveness, the star who became King of Hollywood on his animal magnetism has retained this appeal through the enduring fame of his best-known part, Rhett Butler – a part for which, unlike Vivien Leigh and Hattie McDaniel, he received no Academy Award. In letters and question-naires galore, women described to me their pleasure in 'irresistible' Gable through references to his 'dashing', 'handsome' or 'dead sexy' appearance, 'strong masculine appeal' and 'that twinkle/glint in his eye'. Many women describe being 'in love' with Gable ever since first seeing *GWTW* some fifty years ago: 'I was madly in love with Clark Gable in 1939 – I still think he's rather dishy!' For many, the mere contemplation of Gable induces the kind of weakness that Susan Myrick says came over script girls on the film set. A woman who saw the film in 1970, and claims to have been in love with the star ever since, writes: 'Oooh! it makes me go all gooey-knees just thinking of it.' Another, who saw the film as a teenager, intellectualises her passion:

> I suppose he epitomised/articulated romantic
> fantasies about men I scarcely realised I had.
> He was very sexually attractive to me . . . I knew
> that *underneath* that hard mocking exterior was
> *real* passion.

I believe that for many British women, Gable epito-mises a particularly glamorous and exotic all-American masculinity.

It seems that there was little doubt about Clark Gable playing Rhett Butler. Although contracted to MGM and David Selznick's father-in-law Mayer, from the very first Gable was the public's choice. Even Margaret Mitchell, never very enthusiastic about him, wrote a letter as early as July 25, 1936, acknowledging 'All of my friends are determined that he [Gable] should play this part', and in October that year she wrote that she was also deluged with letters demanding she refuse him the role.[22] Thus Gable was already chosen (or at least argued about) as soon as the novel came out; and apart from a few later critics and a minority of my correspondents, it seems that – in the words of Gerald and Harriet Modell Gardner – 'the perfect actor met the perfect role.'[23]

So 'perfect' was he for the role that David Selznick was able to cast him only because MGM 'loaned' the star and demanded full distribution rights and a sliding scale of gross profits from the completed movie. Gable himself, like Leslie Howard, was reluctant to take the role (among other reasons, he disliked costume parts, David Selznick, and the proposed length of filming) and on set he vehemently disliked George Cukor, known as a 'woman's director'. Because Gable was the undisputed star and had top billing he was able to call several shots, including demanding a change of director. He chose Victor Fleming, his friend and director on *Test Pilot*, a 'man's man' who changed *GWTW*'s emphasis from Cukor's picture about intimate emotions to a grand melodrama. It was perhaps only this confidence between buddies who knew they were 'all men' that enabled Fleming to persuade a reluctant Gable to weep over Bonnie's death. In smaller ways, too, Gable's star status enabled him to dictate terms such as length of working day, a new wardrobe and tailor, and no Southern accent. Although Susan Myrick trained all the actors in appropriate Southern accents, Gable demurred; Myrick later acknowledged, 'I doubt if it matters what he says – the ladies will be swooning at his manly beauty.'[24]

In most of the publicity photos, posters, cards, cinema lobby cards, screen magazine article illustrations and record sleeves, Rhett Butler and Scarlett O'Hara are featured, in erotic or romantic pose. Most reproduced stills (often posed in similar positions to those in the film) are Rhett about to kiss Scarlett on the road to Tara, Rhett embracing Scarlett while proposing to her in Atlanta, and comforting Scarlett after her nightmare during the New Orleans honeymoon.

But easily the most popular image from the film is the famous shot of Rhett with Scarlett in his arms, about to bear her to the bedroom for a night of violent sex. In poster after poster, advertising the film throughout the world (whether it be known as *Gone With the Wind*, *Via col Vento*, *Autant en Emporte le Vent*, or *Tatt av Vinden*), the dominant image is the portrait (not photograph) of Rhett and a very déshabillée Scarlett *en route* to bed. So familiar is it that this masterful figure poring over a saucy, submissive Scarlett has been parodied, on stage, on television and in such items as the cover of Dale Anglund and Janis Hirsch's book *Gone With the Ape*[25] showing Scarlett in the arms of a giant ape, and the now-famous British left-wing *Socialist Worker* poster depicting Ronald Reagan bearing Margaret Thatcher, against the backdrop of nuclear war.[26] In terms of Clark Gable (and the illustration used resembles him far more closely than Vivien Leigh) this repeated image of the film – set against vignettes of Tara and the burning of Atlanta – confirms Clark/Rhett's dominant role in the film, a sexually overpowering star making an erotically intense hero.

Despite all my correspondents' enthusiasm for and belief in Scarlett as the central and dominant figure, there is no doubt that publicity, advertising and memorabilia all celebrate a different mastery – and that Clark-as-Rhett is its vital embodiment. It is hardly surprising that this image – so much reproduced, so much more sensual than any of the film stills (Leigh's pictorial image is one of cleavage and bodice-ripping; in the film her velvet and lace are firmly in place) – is one of my respondents' most frequently recalled memories of the film. And so celebrated is Clark Gable as the sexual heartbeat of *GWTW* that his very first appearance arouses an immediate *frisson*. As Mrs P.E. Buckham wrote to me about her viewing, 'Nearly every woman in the cinema sighed when catching first sight of Clark Gable at the foot of the stairs.' I have heard this often from friends and correspondents; it echoes my own experience of cinema visits.

On Not Giving a Damn

There were several shocking elements in the film of *GWTW* for a 1939 audience, and not least were the final words of Rhett Butler. As he leaves Scarlett, he utters these memorable and much-quoted words in response to her question as to what she should do and where she should go; 'Frankly, my dear, I don't give a damn.' The 'Frankly' is an invention of script-writer Sidney Howard, but the word 'damn' (Mitchell's original) violated the 'Hays Code' ruling about the use of bad language in movies. David Selznick, fully aware of the strict Code, shot two versions (one with Rhett saying 'I just don't care') but he was determined that the force of the original words must remain. With a fine instinct for a good line, Selznick spoke personally to Will Hays, quoted the Oxford English Dictionary and argued that the word was in common usage in publications; he won permission, but had to pay a $5,000 fine. Cheap at the price, Rhett's exit line was – and remains – a triumph.[27]

Mrs Margaret Barlow wrote to me that this line 'was used very romantically among my friends during my growing-up years and was certainly a classic remark to be remembered into my 60s'. Her words are a reminder of how rarely even such a mild expletive as this was uttered by a screen hero. Critic Joan Mellon suggests that Clark Gable is 'never so attractive' as when saying those words, epitomising as he does 'that restless male for whom a woman, any woman, is never finally enough, an image that has become the norm in

American films'.[28] So in that one line, or at least in our response to it, lies a crucial secret of Gable's enduring appeal: he finally withholds love because the woman did not shape up in time, and his absolute masculine superiority, control and thus power are confirmed. No real man is at a woman's mercy, and no hero settles for domesticity on her terms. This was a lesson film-goers were to learn from Gable's successors – James Dean, John Wayne, Clint Eastwood, Robert Redford. . . . For a 1930s and 40s audience, those shocking words broke a screen taboo and confirmed Gable as most thrilling of screen heroes. Scarlett had won him, but did not fully appreciate what she had; for her, as for us viewers, the lesson is clear. The two men – real star and fictional man – converge. Clark/Rhett is unique, irreplaceable, utterly special. He is also unattainable and therefore – like all stars and heroes of romance – deliciously, infinitely appealing.

Joan Didion has written of the appeal John Wayne had for her in childhood, saying that he had 'a sexual authority so strong that even a child could perceive it'. She suggests that in a world which she understood early on to be 'characterized by venality and doubt and paralysing ambiguities', Wayne suggested a different world (mythic or not) in which

> a man could move free, could make his own
> code and live by it; a world in which, if a man did
> what he had to do, he could one day take the
> girl and go riding through the draw and find
> himself home free . . . at the bend in the bright
> river, the cottonwoods shimmering in the early
> morning sun.[29]

This romantic vision is one in which a mysterious and sexually vibrant hero acquires power from his mobility and autonomy and the ability, if he chooses, to convey his chosen woman to a mythic place beyond civilisation.

And in Gable we have a figure of similar power to suggest sexual joy and divine emotional gratification, but one who – in his most resonant role – withholds all from his woman and rides off into the sunset claiming the indifference we have suspected of so many screen heart-throbs as well as real men . . .

The Row and Rape

> Rhett Butler, more than a little drunk, desperately in love with Scarlett, patience shredded, swept up his taunting wife into his strong arms and carried her protesting (to begin with) up those long, deep stairs to be swallowed into the darkness above, end of scene. The rest was left to your imagination (which wouldn't happen today of course) and I had a vivid one, though not necessarily accurate at the time.
> Yes, on reflection it was a husband 'having his way' with his wife, but they had both aroused in me such feelings of romance, love, longing and need that for a long time afterwards I used to secretly watch married couples (my parents as well) to see how they acted to one another.

In that description of her feelings on first seeing *GWTW* in 1957, at the age of fourteen, Irene Beenham encapsulates wonderfully the secret erotic thrill, and yet the troubling quality in Rhett's notorious sweeping of Scarlett off her feet. She also reminds us of the strict censorship governing sexual matters in films of the 1930s, and describes the confused excitement many a teenage girl of the 1950s and early 60s (myself included) felt about a scene suggesting the then socially taboo subject of marital violence and rape.

I have already noted how frequently the illustration

of this scene has been used to publicise the film, and to keep it in popular consciousness. But of all the issues in *GWTW* which arouse strong feelings, Rhett's violent sex with Scarlett is easily the most contentious. In critical and journalistic articles, as well as in the letters and questionnaires I received, it is seen as the erotic climax (in both senses) of book and film, a symbolically crucial scene. Opinions and feelings vary about it enormously, especially among writers of different generations and political positions, as do perceptions of what actually occurs. David Selznick referred to it on the film set as the 'Row and Rape', and several eminent critics of modern fiction – as well as some of my correspondents – believe that Rhett *rapes* Scarlett that night.[30] However, the majority of my correspondents (and I agree) recognise the ambiguous nature of the encounter, and interpret it as a scene of mutually pleasurable rough sex.

That this scene is the subject of controversy and debate came as no surprise. The issues of rape and men's violence toward women – in and out of marriage – have been high on the feminist agenda for many years, and in the last decade have been the subject of much public discussion. The establishment of homes for battered wives, rape crisis centres and rape suites in police stations, 'Reclaim the Night' marches, as well as attacks by women on sex shops, pornography and 'Page Three' nude photos in the tabloid press, have all highlighted the extent of male violence, and the daily fear and vigilance experienced by most women. Feminist debates on and practical measures countering male violence have produced an ideological shift in public perceptions of that violence. Rape, far from being accepted as a primarily *sexual* crime perpetrated on women who 'ask for it' or 'were looking for it' (the dominant view which still influences elderly male rape trial judges) is now discussed seriously by the police and mainstream press as a violent crime by men against women, as an assertion of power, fear, woman-hatred. 'Revolutionary' feminists, following a body of writings from the USA in the 1970s and 80s, took the line of theorist Susan Brownmiller, who saw rape as 'nothing more or less than a conscious process of intimidation by which *all men* keep *all women* in a state of fear'.[31]

One of my correspondents, Elena Bond, reads *GWTW* from a revolutionary feminist perspective. Arguing that Rhett rapes Scarlett and tries to make her have a child, she says:

> To try and make Scarlett finally fall in love with Rhett after all this is the ultimate insult to women, i.e. the green light for men to abuse and humiliate women and if they do so badly enough the women will fall in love with them in return! The author's message seems to be that not only are Scarletts doomed to find Rhetts to humiliate them but in fact should have Rhetts to knock them into shape and break their spirits.

And in her acid, witty article on *GWTW*, Angela Carter describes the 'rape' in terms that offer a revenge fantasy to the Brownmiller apologists:

> Cut to the morning after. Scarlett stretches luxuriously in bed, smiling, singing a happy little song to herself. See? That's just what the bitch needed all the time.
>
> And if you believe that, you will believe anything. But. Perhaps. Perhaps she had broken his kneecaps, at that! Surely that is the only thing that could make her smile, at this juncture!
> And that must be the real reason why he has to go

off to Europe, to visit a good kneecap specialist. Of
course, they can't say that in the script, but
I am sure that is what happened, really.[32]

Critic Kathryn Lee Seidel believes Scarlett's 'maso-
chistic surrender' suggests that 'women secretly desire
to be taken by force'. She reads the scene as a rape in
which Rhett performs the 'ultimate act of domination'
because he is denied 'the privileges he assumes are his
right', and she relates this to the many fictional rapes
in twentieth-century American Southern fiction. She
also points out that Rhett's black looks and animal associations titillate readers with their similarity to those of
the standard black rapist of Southern fantasy and fear,
as represented in nineteenth- and twentieth-century
novels about the Southern belle. But perhaps, in out-
lining a tradition and series of thematic links, Seidel has
become a little carried away. It is possible to interpret
the scene as rape if you do not read the novel too closely,
but to argue that 'the central rationalization' in *GWTW*
is 'the argument that all women wish to be raped' seems
to me a distortion of Mitchell's novel and Selznick's
film.[33] On the contrary, I would suggest that *GWTW*
subverts that very common rape theme by presenting
Scarlett in three situations which – in other Southern
novels and films – would result in violence towards
the female protagonist. What could have been a Union
soldier's rape ends with Scarlett becoming his murderer; the Shantytown near-rape by a black man concludes with Scarlett's rescue by an ex-slave (so not
all black men are rapists . . .). And Rhett, though threatening murder and later confessing to Melanie that he
wanted to hurt Scarlett, in fact finds his willing sexual
match in a Scarlett who is tired of keeping to the
rules and playing polite games in bed as well as out.
My correspondents often expressed ambivalent feelings about Rhett, seeing him as 'nasty-wonderful' in one

respondent's phrase, his roguery very much a 'naughty but nice' element of *GWTW*. Cora Kaplan argued that Scarlett's story is that of a woman who has had lousy sex from two incompetent husbands (a 'boy' and an 'old man', as Rhett reminds her) and knew nothing about women. At last she finds out what *good* sex feels like, even if (or probably because) her first experience takes place in mutual inebriation and a spirit of vengeful anger. Geraldine Kaye made the observation that this is the one psychologically false note in novel and film: since Scarlett revelled in her only night of real passion, Rhett (represented as the one person who understands her thoroughly) would know and would be there in the morning. To apologise and leave, as he does, is out of character; if he does not recognise his achievement in at last showing Scarlett sexual ecstasy, how can he be said to recognise anything else about her? Doris Buckley echoed this sentiment when she wrote that Rhett's leaving the morning after was 'slightly incredible', since 'a man with his experience of women and loving Scarlett so much . . . would have realised what he had awoken in her that night and would have stayed to see if this had indeed been the case.' By far the majority of the women who responded to me saw the episode as erotically exciting, emotionally stirring and profoundly memorable. Few of them referred to it as 'rape'.

Close reading of the novel and viewing of the film gave no indication of an actual rape. Furious with jealousy of Ashley, at whose party Scarlett has had to face the eyes of her peers accusing her of adultery, Rhett *threatens* violence, as he does at other points (he talks of 'riding [her] with a slack rein . . . with curb and spurs just the same' [p. 840], and he has already made it clear that no lock would keep him from the bedroom if he wanted to enter). As they drink downstairs together he frightens Scarlett with those powerful hands on her head, and his threat to smash her skull to get Ashley out of her mind. But threatened or potential violence is not the same as the real thing – and Rhett is always seen as a classic white Southerner in that he kills a Negro and the odd Yankee, but shows no violence to white women.

Of course, the *threat* of violence is disturbing. As Rhett grows menacing towards Scarlett in his cups, he becomes what he was when she first saw him, a stranger; this word is used several times to refer to him throughout the episode. As soon as this 'drunken drawling-voiced stranger' swings Scarlett into his arms and upstairs, he turns into a 'mad' and 'savage' stranger who is associated with 'a black darkness . . . darker than death', an anonymous '*someone, something* stronger than she, *someone* she could neither bully nor break, *someone* who was bullying and breaking her' but who gives her 'a wild thrill such as she had never known' – obviously her first orgasm (pp. 917–18, my emphases). While I believe I interpreted this as rape when reading it in my teens (though I was unsure quite what rape meant), my latest reading reveals more ambiguities. If we remember the codes by which Scarlett has been raised, and the constraints on her sexual freedom, it is not surprising that she dislikes the sex she has had already, nor that she has so far resisted melting gratefully into Rhett's arms, for all his boasts about knowing how to kiss a woman. She has, after all, been raised to consider sex merely a duty of marriage – the less said about it the better: as Frances Newman says in *The Hard-Boiled Virgin* (1926), 'In Georgia, no lady was supposed to know she was a virgin until she had ceased to be one.'[34] In the absence of reliable contraception marital sex inevitably produced babies, and Scarlett, unlike Melanie, resists her biologically determined fate and refuses to have more children. It was thus going to take more than a little technique on Rhett's part to give Scarlett multiple orgasms.

The man who satisfied Scarlett sexually had to satisfy

her *fantasies*, and excite her *imagination*, and this is what Rhett eventually (almost accidentally) does. Normally wary, thoroughly in control, withholding something of himself, the drunken Rhett abandons all reserve and meets Scarlett in a powerful sadomasochistic encounter that gives both of them an experience of dangerous ecstasy and allows each to play out the power relations between them in a manner that pleases Scarlett, but later makes Rhett ashamed. As many critics of romantic fiction have pointed out, the description of sexual activity between a man and a woman is one of eroticised power play set in a timeless space which resolves previous conflicts between them. But in the contemporary mass-market romance (Harlequin, Mills & Boon, and so on) sex is the arena in which the heroine at last *knows* that the hero, hitherto an 'unknowable other, a sexual icon whose magic is maleness',[35] loves her – and then, of course, the story is over.

In Scarlett's case the night of passion proves that Rhett loves her, but it also gives Scarlett a great sense of power over him. Although none of this comes through in the film, in the novel Scarlett revels in the thought that 'she had him at last', that her early desire to 'hold the whip over his insolent black head' was now fulfilled, since she 'knew the weakness of his armour' and could 'make him jump through any hoops she cared to hold' (pp. 918–19). Far from being the thoughts of a victim of rape, or the tones of a woman at peace with the husband who has humiliated her, this is the language of the slave-owner who is coolly sure of – and gets a sadomasochistic charge from – his absolute power. Here, Scarlett is more clearly equated with the cruel male planter of Southern fiction than the passive frightened girl so prevalent in the 'female gothic' novel; a product of her class and race, who has used male tactics and adopted masculine traits, she has internalised a white upper-class male confidence. What she has learned about power play between black and white comes in handy when dealing with an uppity white though significantly swarthy dark lover.

For, of course, Rhett has fled. As I have indicated, a few women saw this as a false note, but I believe it is a psychologically astute narrative twist. Rhett, after all, has uncharacteristically abandoned his self-restraint and sardonic manner and expressed the full force of his jealousy, anger, passion and longing – then run back to Belle Watling, over whom (unlike Scarlett) he has total financial and sexual control (this is omitted from the film, probably to avoid alienating our sympathy for him). And Rhett suddenly looks very weak and vulnerable. Far from using that night to confirm his power over Scarlett, and to let her see what a great lay she has been missing, Rhett seems to me a frightened and jealous man who needed to be brutal towards Scarlett to allay fears of his impotence and inadequacy. No wonder he sneaked away before breakfast.

What all these different readings of the rape/seduction reveal is the different lines intepretation can take when a contentious issue is at stake within a text. While rape in marriage was not a matter of public discussion until very recently (and its legality has only very lately been challenged), the 'Row and Rape' has been received as erotically satisfying or not, depending on the reader-viewer's response to sadomasochistic sex and the nature of her interpretation of the characters and screen actors. It did not surprise me that women over fifty mostly found the scene very exciting and pleasurable and that criticisms of both it and the figure of Rhett emanated mainly from younger women, especially those identifying themselves as feminists. And several expressed the kind of contradictory and muddled sentiments I myself share about this show of male force.

Feminist theorist Lynne Segal's words are of relevance here. Drawing on psychoanalytic readings of sexuality, she suggests:[36]

> the idea of power and submission is built into
> the language and imagery of heterosexual
> encounter . . . How does a feminist handle the
> fantasy of desire for sexual mastery from men
> alongside the day-to-day struggle to combat men's
> power in every sphere of life? . . . Neither women's
> nor men's sexual fantasies reflect simply the reality
> of male dominance and misogyny (although they
> are influenced by this reality). They draw upon all
> manner of infantile sexual wishes, active and
> passive, loving and hating, all the way back to our
> very earliest feelings of desire and pleasure in
> childhood.

So, whatever perverse 'pleasure' fantasies of surrender, submission and rape may bring to women, the act of rape itself – as Segal and many others emphasise – is *not* pleasurable for them. A vicarious enjoyment of Rhett's violent passion that brings 'surrender to arms that were too strong, lips too bruising, fate that moved too fast' (p. 918) is no indication that a reader-viewer condones male violence, or indeed secretly wishes to be treated in such a way in order to achieve her own sexual fulfilment.

*   *   *

I have concentrated on the figure of Rhett Butler because my correspondents did, obsessively, and because he seems to be the prototype of the modern romantic hero: enigma and cad, but also mother, father and counsellor rolled into one. I have argued that in many ways he is a composite rather than an original figure. It is undoubtedly true, as biographer Anne Edwards demonstrates, that Mitchell used some characteristics of her first husband, 'Red' Upshaw (whose name perhaps suggested Rhett's) and that her hero's emotional power may derive from

Mitchell's profoundly ambivalent feelings about her charismatic but violent partner. But he was already a familiar type in romantic and Victorian poetry, novels and plays – Mitchell acknowledged that *GWTW* was 'probably as Victorian a novel as was ever written'[37] – and had remained a popular stereotype in British and American fiction and drama. Thus the portrayal of Rhett drew on and deliberately departed from elements of real people and earlier representations to emerge as the resonant and memorable character he is now considered by most reader-viewers.

And Rhett is a peculiarly *modern* hero, one who is emulated more by Jacqueline Susann than Barbara Cartland. Because *GWTW* is a historical epic and version of the family saga, his fate is not simply to capitulate finally to his beloved, in bed and/or marriage; he and Scarlett marry three-quarters of the way through, and then their real problems begin. Although in some ways he is the 'older man, a dark, magnetic, powerful brooding, sardonic *Super-Male*' of gothic fiction, Scarlett is far from the shy, inexperienced and frightened female counterpart of that genre.[38] She is already her own woman, and even in the 'Row and Rape' episode she remains so. For the sexual climaxes or decisive moments of romantic or gothic fiction *result in* marriage, the tender kiss or (in contemporary fiction) the sexual act sealing, once and for all, compatibility and harmony between the lovers. In *GWTW*, as in many later family sagas, marriage *precedes* sexual and emotional knowledge. Scarlett marries Rhett for dubious mixed motives, but remains fearful of that sexual power he has always offered or held over her. The recognition of her desire and love for him follows only from a night when each becomes again unknown and anonymous, and can explore unconscious and repressed desires without inhibiting restraints. Sex here is not presented in agony-column terms, as a way of getting to know your partner with the light on; on the contrary, it is a means by which lovers can become estranged from each other in the dark in order to explore their most delicious and forbidden (thus liberating) fantasies. No wonder it is a scene that stays in the imagination, one which Hollywood publicists used repeatedly to promote the film. And while one may fault various aspects of Clark Gable's performance as Rhett, for most women he – with his already powerful sexual charisma as star – was able to represent the *sexual* truth about the romantic hero.

In some ways, popular judgements of Rhett and Ashley suggest that *GWTW* invites depressingly orthodox and reactionary verdicts on men and masculinity. Virtually to a woman, my correspondents condemned Ashley Wilkes for his 'wimpishness', without acknowledging that tortured idealism and very human agony he suffers in a period of change he barely understands. It seems that any generosity of spirit which might have accrued to Ashley is absorbed completely by Rhett who, though initially very different, gradually takes over Ashley's best qualities and even adopts his anguish. As the novel – and even more the film – focuses in on Rhett as unrequited lover, bounder-turned-conservative idealist, and finally unattainable love object, Rhett takes over all Ashley's fictional and filmic space and is transformed into one of the most versatile and multidimensional of epic romantic figures. Swashbuckler and tough guy; entrepreneur and war hero; enigmatic stranger and relaxing confidant; sexual wizard and tender parent; wanderer and home-lover; iconoclast and visionary. Is it any wonder he is the stuff female heterosexual fantasy is made of, or that so many women find his final parting so profoundly tear-jerking?

6

Tomorrow is Another Day:
Gone With the Wind's Ambiguous Ending

Eat your heart out Conran, Krantz, Robbins *et al*. The most memorable sexual relationships are not those which are resolved before the reader's eyes, but those which never reach fulfilment. (Lesley Garner, 'The greatest love story yet to be told')

As every *Gone With the Wind* fan knows, the novel and film offer no comfortable happy ending. After more than 1,000 pages or nearly four hours of following the complex trials and tribulations of the female and male protagonists, we are further than ever from that clash of cymbals and stirring violin strains which should signal a passionate reconciliatory mutual declaration by Scarlett and Rhett. Unusual among popular realist novels, departing from its nineteenth- and early-twentieth-century literary models, and very different from classic 1930s Hollywood films, *GWTW* denies the wish of reader and film-goer that the cat-and-mouse defensive game between lovers should be settled once and for all. Following the handful of ambiguous nineteenth-century novels such as *Great Expectations* and *Villette*, and the experimental open endings of writers such as Henry James and Virginia Woolf, *GWTW* frustrates popular narrative expectations and offers instead a series of possible scenarios. No wonder so many of my correspondents assume – absolutely wrongly – that Margaret Mitchell intended to write a sequel, and was simply offering a tempting ending to ensure interest in a *GWTW Part Two*.

Margaret Mitchell wrote the novel's last chapter first,

the first chapter last. She always denied vehemently that she had a sequel in mind, and refused every request to reveal what happened after the story's end. 'I do not have a notion of what happened to them and I left them to their ultimate fate'[1] is typical of her remarks to correspondents, while she joked about a sequel called *Back With the Breeze*, 'a highly moral tract in which everyone, including Belle Watling, underwent a change of heart and character and reeked with sanctimonious dullness'.[2] When she wrote that final chapter first, Mitchell laid out the series of complex overlapping themes she would go on to explore in the rest of the novel: the relationship of land and woman, woman and mother or mother-figures, the nature of hope and despair after bitter experiences, including deaths, the quality and endurability of love, the power of tradition, old loyalties and roots, the problem of human beings understanding one another, and the key issue of survival. All these are concentrated in a wistful, sad conversation between Scarlett, newly aware of her love for Rhett, and Rhett himself – battle-scarred, tired of emotion and patience, ready to leave in search of 'the things he's thrown away so lightly in youth, the clannishness of families, honour and security, roots that go deep' (p. 1008). That is, after uttering possibly the most famous exit line in literature: 'My dear, I don't give a damn.'

And it is in this final chapter that all the various elements and meanings of Scarlett O'Hara come together to produce an anguished intensity of panic, frustration, thwarted desire and loss: an amalgam of personal, political, familial and racial lost causes. Just at the moment she understands her recurrent nightmare of running through the fog, realising finally that Rhett was the only enduring love she had known, he asserts his masculine power and withdraws those enfolding maternal arms to deny us all – Scarlett, readers and viewers – the grand finale we have come to expect.

And David Selznick was brave to follow the book faithfully, without firming up the ending. A large number of my correspondents note the fact that 1930s and 40s films always ended clearly, and that romantic epics would invariably offer a happy ending. Mrs Margery Owen recalled that even David Lean's film of *Great Expectations* (1946) ended – inaccurately in terms of Dickens's story – with Pip and Estella marrying. She writes: 'No matter what vicissitudes went on beforehand, it was *de rigueur* for the hero and heroine to end in a clinch, especially in the popular dramas.' She recalls seeing *GWTW* several times during the war. Each time, at the point when Melanie tells Scarlett that Rhett loves her and Scarlett runs towards her house to his arms, many people in the audience leapt to their feet to get home before the next air-raid, certain of the happy ending conventional in romantic films. As she notes wryly, 'During the War there must have been large numbers of people all over the country who saw *GWTW* and *probably never realised that it did not end happily.*'

And some of them would no doubt have been devastated. A certain number of my respondents describe feeling bereft, distraught or extremely vexed at the inconclusiveness. The critic Cora Kaplan wrote powerfully of her own 'despair and near hysteria' after finishing the book at the age of approximately fourteen. The daughter of left-wing Jewish intellectual parents who disapproved of it, she explains her frustration at the author's refusal of a happy ending:

> *Gone With the Wind* brought home to me what I already knew at a social and political level, had felt powerfully the day the Rosenbergs were executed, that life was, could be unfair and I met this realization with howls of rage and pain.[3]

Many women (though a minority of my correspondents) ticked the box which asked if they felt 'cheated' of a happy ending, but many more said they fully expected it and were nonplussed at the irresolution (a 'feeling of utter emptiness', as one put it). Witnessing a happy ending is clearly a cherished pleasure, and several women in their fifties and older described themselves as being 'of a generation that expected' happy – or 'tidy', as a few put it – endings. One such woman expressed the vexed initial reaction that reluctantly turned to admiration for the author: 'The ending shocked me at first – it just couldn't end there – all the books I had read finished with the heroine locked in the hero's arms. How clever to end a book like that.'

The ending is viewed with less surprise and shock by generations of women raised on postwar fiction and film, with its uncertain or open endings reflecting a modernist and post-modernist age in which comfortable certainties are regarded as suspect – or at least, the province of only particular genres like the popular detective and romantic novel and film. While many younger reader-viewers are dismayed at being cheated of a final clinch, they usually express exhilaration at the 'open, forward-looking ending . . . a sense of possibility'. While one respondent felt that the ending was not fair, and was 'like a symphony without a final movement', she saw the unresolved conflicts as 'part of its haunting resonance. Because the characters are not safely tucked up in bed together they stay with you'. The very openness of the ending has allowed many to speculate over what has gone before, to imagine deliciously different scenarios, or to fantasise over how *they* would succeed in getting Rhett back.

For at least two readers, who lapped it up in their early teenage years, the lack of resolution made them feel they had entered an adult emotional world. One, who read it at thirteen in 1959, said it 'seemed very "sophisticated" ', while another ex-convent school pupil 'felt "grown up" at not being spoonfed false resolutions'. For others, an adolescent reading or viewing has been followed by many more in adult life, with different responses and associations each time. A much-repeated experience is of reading-viewing when young and romantic, then feeling, as one grew older, that life offers precious few happy endings – so the older reader-viewer finds the conclusion more believable (if not very consoling). One correspondent expressed this poignantly: 'In those days as a prewar young lady we were all romantically inclined. My reaction now would probably be quite different, having had a very varied life!' And for some women, each experience of *GWTW* changes their minds about events after the close of book and film. 'It's fun to imagine a different outcome each time,' said one, while Norma Miller goes into more detail:

> Scarlett usually got what she wanted (except Ashley) and when she said she would return to Tara I think we are led to believe that she got Rhett back. On the other hand, were we meant to believe that this was the one occasion when Scarlett did not get what she wanted? The times I have discussed this!

Like many other women, Norma Miller defers to the author's intention ('were we meant to believe . . .') rather than trusting her own judgement, and there is some nervousness among women about the validity of their interpretations of the ending. On the whole, however, there is delight in the active participation demanded of reader-viewers; far from wanting all loose ends tied up, women derive renewed pleasure on each occasion from drawing on their current emotional experience and perspectives in order to imagine the eventual destiny of Scarlett and Rhett, not to mention the wimpish widower Ashley and boy Beau. And, as with other aspects of *GWTW*, the ending provides a debating point between mothers and daughters, friends and colleagues. Indeed, the uncertain conclusion has offered women the excuse to reread and re-view, as in a dream repeating the story without ever reaching a resolution which might seem like an anticlimax, or a small death.

Imaginative involvement in *GWTW*, determined as it is by each enthusiast's particular experiences – of life as well as fiction and film – led to an interesting variety of responses to my questionnaire query:

> At the end of the book [and film], it's not clear whether Scarlett gets Rhett back.
> Do you: think she does?
>   think she doesn't?
>   not care?
>   feel cheated of a happy ending?

In response to the first two questions (does she or doesn't she?) I received almost equal numbers of crosses. Margaret Mitchell played that one cleverly! In terms of psychological verisimilitude, it seems that Scarlett and Rhett are portrayed as sufficiently complex to have the potential for more than one fate, and my correspondents give a convincing variety of explanations for their interpretations. As with all critical responses, these told me a certain amount about every respondent's emotional life, philosophy, and especially attitude to the possible transcendental properties of romantic love. In each case, reader-viewers' most cherished fantasies, deepest fears and the wisdom of years of life and love are brought to bear on the questions posed by novel and film. Unlike a definite ending, which might satisfy expectation and close off thought, the ambiguity of *GWTW*'s last page and screen minutes prevents passive reception and demands a creative imaginative response from each person.

Below are selected representative quotations from correspondents explaining why they believe Scarlett does, or does not, get Rhett back:

SCARLETT DOES . . .   SCARLETT DOESN'T . . .

(I) *LOVE CONQUERS ALL*

They were made for each other.

Rhett is ready to move on to someone else, softer and more caring.

They were two of a kind.

They're both too stubborn/pigheaded.

Their relationship would always be a stormy one, but somehow I think it would endure all that fate threw at them.

Their lives have been so dependent on each other and with the onset of age and maturity bitter memories will fade.

(II) *RHETT AS STABLE SUPPORT AND IN CONTROL*

Rhett would keep himself informed as to how Scarlett and Tara were doing. He would go to her if she was in trouble.

I think Rhett had fallen out of love, or maybe his love had been killed.

Rhett has had enough of Scarlett's tantrums and caprices . . . I prefer to think or hope that when he thinks Scarlett has been chastised or punished enough he'll make her crawl back to him.

I prefer to think that Rhett, having washed his hands of [Scarlett], went off and found happiness in his old age with kindly Belle, which they both deserved.

SCARLETT DOES . . .	SCARLETT DOESN'T . . .
I like to think that Rhett's final uncaring attitude is just a shell.	If Scarlett did get Rhett back it would be a tired middle-aged man who wanted a bit of home comfort.

(III) SCARLETT'S INDEPENDENCE

Scarlett, rather like our present Prime Minister, gets her own way.	Scarlett would take a deep breath, replenish her wardrobe, and find someone or something to fill her life.
She's a tough cookie.	Strong women in her time tended to be left on their own.
Having triumphed over so many emotional disasters, she will with characteristic determination set about turning the situation to her own advantage.	Having ridden roughshod over weak men, Scarlett finally came up against a man who could resist her.
	Scarlett has a constant longing for the mother, the feminine. Will she – post-return to Tara – end her days as a lesbian?

(IV) TARA

I think Tara is what Scarlett wants – men have not lived up to her expectations.

SCARLETT DOES . . .	SCARLETT DOESN'T . . .
	I think Scarlett loves property more than Rhett.

(V) *READER–VIEWER EXPERIENCES/PERSPECTIVES*

I like happy endings and I think Rhett and Scarlett deserved to be happy. I can't believe it was all too late!	That's what life is like. There are no happy endings.
This way it leaves you with hope of tremendous happiness.	I want her to be an independent and single woman.
I constructed imaginative scenarios about what *I* would do if I were to get him back . . .	

In these responses – typical of many more – reader-viewer explanations and rationalisations for their opinions vary from a reference to the text's internal evidence (the logic of characterisation, themes, and so on) to an expression of personal need and desire ('That's what life is like'). Thus, *GWTW* enthusiasts familiar with book and film produce cogent and coherent reasons for Rhett's losing patience with and passion for Scarlett, especially in view of her lack of self-knowledge and realisation of feelings 'too late'. The justice of Rhett's desertion and its logic in terms of the text's recurrent themes of betrayal, loss, the importance of origins and security . . . all these make

sense to those who explain why they feel Rhett will not
return, or only after a period of years.

Reading in sequence the responses to my question
about the ending, what struck me most was how hard
everyone is on Scarlett, and how indulgent towards Rhett
(and hardly anyone attributes blame or responsibility
to Ashley). Although, as I demonstrated in chapter 4,
in general Scarlett is much admired and excused by
reader-viewers, she is also without doubt the target
of considerable hostility. While, as the columns above
indicate, many correspondents found much to praise in
Rhett, feeling that he was worthy to find peace at last,
comments on Scarlett were sharp, rather ungenerous
and judgemental: 'she got what she deserved'; 'deserved
her comeuppance'; 'doesn't realise what she's missing!'
Women of all ages and classes seemed to find themselves
rather more sympathetic to Rhett than to Scarlett at the
close of GWTW.

In relation to the 'romantic' or 'happy' ending, this
is intriguing. In the classic romantic novel, from Jane
Austen through Charlotte Brontë to Barbara Cartland,
the final declaration of love between two people who
have misunderstood their own feelings and motives provides the climax of the novel, and usually culminates in
marriage. In most cases, it is the *man* rather than the
woman who has resisted his feelings; in the standard
Mills & Boon plot, he is often brutal and offhand –
until, that is, the overwhelming force of his feelings
for the female protagonist breaks down his defences and
makes him recognise the reasons in his upbringing or past
relations with women which have prevented the expression of his truly caring nurturance towards his beloved. In
family sagas and blockbusters, because marriage occurs
long before the end, there is no simple affirmative climax and no clear-cut contrast between patient, loving
heroine and cruel, misguided hero. Often the heroine
makes several marriages – each ending, like Scarlett's,

in death or (on a more contemporary note) divorce, and so the affirmation of the first kiss, sexual encounter or marriage proposal is no longer possible as an ending. In most cases, because women characters are at the centre of these texts, readers are caught up in the ways women handle or mismanage their relationships in and out of marriage and motherhood, and it is the woman's character and spirit which are most visible, most on trial.

GWTW is perhaps the first and most sustained novel/film to present a heroine more in touch with her practical, pragmatic and entrepreneurial qualities than her emotional needs – no wonder Margaret Thatcher's name is invoked more than once! And it seems that my correspondents judge her harshly for not being in touch with her own feminine qualities and limitations; for reader-viewers deeply involved with this narrative, it seems, that is the most threatening aspect of Scarlett O'Hara. The fragility of feminine charms and the problems of reconciling different aspects of a woman's life are something of which we are all acutely aware. On the one hand, my respondents admire Scarlett's resilience and ability to make her own life – and a minority feel strongly that she does not need a man at all (one even suggesting that her obsession with maternal loss might lead her to a lesbian future). On the other, however, they know that Rhett has responded to and brought out the female vulnerability in her, giving her her first orgasm, the first of her children she has really loved, and the first pregnancy she has desired, as well as offering her the first true adult love she has known. The preciousness of such a man, who reciprocates love and desire, is good in the nursery as well as in bed, knowledgeable about bonnets *and* the female body . . . no wonder my correspondents blame Scarlett for looking a gift horse in the mouth.

Also, as in all romance, the primary emotional responsibility lies with the woman: the majority of my contacts lay blame for the failed marriage at Scarlett's door. Only a few point to Rhett's unsavoury and unreliable sexual and emotional career; his apparently casual murder of an 'uppity nigger' and Yankee cavalryman in a bar-room; his drunken violence; his excessive love for and spoiling of Bonnie, which lead indirectly to her death; his inability to comfort Scarlett after Bonnie dies; his contribution to Scarlett's miscarriage; and most unforgivable of all, perhaps, leaving her the morning after both have enjoyed their first truly abandoned and satisfying sexual experience together. Though I have discussed this latter insensitivity with several women, only one correspondent described it in response to my question about the ending. With great acuity, Joy Adams wrote:

> Rhett misinterpreted Scarlett's revised appraisal of Ashley as her lover and breadwinner, and walked away too quickly. He had already made us aware, after the 'rape' scene, that he isn't quite as intuitive about Scarlett's reactions [as he thinks].

For the majority of women, the orthodoxy of true femininity demands that women, supposedly more in touch with their feelings and the emotional demands of men and children, are responsible for holding together marriage and family and – if those fall apart – bearing the main burden of blame. Scarlett O'Hara Butler is acknowledged as a fighter and schemer, and roughly half my sample believe she will get Rhett back eventually, but most women who went into any detail revealed what I consider excessively adverse critical judgement of her character and actions. Perhaps, in the late 1980s when I asked for reader-viewer reactions, with media celebration of that creature I, for one, have never met – 'post-feminist woman', who 'has it all': career, husband, children, a trim waistline, clean floors and multiple orgasms (with feminism and unglamorous real women parenthesised and marginalised) – Scarlett is likely to be more heavily judged than ever. It's OK to keep Tara, the store and your vulgar Peachtree Street house going, but whatever you do don't let your husband's needs slip. Marriage must be worked at and you, Scarlett, should have worked harder . . .

None the less, however my correspondents judged Scarlett and answered the 'does she, doesn't she?' question, very few of them 'didn't care'. The crisis in the Butlers' marriage and the uncertain nature of their separation apparently speak meaningfully to women about our own failed relationships, unsatisfactory marriages, and estrangements from those we love most. And the return to Tara and Mammy's bosom, while it is a poor substitute for reconciliation in Rhett's arms, suggests women's ability to survive rejection and despair, and also the importance of secure roots and female networks to protect us all from men's withdrawal of love and support.

For Scarlett's sexual powers can seem to mean nothing when they are no longer recognised and appreciated by men. Until Melanie's death Scarlett had always enjoyed Rhett's admiration and love, as well as Ashley's sheepish repressed desire (mistaken for love). As she comes to terms with Ashley's true love for Melanie and his superficial sexual attraction to herself – she has long served as his parent – she must then face her husband, who, in the most chilling rebuff in popular fiction, tells her he doesn't give a damn. Rhett's desertion, I would suggest, is blamed by many women on Scarlett because for a woman to lose the attentive recognition of men is indicative of the loss of her femininity. Rhett's freedom to go to London, Paris or Charleston is not for Scarlett; as a woman in the late-nineteenth-century South she is constrained by social and sexual mores which forbid easy mobility. And of course she, unlike Rhett, is lumbered with Ashley, Beau and her own – albeit neglected – children, Wade and Ella (the latter absent from the film, so her splendid isolation seems greater). Since to wander Europe would be worse for her reputation than driving a buggy alone through Shanty Town, Scarlett has no alternative but to go home – in all senses of the word. Back to her origins, her childhood home, where familial, social and race relations seem to remain intact, war or no war; to the white house with white curtains; to the bosom of black Mammy, loyal and eternally maternal ex-slave, 'the last link with the old days'. Back at home, where everything has symbolically gone full circle and been restored to the status quo, she can regain a childlike status free of the complications of adult female sexuality, becoming again a Southern belle who plans a campaign to get the man she wants.

So why the appeal for women readers of this ending which is not a proper ending, which takes us right back to Tara's white and black contrasts but also addresses the problem of Scarlett saving the only good marriage she ever had? First, perhaps, it satisfies our sense of rough justice and our desire as reader-viewers to see Scarlett punished for that major crime in fictional texts, her lack of self-knowledge and misrecognition of love. Second, it demonstrates with alarming power the perilousness of the female condition, especially when a woman departs radically from feminine responses and responsibilities, and loses touch with her real needs. Finally, it may satisfy all our urges to give up the struggle for true understanding and recognition (usually called love) and to return literally and metaphorically to our origins, especially to a symbolic mother who will (rather unlike most real mothers) accept us fully and unconditionally for what we are – and help us gently and cossetingly to return to the adult fray, where we can also be accepted despite and because of what we have become. As Cora Kaplan says, 'Gone With the Wind encourages the reader to regress, insists that she moves on.'[4] The ending comforts and disturbs (and in serial readings, sometimes one after the other) and leaves open an imaginative space in which each reader-viewer may examine her own relationship to past and future, the urge to retreat and the compulsion to try again.

'Back With the Breeze': the Sequel to
Gone With the Wind

So the apparently open, ambiguous ending of both book and film is a tease to reader and viewer alike, an apparent signal of a *GWTW–2* to come. Certainly publishers, novelists, film-makers and screen-writers have seen the inconclusive ending as offering a tempting invitation to step in with sequels. Until recently they have all been frustrated by Margaret Mitchell's adamant proscription of these, a wish honoured until just before his death in 1983 by her brother and heir, Stephens Mitchell. It seems that Stephens and his sons realised that the copyright on *GWTW* would run out in the year 2011, after which time anyone could produce a sequel – however dreadful and tangentially related to the original – and they might not approve. So, in an elaborate deal masterminded by the William Morris Agency, the Margaret Mitchell Estate finally contracted South Carolina author Alexandra Ripley to produce the sequel novel, which will be used as the basis for the *GWTW–2* film.

The Estate's choice must have disappointed many an aspiring novelist and sequel-writer (not to mention millionairess – Ripley's book sales, together with film rights will virtually guarantee that she never need work again!). Many hopeful unknowns have written their versions of the sequel, including a psychic who claimed that Margaret Mitchell dictated each word through a Ouija board.[5] And although the sequel rights were shrouded in secrecy, it is certain that other well-known novelists put in bids. Two possibles cited in the US press were the unlikely duo of Barbara Cartland, Britain's queen of the virginal romance, and Rita Mae Brown, author of the lesbian feminist comic classic *Rubyfruit Jungle*. Most frustrated of all must be Margaret Mitchell's and Vivien Leigh's biographer, Anne Edwards, who was commissioned in the late 1970s to write a sequel novel for film producers Richard Zanuck and David Brown (producers of *The Sting* and *Jaws*). Her completed novel, called 'Tara: The Continuation of Gone With the Wind', was turned into a screenplay of the same name by James Goldman. These versions ran into various problems in Hollywood and with the Mitchell Estate; both will presumably now bite the dust.

The choice of Alexandra Ripley was hailed as a major event of international significance. Her appointment to the awesome task of satisfying the desires of millions to know what happened in the 'tomorrow' that is 'another day' featured prominently in the international press, television and radio and accorded her the honour of a cover article in the American *Life* Magazine. Beneath headlines such as 'Going for Scarlett and gold' and '$6m bids for unwritten Scarlett sequel', Ms Ripley's track record and qualifications were carefully inspected for her worthiness to be what *The Times* called 'custodian of a great American myth'.

I am writing before the appearance of Ripley's book, so it is impossible to predict the full impact it will make, but at present she seems to be regarded as a safe bet – as safe as anyone can be who takes on an international institution, a task many feel to be impossible since feelings about *GWTW* run so high. It seems the Estate has gone for a conservative choice, someone who can be trusted to adhere faithfully to the spirit and tone of the original without radically transforming story or character and without overstepping sexual, racial and linguistic bounds. While we may speculate as to what Rita Mae Brown might have done with Scarlett (turned her from the unreliable vagaries of men to a passionate lesbian affair with the voluptuous Belle Watling, perhaps?)

what we will get is a version from a Southern romance-writer, native of fictional Rhett Butler's Charleston. As a child she sold directions to tourists to 'Rhett Butler's grave', and later went to the women's college Vassar on a scholarship from the ultra-conservative United Daughters of the Confederacy. 'Why was I chosen?' she asked. 'Because I'm a woman writer and I have the right amount of Southernness.' Like Mitchell, she has been married twice; has worked in the commercial world – in her case, publishing and airline publicity; and is an expert on the American Civil War period. She may prove a popular choice with British fans, since she is the descendant of seventeenth-century British immigrants and a known Anglophile.

Ripley's first two novels, written in her forties and published in the 1980s, are popular historical romances entitled *Charleston* and *New Orleans Legacy*. *Charleston* was a good dry run for *GWTW–2*: a story of the South Carolina city between 1863 and 1898, and one family's fortunes through a turbulent period. Its heroine, Lizzie Tradd, shares Scarlett's courage, grit and love of birthplace; indeed, the US book jacket, illustrated with the inevitable magnolia and dogwood blossoms, Southern belles and wounded beaux, calls the novel 'a Gone With the Wind flavored with rice and pluff [*sic*] rather than upland cotton and red clay'.[6] In order to prepare herself for the sequel, Ripley has not only read *GWTW* six or seven times but has copied out 200 pages in longhand in order to get into the Mitchell spirit. Although she will not divulge her own ending, claiming that she has two options between which she has not yet decided, she has admitted that there will be more extramarital sex (though nothing too explicit – she is 'of the three-dot school'), a few 'hells' to add to the original Rhett's shocking 'damn', and sensitive treatment of black characters. She also cannot bring herself to give Scarlett the expression 'Fiddle-de-dee'.

Although there are significant differences between Ripley and Margaret Mitchell, both temperamentally and because of the different times in which they have written, the two share some qualities and similar problems. A somewhat self-effacing and publicity-shy writer like her mentor, Ripley has to date avoided the kind of multimedia exposure which Mitchell would have endured in a television age, had she lived beyond 1949. When the book appears, she will have to decide whether to hire secretaries and minders, and build high walls round and install guard dogs within her eighteenth-century farmhouse home to avoid the kind of press interest that distressed and obsessed Mitchell for the last thirteen years of her life. And Ripley is already being warned about the problem of plagiarism threats which Margaret Mitchell suffered; she is being advised not to open her mail in case a correspondent suggests a plot line she then adopts. Like Mitchell, too, she will almost certainly be plagued by begging letters and new fine-weather friends (and maybe demands for a further sequel!). The problem of taking on such a sequel, however, especially to a book which was a surprise success by an unknown writer at a time when books and writers had a glamour that has since been superseded by visual media writers and producers, is that both she and the novel will be all too familiar before they appear, following closely as they will the fiftieth anniversary of the film. While *GWTW–2* is bound to make a great deal of money for its creator, it will also be scrutinised mercilessly by a public very loyal to and protective towards its antecedent. I do not envy Ms Ripley's breakfast-time reading of the first reviews, all the more since some of them will no doubt pour from the poisoned pens of disappointed sequel-writers . . .

For that luscious celebration of the past which suffuses *GWTW* itself, and which it summons up in its reader-viewers, allows scarce generosity towards a sequel that will definitively answer those questions which are for many fans part of the tantalising pleasure of the open ending. Those who publicly oppose any sequel refer usually to the film; their resistance derives from a nostalgia not only for *GWTW* as 'the greatest daddy of them all' but also for the golden age of Hollywood, of which it is seen as the culmination and, significantly, the final curtain. The most celebrated British example is this country's best-known film critic Barry Norman, respected as a knowledgeable aficionado of Hollywood. In his frequent television appearances *GWTW* is always referred to lovingly in superlatives, and Norman has written at least three syndicated newspaper articles in three years deploring the very idea of a sequel. Under such headlines as 'Nasty rumours that blow in the wind' (Birmingham *Evening News*, October 30, 1986), 'Leave Rhett and Scarlett alone' (Bristol *Evening Post*, March 1987) and 'The new Scarlett MUST be good' (*Evening Post*, 4 July, 1988), he records the rumour that Sergio Leone wants to remake *GWTW* ('about as sensible as, say, David Hockney trying to repaint the Mona Lisa'); the US newspaper polls' verdict on which actors should play Scarlett and Rhett in any proposed sequel; and finally the choice of Alexandra Ripley as *GWTW–2* writer, accompanied by his scepticism that any film sequel could possibly succeed. Echoing, as he does well, the feelings of many readers, he refers to the original *GWTW* as 'one of the few, true classics of the cinema'; 'as near perfect a film of its kind as it is possible to make'; 'created for posterity, for ever'. In the questionnaire he completed for me, he described it as 'the high water mark of American cinema in the 1930s . . . the most perfect epic ever made'. For him, the original actors *were* the parts, and no other actors could play Scarlett, Rhett, Ashley or Melanie (although, of course, by the sequel she is dead) 'without arousing scorn, derision and rage'.

His injunction to Hollywood to 'leave the damn thing alone' has found many supporters, and letters to editors at the time when the sequel was aired in the media confirm his sense that this 'unique classic' should not be emulated. Richard Boyett of Henbury, Bristol, wrote to the *Western Daily Press* in March 1986 to protest that modern films are 'in the main inferior to the best films made in the golden era of Hollywood and so are the actors and actresses'. Referring to golden actors Judy Garland, Cary Grant, Bette Davis and so on, he mouths a familiar Norman theme: 'They just don't make 'em like that any more!' On the same Letters Page, Joy Hyslop argues for a return to romance; citing Rhett's carrying Scarlett upstairs as 'the most sexually romantic part of a movie I have ever seen', she imagines a sequel filled with what she calls the five Bs, 'Bed, Belly, Boobs, Bum and Blood to draw the audience'.

Many of my correspondents echoed these sentiments, suggesting, like Barry Norman, that any sequel would be an anticlimax, and no actors could replace the originals; or, like Joy Hyslop, that a modern rewrite would inevitably go for explicit sexual detail that would be far less erotic than the original. Many felt that the television mini-series and glitz-serial would greatly influence contemporary writers, one male correspondent envisaging 'something that resembles *Dallas* or *Dynasty* in fancy dress, full of steamy bedroom scenes and ludicrous big-business contrivances', another (female) regretting the whole project:

> There is nothing more to say: the war is over, Scarlett has Tara back, Rhett is *bound* to have got over his sulk by now, so enough already. Yuk. Knowing Hollywood writers, they'd probably have Rhett opening up a children's riding school and Scarlett would go into curtain and dress design.

Pithily, this correspondent voiced the view of many about anyone following Vivien Leigh: 'Who could fill her shoes? That would be like one of the ugly sisters squeezing into the glass slipper.'

But as with all the sequels to *Jaws*, *Rocky* and *Crocodile Dundee*, and remakes of Hollywood classics such as *The Big Sleep*, *The Postman Always Rings Twice* and *A Star is Born*, the possibilities of huge profits deriving from more-of-the-same, an updated or continued version of a popular success has its own economic logic. However much Barry Norman and many of my correspondents deplore the fact, Ripley's novel will be a best-seller and will be closely followed by an inevitably money-spinning film sequel. So already the media circus is whipping up the kind of enthusiasm for public participation in casting that characterised the legendary 1930s 'Search for Scarlett'.

In March 1987 the press reported US newspaper polls of favourite actors to play the new Scarlett and Rhett. Apparently, arguing that the actors needed 'umph' and 'fieriness', they opted for the British Jane Seymour or American Kathleen Turner as Scarlett, Tom Selleck (television's Magnum), Stacy Keach (Mr Steele in the American mini-series on the Civil War, *The Blue and the Gray*) or Harrison Ford as Rhett. *GWTW* 'experts' were reported as feeling that the new stars lacked the requisite romantic qualities, so they held that only an experienced actress such as Elizabeth Taylor could handle the older, wiser Scarlett – but, although she is British and greatly resembling the late Vivien Leigh, she is at least twenty years too old. Their choices for the rather older Rhett, however, were the eternally youthful Robert Redford and Clint Eastwood. These experts, like others nostalgic for Hollywood's past, pointedly chose 'classic' actors to take on these legendary roles. Alexandra Ripley, evidently of the Old School, cannot imagine who could play Scarlett 'short of digging up Vivien Leigh'.

Sequels, Influences and Quotations

It is perhaps inevitable that a demand for 'more *Gone With the Wind*' should result in a sequel commissioned from a writer as close to the original author as possible and that a sequel film should be imagined in the same terms as the golden oldie, with public and critics searching for Vivien Leigh and Clark Gable look-alikes to repeat the original experience. The most conservative elements of the book trade, film production and star system are being invoked; it is difficult to imagine a very exciting, radical or disturbing sequel resulting from this all too predictable process.

Of course, *GWTW* has by no means gone underground in the last fifty years, and its 'survival' will not depend on any sequel. It has influenced writers and film-makers galore, and it is reworked, cited and quoted in an astonishing variety of contexts. All writers and film-makers use earlier novels and films for inspiration and model, and the history of fiction and movies is in many ways a history of influences. Novelists and producers create texts which comment on, argue with and take further debates and themes within earlier works, and supremely successful fictions like *GWTW* can hardly be ignored. So *GWTW* (sequel or no) lives on in its many reinterpretations, meant to complement or refute its perspectives and polemic. And any writer of novel or script who engages with the American South's history between 1860 and 1900 cannot fail to take on *GWTW*'s immense popular power and significance. As Harriet Beecher Stowe's *Uncle Tom's Cabin* was a reference point in the nineteenth and early twentieth centuries for all white and black writing about slavery (however reluctantly, especially in the case of radical black writers)[7] and *The Birth of a Nation* was the reference point for Southern films, including *GWTW*, so since the 1930s *GWTW* has taken their place. Although Margaret Mitchell herself drew on and quoted from many earlier novels by white men and women (conspicuously, no slave narratives or black fiction), her book, and even more so its film intepretation, have become the staple reference point for all representations of the slaveocracy and Southern white middle-class experience of the Civil War.

Indeed, *GWTW* – a story about a woman deeply committed to her home and native soil, wrenched by historical necessity on to a wider and more complex canvas, encountering love, death, passion, disaster, and challenges of all kinds – is the prototype of certain kinds of modern fiction written by women. Its influence has been strongest on American and British women writers of genres such as the popular historical romance, the family saga, and the 'Superwoman' novel.[8]

GWTW is referred to within novels, directly or allusively through plot lines, character names or types, in a range of contemporary fiction by some black – but especially white – middle-class women (and a few men). The family saga set around the Civil War has remained a popular topic, treated by best-selling established writers such as Frank Yerby (the first was *The Foxes of Harrow*, 1947) and John Jakes (*North and South*, 1982), as well as newer saga-writers such as Marie de Jourlet (*Legacy of Windhaven*, 1984), Elizabeth Kary (*Let No Man Divide*, 1987) and *GWTW* sequel-writer Alexandra Ripley. Furthermore, many novels by women assume their readers' intimate knowledge of *GWTW*, a knowledge not assumed of any other work. Jacqueline Susann, in *Valley of the Dolls* (1967), mentions it by name, among other references using O'Hara as character Neely's stage name. Judith Krantz refers to *GWTW*'s main characters by name in *Scruples* (1978), while in *Princess Daisy* (1980) Francesca Valensky is horrified at the thought of a drug-free child-birth, since Melanie's fictional agonised birth is the only one she knows.[9] In Barbara Taylor Bradford's *A Woman of Substance* (1981), Emma Harte is given Scarlett's green eyes (to denote determination and striking looks). Sally Beauman, in *Destiny* (1987), expects us to know what Southern rogue Ned Calvert looks like when comparing him with Clark Gable as Rhett, and she uses the story of beloved daughter jumping an untamed horse to create narrative surprise: unlike the outcome in *GWTW*, the girl is not killed; instead the husband commits suicide in his car.

The classic status *GWTW* has assumed in the world of the fictional saga is clearly demonstrated through constant publicity and review references to it as a measure against which later texts are judged. For instance, as early as 1945 Kathleen Winsor's *Forever Amber*, the saucy best-seller about the English Restoration (edited by Harold Latham, *GWTW*'s editor), was marketed as 'the new *Gone With the Wind*'; and in the last ten years or so this comparison has increased. Colleen McCullough's smash hit *The Thorn Birds* (1978), described by critic John Sutherland as a 'birth of the nation' epic in the mould of novels by James Michener and Leon Uris, was praised in reviews as 'the Australian answer to *Gone With the Wind*',[10] while Régine Desforges's first volume of *The Blue Bicycle* (1982) was dubbed 'the Gallic answer . . .'. Reay Tannahill's dynastic saga *A Dark and Distant Shore* (1983), about a Scottish castle in the early nineteenth century, is celebrated on the cover as 'a marvellous blend of *Gone With the Wind* and *The Thorn Birds*'. And it would seem strange to publish a novel about the Old South and a family's varied experiences without a blurb claiming that it has 'the grandeur of *Gone With the Wind*' (back cover, Eugenia Price, *Savannah*, 1983). Even when *GWTW* is *not* cited as a literary antecedent, themes, style and presentation of material echo Margaret Mitchell's original. The rows of plantation blockbusters, birth-of-a-nation romances and 'bodice-rippers' which fill American bookstores, proudly boasting of their well-researched historical accuracy and set somewhere in the steamy Southern states, testify to *GWTW*'s enduring influence on the market.[11]

Indeed, the critic Madonne M. Miner traces a 'matrilineal tradition' of women's writing from Mitchell's *GWTW*, through four other representative – and much-imitated – novels of different decades written by and for white middle-class American readers: Winsor's *Forever Amber* (1944), Grace Metalious's *Peyton Place* (1956), Susann's *Valley of the Dolls* and Judith Krantz's *Scruples*. Referring to feminist psychoanalytic thought as represented by Nancy Chodorow, Miner argues that all five portray daughters bound closely to their mothers but turning to father-lovers, and that they

> allow a female reader to repeat the most ambivalent relationship of her childhood, that relationship with the woman upon whom she depended for sustenance and love, but from whom she eventually needed to distance herself.[12]

Thus she reads all the texts in terms of women's need to come to terms with their mothers, and their own potential capacity as mothers, all the while establishing a separate identity; as I have discussed, very much my own feeling about the power of *GWTW*. All five – and other novels within this matrilineal tradition – are described as being 'in an extended conversation about the appetites of women', and Miner suggests that they are popular with women readers because their pages offer sustenance: 'a meal composed of dreams, nightmares, psychic and social structures affecting the lives of women – mothers and daughters – in twentieth-century American culture'[13] (and, one might add, other cultures too . . .).

If we read *GWTW* as a family romance, this interpretation is both satisfying and convincing, and Miner's tracing of a tradition of women's writing gives a fascinating perspective on its influence. But *GWTW* also feeds into other traditions, which may help explain its impact on male writers and readers too: notably the historical novel, the Southern epic, as well as those genres which *GWTW* plays with and transforms – the Southern gothic and Victorian Southern belle saga. And although *GWTW* has launched a tradition of white middle-class women's writing, it has undoubtedly influenced black writers, who have deliberately rewritten the Civil War and Reconstruction period from a black perspective in order to repudiate Mitchell's apparently authoritative version. The best-known response of all is the enormously successful novel and television series *Roots* (written by Alex Haley in 1976, dedicated to the United States in its Bicentennial Year), which is an argument with Mitchell's version of race relations as harmonious before, tragically shattered after the Civil War. For the first time a black fictional history of the USA became a huge best-seller, while its televised version broke prime-time viewing records.

And what of the influence of *Gone With the Wind* on celluloid? This Technicolor representation of a genteel, ordered antebellum South of white-columned plantation houses, cotton fields full of happy slaves and dashing cavalier beaux with their fluttering belles (far more than the images of suffering and destruction after the War) has endured in popular imagination as a legendary 'truth'. After 1939, images, themes and actors from *GWTW* were used in and as publicity for other Southern films. Vivien Leigh was used to great effect as neurotic belle in *A Streetcar Named Desire* (1951); Clark Gable's part as plantation owner in *Band of Angels* (1957) is described by film critic Leslie Halliwell as 'reinforc[ing] the impression of sitting through the ghost of *Gone With the Wind*'.[14] Walt Disney's nostalgic, racially offensive Uncle Remus plantation romp, *Song of the South*, featuring Hattie McDaniel as another comic servant and using *GWTW*'s worst clichés, was issued in 1945 and reissued in 1972 – hard on the heels of the 1971 reissue of *GWTW*. Jack Warner's 1940 film *All This And Heaven Too*, starring Bette 'Jezebel' Davis, traded on *GWTW*'s success by using Max Steiner music, emulating *GWTW* advertisements, and attempting (unsuccessfully) to sell on its initials, *ATAHT*.

The resonant staircase of the Butlers' Atlanta house must be one of the most familiar visual memories of film-goers; the artist who designed the original poster of Rhett carrying Scarlett up those scarlet stairs was hired to produce an imitation to promote Dino de Laurentiis's 1975 film about a Louisiana slave-breeding plantation, *Mandingo*, with the master carrying his black concubine while his own wife is borne in the arms of his prize slave. Even Steven Spielberg's much-praised film of black writer Alice Walker's novel *The Color Purple* (1985) – in terms of use of image, colour, music and logo – is very much a liberal tribute to *GWTW*. The television mini-series of the 1980s – *Beulah Land* (1980), *The Blue and the Gray* (1983) and *North and South* (1985–6) – rely on audiences' knowledge of *GWTW*'s version of the War and Reconstruction. So intimate is the viewing public with this one work that numerous parodies have appeared, often by stars such as Joanne Woodward, Carol Burnett and Stanley Baxter, ensuring a warm, largely uncritical popular image of this work that seems to run and run. Because of film and television versions in different decades, with different emphases since the 1939 *GWTW* film, the survival of the South as a separate section of the United States, and a romantic, mythic version of the Old South, owe a great deal to Hollywood, probably more than any other source, and to *GWTW* as the supreme film version.[15]

In many ways, then, by drawing on and using in imaginative new ways so many literary and filmic traditions and stereotypes, as well as creating a powerful mythic epic of America's tragic Civil War, the relations between men and women, black and white, mothers and daughters, individuals and the land, *GWTW* has become the prototype of many subsequent fictions – novels, films and television series. It needs no sequel to continue to live – as a model text on which writers and film-makers may draw, or against which they may argue. At present, it reigns supreme. And when the sequel – and, perhaps, the sequel's sequels – appear, a whole new dimension of life will undoubtedly accrue to this work.

7

The Mammy of Them All:
Gone With the Wind and Race

When reading the book I remember wincing at the strangeness of owning people, but being surprised and very interested at the mutual trust and regard that could evidently occur between individuals despite this. (Ms C.M. Ford)

I find the racism inherent in the story so repellent that I can scarcely read it for nausea. The apologia for the activities of the Ku Klux Klan is shameful. The only way I can make it even faintly palatable is to reflect that it is probably a historically correct, though not honestly slanted, record of the attitudes of those times and that those attitudes were as much a part of the period as Scarlett's seventeen-inch waist and pantalettes. God knows, the world still suffers because of racism, but to make it sound so attractive, so honourable, so reasonable is very sinister. (Pat Read)

If you drove today along one of the main highways out of Natchez, Mississippi, you could not miss an extra-ordinary sight. Towering at least twenty feet above the road is a vast, grinning, turbaned, earringed, tray-carrying Mammy. At first sight she appears to be a monument, until you see the signs for a petrol station, public phone and café. In order to eat, you enter a door in her voluminous skirts and order your hominy grits and black-eyed peas within her warm, welcoming body.

This icon to the Mammy of history and myth is sym-bolically interesting. Standing proud, she offers her many services on a tray and is the daily dispenser of nourishment to all who enter her; her very body invites invasion and knows no privacy. Like commercial 'Aunt Jemima' pancake mix, this figure embodies one of the white South's favourite legendary characters: the omnipresent, cow-like, asexual, obese provider – eternally associated with biscuit dough, a veritable 'grain goddess'.[1] For over a century she has been celebrated in poem, novel, play and film. In 1869 a journal published a poetic tribute to her from devoted Whites:

> *All* to her is dear devotion whom the angels
> bend to bless,
> All our thoughts of her are blended with
> a holy tenderness.[2]

In 1923 the United Daughters of the Confederacy asked the US Congress to allow them to erect a monument in Washington to 'Mammy'. If you wander the streets of New Orleans you will see in shops an array of dolls, ashtrays, mock plantation bells and cookie jars shaped like a figure who, in the United States at least, has been seen as 'the Great Black Mother of us all'.[3]

This revered Mammy figure has been the stuff of white idealisation since the early Southern novels, in which she was described as central to harmonious relations on the happy plantation. Harriet Beecher Stowe put her on the map in the world-famous *Uncle Tom's Cabin*, and in novels as different as Thomas Nelson Page's *Red Rock* (1898), Ellen Glasgow's *Virginia* (1913) and William Faulkner's *The Sound and the Fury* (1929) – as well as films from *The Birth of a Nation* (1915) to *Guess Who's Coming to Dinner* (1967) – she is a solid, enduring presence. Passive, patient, with no apparent needs or desires of her own, she is loyal to 'her' white 'family', hostile to Yankees, white trash and uppity Negroes, and a constant source of emotional and physical solace. She is favourably compared with her opposite number, Sapphire – the shrewish, stubborn, dissatisfied

nag made famous in the 'Amos 'n' Andy' radio and television shows.[4]

Historically speaking, Mammy was far from being a
mature, sexless older woman of infinite wisdom, treated
with awesome respect. She was usually a young woman –
her tasks were too heavy for an overweight older woman
to perform! Indeed, she would rarely have grown fat
and happy on the meagre diet allowed to slaves, even
privileged house workers, and she got little for her
pains from even the most sympathetic planter family.
Frederick Douglass, a slave who escaped to the North
to become a major figure in the Abolition movement
of the mid nineteenth century, wrote poignantly of his
grandmother's fate:

> She had served my old master faithfully from youth
> to old age. She had been the source of all his
> wealth; she had peopled his plantation with slaves;
> she had become a great-grandmother in his
> service. She had rocked him in infancy, attended
> him in childhood, served him through life, and at
> his death wiped from his icy brow the cold
> death-sweat, and closed his eyes forever. She was
> nevertheless left a slave – a slave for life – a slave
> in the hands of strangers; and in their hands she
> saw her children, her grandchildren, and her great-
> grandchildren, divided, like so many sheep, without
> being gratified with the small privilege of a
> single word, as to their or her own destiny . . .
> [in old age] they took her to the woods, built her
> a little hut, put up a little mud-chimney, and then
> made her welcome to the privilege of supporting
> herself there in perfect loneliness; thus virtually
> turning her out to die![5]

A contemporary black novelist, Gloria Naylor, referring
to the 'myth of the matriarch' which is found in white

fiction, analyses the significance to Whites of such an idealised character:

> Her unstinting devotion assuaged any women
> that slaves were discontented or harbored any
> potential for revolt. Her very dark skin belied any
> suspicions of past interracial liaisons, while her
> obesity and advanced age removed any sexual threat.
> Earth Mother, nursemaid and cook, the mammy
> existed without a history or a future.[6]

For *black* writers and critics, then, the Mammy is a useful and taken-for-granted workhorse, used to reassure frightened Whites that there is a 'good' black woman they can admire and indeed worship, precisely because she is happy to subordinate her own identity as a black woman – slave or free – to her white masters or superiors. 'Good Nigger-in-Chief', as Leslie Fiedler dubs her, she stands as a model for all 'bad' Blacks who might presume to challenge white dominance. Hosea Williams, an Atlanta-based civil rights activist, bears on his office wall an Aunt Jemima poster-with-a-twist. V.S. Naipaul described it: 'The big black woman didn't smile; she offered a big black fist; and the words were "No more" and "Net Weight 1,000 lbs".'[7]

Gone With the Wind was by no means the first book and film to feature the Mammy (and her young successor Prissy) but it certainly sealed her fate in racial myth. Margaret Mitchell used many literary clichés, and David Selznick added a few of his own. The book's Mammy is huge, 'shining black, pure African' (no hint of mixed-blood hanky-panky, of course), devoted 'to her last drop of blood' to the O'Hara family, and – though a slave – completely in command, virtually her masters' owner: she 'felt that she owned the O'Haras, body and soul, that their secrets were her secrets' (p. 24). She is described in terms of an elephant, a savage, a child; like the good maternal provider she is, she has a 'ponderous' body and 'monumental, sagging breasts' (p. 532). She speaks in a dialect which renders her comments and scolding comical – as readers, we smile at her rendition of 'gentlemen' as 'gempmum', while in the film we laugh at her muttered 'It ain' fittin' '.

Far more than Ellen O'Hara herself, Mammy voices the conservative views and values of her mistress, usually in order to scold or express shock at Scarlett – whether over a choice of dress ('You kain show yo' buzzum befo' three o'clock', p. 79), a purchase of rouge ('Paintin' yo' face lak a — ', p. 585), or marrying Rhett Butler ('Mahyin' trash!', p. 826). And most of all, in the absence of any name or family of her own, she cares passionately for 'her' white family's welfare, wealth, physical and moral health. A substitute mother, given her close daily contact with her charges, she is a fixed point throughout all the turbulences of the O'Hara family and her own race. Emancipation does not affect Mammy; her attitude to the family, and theirs to her, and her own status in employment (is she paid when freed? we never know) all remain unchanged. We see how *white* families adapt, change and grow in stature as a result of the major political and social upheavals; but Mammy, who – in Gloria Naylor's words – 'existed without a history or a future', is the eternal and unchanging. In the book (though significantly not the film) Scarlett can think of returning to Tara to plan her strategy of getting Rhett back only because 'Mammy would be there'. With her broad bosom and gnarled black hand to comfort Scarlett, she remains 'the last link with the old days'(p. 1011).

David Selznick humanised Mammy, giving her more to do than she has in Mitchell's novel, demonstrating the intimacy of black–white slave–mistress relations through several key scenes – again more than in the book, presumably to give Hattie McDaniel a more significant part. Mammy sees Scarlett at her most revealing moments, and participates in her joys and humiliations: lacing her into corsets as a flirtatious party-goer and after childbirth; making an outfit from Tara's curtains to capture Rhett's heart and money; preparing her to woo Frank Kennedy's fortune. Selznick elaborates on the book, making Mammy watch the newly widowed Scarlett try on a frivolous hat instead of her dull mourning garb, pick up her scarlet dress after the disastrous party, and (instead of the book's Will Benteen) caution Scarlett, when Ashley returns from war, that he is Melanie's husband, not hers.

Mammy is Scarlett's conscience, counsellor, best friend. She expects – and gets – no gratitude, and as a freed slave (or 'servant', as the film always refers to the Blacks) carries on opening the front door and organising all domestic arrangements. Furthermore, she makes her last appearance in the film as a distraught figure entreating Melanie to persuade Rhett that Bonnie Blue should be buried; hers is not one of the voices which recalls Scarlett to Tara's importance in her life. This exclusion of Mammy from the final act of the film has the effect of silencing and marginalising her even more thoroughly than before. Mammy's authority goes so far and no further. For Selznick and his script-writers, as she lies across the stairs wondering what to do next, Scarlett responds to the recalled authoritative tones of three *white men*, Gerald, Ashley and Rhett, calling her back to 'the old days' and Tara. That said, Selznick may also have wished Hattie McDaniel's finest scene to be her last. Her extended semi-monologue as she climbs the stairs with Melanie, describing the terrible recriminations and distress caused by Bonnie's death, affords the actress the opportunity to display a tragic depth and melodramatic range which none of her other 'maid' roles allowed.

Hattie and Mammy

Hattie McDaniel had had considerable practice at playing 'Mammy', and was to get even more. Throughout her Hollywood career, which followed a successful period as a singer in a 'Colored Orchestra', she established herself as the archetypal screen mammy. She played it all her life; in the year *GWTW* was made she acted the role in no fewer than twelve films. It is perhaps no wonder that Susan Myrick, who coached McDaniel into an appropriate Southern dialect, reported that on set she was 'Mammy in real life': tap-dancing, singing songs from a vaudeville tour, and administering home-made cough syrup to ailing crew members.[8] Myrick's identification of the two is particularly significant when you know that the *GWTW* set had separate 'Whites' and 'Coloreds' lavatories until a protest integrated them, and that – although she was in Atlanta at the time – Hattie McDaniel was not invited to the all-white première of the film.

Selznick's choice of McDaniel, made after a considerable number of others had been tested, seems inevitable. Although he first wrote to Margaret Mitchell that McDaniel lacked dignity, age, nobility and the right face, he chose well.[9] For not only was she rewarded with the first Academy Award ever given to a black actor (and there have been few since), but her performance helped to quell a certain amount of the adverse criticism which the film faced on its release. While black and liberal groups and individuals questioned the wisdom of Ms McDaniel's often-repeated role, they had to agree that her award at least acknowledged her acting ability – and the fact that she did not merely fit the role *naturally*. Furthermore, the logic of her own position could hardly be faulted: 'Why', she asked, 'should I complain about making seven thousand dollars a week playing a maid? If I didn't, I'd be making seven dollars a week actually being one.'[10] (She was exaggerating; in fact, she made $450 a week in *GWTW* — still an enormous wage for a black woman in 1939.)

There are problems about this, however. First, as Jim Pines points out, Hollywood was probably sensitive to civil rights attacks on this film — as on the controversial *Birth of a Nation* — so McDaniel was awarded an Oscar to defray criticism, successfully as it turned out. Thus the Award itself may have been a political rather than an artistic decision. Second, the acclaim for and ensuing celebrity of this actress could not compensate for and did little to improve the dire lack of alternative acting roles for black women in Hollywood movies. Hattie McDaniel herself was forever typecast, while Butterfly McQueen, who played Prissy, resented her post-*GWTW* offers. She refused to repeat what she called 'handkerchief head' maid roles, and after *Duel in the Sun* (1946) said she had had enough. Producers boycotted her and thus ended her film career; she went on to do a variety of jobs, including working as a maid . . . And in case we are tempted to say that times have changed and such outrage is out of date, it is instructive to read a comment by black British actress Judith Jacobs, one of the few black women to have starred in a British soap opera. Playing 'Carmel' in 'EastEnders' during the late 1980s, Jacobs is unusual in having a regular role as a professional health worker, rather than the more available 'subservient, stupid or morally dubious' black parts:

> The main reason why black people play so many negative roles is because they are the only ones they are offered . . . I would never play the archetypal maid, who had no sense, but there will be black people who will take those roles.[11]

Since the 1960s, mixed feelings have been expressed about Hattie McDaniel's role as Mammy. *Time* Magazine, giving the film a 'revisitation' review, in 1961, wrote with patronising benevolence, 'Scarlett's hammy old mammy just about waddles off with the show', but then acknowledged that the 'Jim Crow humor', fine for most audiences in 1939, 'will embarrass the average moviegoer today'. And writing in the 1970s, black American critics Daniel J. Leab and Thomas Cripps both recognised McDaniel's typecasting but also celebrated her success. Jim Pines is one of the rare black voices raised against this characterisation. He says that her 'apparently assertive and articulate servant role . . . [is] greatly puffed up by the grandeur of the film's romantic love theme [to make it appear] untypically significant.' In fact, he says, it is typical of the genre and quite mundane.[12] If you sit and watch a selection of 'Southern' films in which Hattie McDaniel plays her mammy part, it is indeed hard to see how the *GWTW* role differs significantly. The sentimentality, shrill, scolding comic dialogue, and the clumsy movements of an obese body are mostly there in *The Littlest Rebel*, *The Little Colonel*, *The Song of the South*. Even if those parts are far smaller, and never require the emotional range which the tragic melodrama of the second half briefly calls from her, they all seem identical – it is hard to recall the details of one as distinct from another.

My correspondents felt warmly towards Mammy. Twenty-two named her as their favourite character (half as many as Melanie, six more than Ashley), and her positive qualities were well recognised. She was seen as exceptionally powerful (something which, historically speaking, she could never be): one woman described her as Scarlett's 'matriarchal support', another as 'the mainstay at Tara', and a third accorded her the historically impossible quality of 'the archetypal aristo-crat'. Yet another saw her as 'the eternal mother figure', black *or* white. She was admired for being 'maternal and loving, dignified and wise', and her 'intelligence' was seen as 'confirming the need for abolition of slavery'. A few correspondents expressed discomfort at the way Mammy is 'patronised' and made into a comic figure, and a few pointed to the curious contradiction displayed by Whites who entrusted their lives and homes to Mammy, but also condescended to her and felt no compunction about keeping her enslaved. One thing is clear, however: my correspondents were certain that Mammy was accorded a dignity and nobility which were entirely lacking in the figure of poor Prissy.

Prissy and Butterfly

It seems sad that Butterfly McQueen, who made such a brave stand in her own career, should be remembered for nothing besides Prissy. Although in 1967 she had objected to MGM's reissuing the film in the era of civil rights legislation, a decade later, on a US panel show, she agreed to recite the line from the film about 'birthin' babies', and in 1986 returned to Atlanta to celebrate the novel's fiftieth birthday. However, she still maintained a healthy contempt for the time when, as a woman of twenty-eight, she had to play a twelve-year-old maid. In her one-woman show in New York, in 1978, she said of *GWTW*:

> I was suffering the whole time. I didn't know that they were going to make the movie so authentic, that I'd have to be just a stupid little slave. I'd do anything they asked, but I wouldn't let Scarlett slap me [in the cotton field], and I wouldn't eat watermelon . . . Of course, thinking about it now, I probably could have had fun eating that watermelon and spitting out the pips while everyone went by.[13]

It is certainly McQueen's role as Prissy which deeply

upset or annoyed black viewers. While a few of my correspondents expressed great pleasure in her performance, most who commented on her saw the portrayal as 'foolish' and thus 'insulting' (hardly anyone commented on her in the *novel*, where she is far less prominent). On the questionnaires, many women distinguished between Mammy's 'dignified' and 'loyal', and Prissy's 'foolish' qualities. For black viewers, however, Prissy – dumb, irresponsible, squeaky-voiced and comical, the recipient of a slap from a white woman – takes on a different hue. Black revolutionary Malcolm X described in his *Autobiography* going to see the film in his home town, Mason, Michigan: 'I was the only Negro in the theater, and when Butterfly McQueen went into her act, I felt like crawling under the rug.' Two decades later, writer Alice Walker rebuked a feminist friend for appearing at a women's ball ('Come as the feminist you most admire') dressed as Scarlett O'Hara:

> My trouble with Scarlett was always the forced
> buffoonery of Prissy, whose strained, slavish voice,
> as Miz Scarlett pushed her so masterfully up the
> stairs, I could never get out of my head.[14]

The character of Prissy is, in historical terms, nearer the age of the average 'mammy' than her elephantine superior. She is young, inefficient and irritating (also part-Indian, so she has the reputed unreliability of the mixed race). Though merely a child, she is annoyingly incompetent at those skills a budding mammy should have acquired – remaining calm in crises, being practical and efficient. We are told she is the first 'darky' Scarlett has ever hit, and she gets it twice – from Scarlett's hand and then from a tree-limb whip. Boasting that she can 'bring babies', she is revealed as a liar and proceeds to misplace the scissors, spill water on Melanie's bed, and drop the newborn baby. In the film she is yet another stereotype, the superstitious slave, suggesting that a knife under the bed cuts the pain in half. Such behaviour confirms Scarlett in feeling: 'And the Yankees wanted to free the negroes! Well, the Yankees were welcome to them' (p. 363). It is perhaps ironic that Prissy, a 'little girl' of about eleven or twelve, is supposed to be fully competent to deliver babies – and even more poignant that she should be played by an actress more than twice her age.

But Prissy is not just incompetent. She is the embodiment of black childlike inefficiency which works against white interests, and also comes near to defying them. As Claire Meyer wrote on her questionnaire:

> At times Prissy seems to be the bridging point
> between the negro masses of whom Scarlett is
> afraid and the old guard like Mammy. One
> feels she is not staying with Scarlett out of loyalty
> but because it is a more comfortable course
> of action.

Certainly, Prissy comes close to the 'insolent', 'bad' Negro who must be distrusted – and sternly disciplined. A few of my correspondents wanted to give her a good slap; Margaret Mitchell says the same thing in a letter.[15] Prissy irritates precisely because she is *not* Mammy, and cannot be ignored and left to get on with all the tasks Whites would rather not do for themselves. Like the independent, insubordinate Negroes in Reconstruction (though Prissy never runs away or identifies with them) she expresses through her clumsiness a kind of resistance to white domination and is thus a potentially threatening figure. Within the context of the book, if we reader-viewers were to identify closely or sympathise much with Prissy, the cosy hierarchical structure on which the work's foundations lie would be called into question. No wonder it is *Prissy* who is seen as the most offensive stereotype by black critics.

Gone With the Wind and the Klan

Of course, the figures of Mammy and Prissy must be seen within and defined against the wider context of racial issues in both book and film, especially the controversial treatment of the Ku Klux Klan. A revealing letter on this topic came to me from Leslie Dick, an American writer currently living in London. Leslie described her first reading of *GWTW* at the age of eight in 1963, followed by an incident at school in New York a few months later:

> *Life* Magazine had a photo essay on the revival
> of the Ku Klux Klan. In *GWTW*, the Klan
> is presented as a group of heroic white gentlemen
> who ride round protecting the ladies from rape
> and other terrors. At school, in class, I said 'Isn't it
> wonderful that the Ku Klux Klan is being revived!'
> My teacher Miss Crawford was horrified. She
> actually stopped the class, told everyone to get on
> with their reading, and came and sat at my
> desk to gaze into my eyes and tell me how wrong I
> was. What I remember her saying is: 'If you
> were a little black girl in Alabama and lots of men
> in white hoods came and burned a cross in your
> back yard, it wouldn't seem so romantic, would it?'
> She was very vehement, and I was scared, and
> unhappy to have got it so wrong, but terribly
> confused also, because I'd taken the portrayal of
> events, of who's a goodie, and who's a baddie,
> from the novel [*GWTW*] and knew almost nothing
> about real life.

This account of the confusion between fiction and fact, political realitites and myths, and the still-live tensions between North and South, all of which the eight-year-old Leslie Dick encountered in that classroom during a crucial year of civil rights activities, helps remind

us that in its fifty years of success, *GWTW* has hit many
raw nerves and roused much strong feeling. For although
this one white middle-class child had learned what she
thought was an objective historical lesson from her reading of fiction, she was not alone in feeling that the Klan's
formation as the protector of women from black rape
and attack was positive, and that *GWTW*'s version of
its successful first phase in the Reconstruction period
was indisputable. The Klan, from the 1860s onwards,
has always defended itself in terms of *moral* crusade
rather than political or racial campaign; and in *The Birth
of a Nation* and *GWTW* it has been exceptionally lucky
in receiving two magnificent, successful film tributes
(even if it is never actually named in *GWTW*). Leslie's
teacher reminded her that the Klan's agenda was first and
foremost political and racist, and perhaps suggests that
that 'little black girl in Alabama', now grown up, might
have something very negative to say about *GWTW*'s
implied glorification of a Negro-hating organisation.

When I began researching the Klan in order to understand Margaret Mitchell's portrayal in the book, I was
surprised to find that far from being a historically
remote and outmoded group, it was still exerting political and ideological influence. Of course the conflicts
and debates about race in the USA and elsewhere are
infinitely more complex than the Klan's agenda allows.
Besides, members of individual 'klaverns' may seem relatively insignificant obstacles to the well-being of blacks
and other ethnic minorities in the USA, especially in
the light of harsh welfare policies, high unemployment
and poverty, drug abuse and associated crime. However,
the Klan's clear, unequivocal, populist rhetoric and sym-
bolism stand as a beacon to all racist groups, political
parties and individuals, and it is still the most vociferous
and highly publicised model of racial intolerance. Wyn
Craig Wade calls the Klan 'an inversion, or shadow, of
American democracy', and he argues that with its new

emphasis on sophisticated technology and disciplined militarism, it is possibly 'in a nascent, transitory state and could burgeon when the time was right'.[16] And maybe that time is close at hand. Several commentators noted the ominous frequency with which George Bush's 1988 presidential campaign referred to Willie Horton, the black murderer who (in Democratic candidate Governor Dukakis's home state, Massachusetts) raped a woman and stabbed her fiancé while on weekend parole. 'Willie Horton has endorsed Dukakis. It's lucky he's in jail, otherwise he'd be going door-to-door now.'[17] The crudest, most emotive rhetoric of the Klan – 'Every black man a potential rapist or murderer' – was back on the agenda, with the capacity dramatically to influence the result of a presidential election.

Since the 1920s, the Klan's fortunes have waxed and waned; it has folded through virtual bankruptcy; there have been internecine struggles and two major Congressional investigations. But it has survived and still operates in both North and South, building links with other neo-fascist groups in Europe and elsewhere. An all-male organisation which attacked Catholics in the 1920s, it now embraces women and Catholics, both of whom have joined in increasing numbers. Indeed, in August 1986 the British magazine *Woman* ran a report on a small town in the Northern state of Connecticut which had seen a faster rise in membership of women than men. One woman, Denise, had joined 'when they started teaching us at school that we were equal to the nigger' and she now participates in sending hate mail to Blacks who live in white areas, victimising Jewish children at local schools, and attending Klan rallies and cross-burning (the mark of terror).[18]

The Klan has been an important point of reference for many major twentieth-century figures. Marcus Garvey, the Jamaican black nationalist active in the 1920s, agreed with the Klan that American Blacks' only future hope lay in emigrating to Africa (he was bitterly condemned by other black leaders such as W.E.B. DuBois). The Democratic 'New Deal' President Franklin D. Roosevelt saw the Klan as a major national threat and temporarily crippled it with a huge tax bill in 1944. After the war, President Harry Truman created a human rights commission to try to prevent its revival. In the 1950s, black civil rights leader Martin Luther King adopted Gandhian methods of non-violence and contrasted them with the Klan's violent activities. A Klan leader, recognising his growing authority, dubbed him 'Martin Lucifer Coon' and the Klan bombed a hotel he had just left, as well as his brother's home.[19] He is still one of their *bêtes noires*; in a 1987 march Klansmen held up posters saying 'King was a Commie, pinko faggot'.

Since the early 1960s, the Klan has tried to reverse the triumph of those civil rights struggles which culminated in Lyndon Johnson's signing the Civil Rights Act in 1964. Klansmen had been delighted at John F. Kennedy's assassination in 1963, hoping that this Act would never see the light of day; they had resisted it strongly through attacks on and murders of 'freedom riders' who came South to help Blacks register to vote, as well as violent resistance against any attempts to integrate schools and universities. And in the 1970s and 80s, during Ronald Reagan's terms of presidency and the rise of the Moral Majority, the Klan has turned again to white supremacist rhetoric and activity, as well as joining homophobic New Right attacks on gay rights. Their targets are the familiar ones of school buses and individual Blacks, but now also gay bars and individual gay men.

In the 1980s, visiting key sites in the Deep South, novelist V.S. Naipaul reported the now notorious marches through all-white Georgia's Forsyth County, from which, after the rape and murder of a white girl in 1912, Blacks had been chased out and never allowed to return. Forsyth County had been chosen by the Klan for its march in

January 1986 to protest against the public holiday for Martin Luther King. Exactly two years later, in January 1988, a 'Walk for Brotherhood' was organised through Forsyth to mark with respect the anniversaries of King's birthday and also the assassination of Mahatma Gandhi; a week later, because of Klan attacks on and disruption of this march, between twenty and forty thousand people turned up to march through Forsyth in a second white and black 'Brotherhood' celebration. During the first march, led by black Atlanta city councillor Hosea Williams, an associate of Martin Luther King (and owner of the defiant 'Aunt Jemima' poster), Klansmen rallied to the cry, 'Kill the niggers! Run the niggers back to the Atlanta watermelon field.' An unusually large number of Klanswomen with children screamed, 'The niggers get AIDS!' Atlanta's black mayor Andrew Young commented that this Klan action had a class and economic basis: 'the desperate acts of people who find that history is leaving them behind'. He described Georgia's current problem as one of the 'underclass' – a black underclass involved in drugs and crime, a white in drugs, crime and the Klan. Hosea Williams, a worthy successor to King, told Naipaul: 'Racism is coming back, man. Just like it did after the Civil War.'[20]

And while all this may seem a long way from home to us in Britain, the rise of neo-fascist groups and of violent attacks on ethnic minority groups here must prevent complacency. When David Duke, the 'National Director' (the new name for Imperial Wizard) of a revived Ku Klux Klan visited Britain in 1978, he was interviewed by the BBC and spoke to large gatherings in several cities. Although the Home Secretary eventually signed a deportation order, Duke stayed in the country for some weeks before leaving. He undoubtedly found friends in overtly racist groups such as the National Front, as well as among Members of Parliament and groups actively advocating repatriation of black and Asian Britons and supporting

South Africa's apartheid policies. The British record on immigration policy, housing, employment, education and indeed tolerance of ethnic minorities is a shabby one; racism and racial fear are by no means confined to the American South and racist groups.

Contemporary Criticisms and the Four M's

Because of her own family's history, Margaret Mitchell was well aware that she had written a politically controversial account of the rise of the Ku Klux Klan.[21] It came as no surprise to her when the radical left press attacked GWTW, but she had little need for worry since these hostile criticisms were drowned in a chorus of applause from everyone else. The left press was unanimous in its condemnation – from *The New Republic* and *New Masses* to the Communist Party's *Daily Worker*. All their book critics frowned on its reactionary politics, especially its racism, and *The New Republic* went on to publish several attacks on GWTW between the 1930s and 1970s. The first, by Malcolm Cowley in September 1936, has remained the most influential negative opinion of the book over the last fifty years; he called it 'an encyclopedia of the plantation legend' with its 'every last bale of cotton and bushel of moonlight, every last measure of Southern female devotion working its lilywhite fingers uncomplainingly to the lilywhite bone'.[22] Other distinguished white writers such as W.J. Cash and Lillian Smith echoed his condemnation, and in recent times black writers like James Baldwin have joined the chorus of dissent.

As for the film, in many ways *Gone With the Wind* benefited from following *The Birth of a Nation*, which had been a major target for black groups such as the NAACP and had been generally regarded by left and liberal critics as an appalling insult to black people. (The absence of real Blacks playing black roles did not help to quell the uproar.) The response to the less offensive *GWTW*, therefore, was – and still remains – mixed, while it was recognised as avoiding the racist excesses of its famous predecessor. Furthermore, Jewish David Selznick, well aware of the persecution of his own race and the rise of fascism in the 1930s, had learned lessons from the critical reception of *Birth* and was ready to listen to the NAACP and others. Throughout the making of the film he had a file labelled 'The Negro Problem'; he wrote to ask script-writer Sidney Howard to ensure 'the Negroes come out decidedly on the right side of the ledger'; and he excised all script references to the Ku Klux Klan, in case they gave an 'unintentional advertisement for intolerant societies in these fascist-ridden times'. He made small but significant alterations to the script, such as changing the book's black to a white man's attempted rape of Scarlett in Shantytown, giving the word 'nigger' to black characters only, cutting the slap Scarlett was to give Prissy for laziness in Tara's cotton field, and making Prissy cut open, but not eat a watermelon – that fruit so often associated (as in Forsyth County) with a caricatured dumb Negro. He also bowed to the Production Code Administration's objection to Sidney Howard's use of 'obviously offensive' words to describe Negroes.[23]

However, these tinkerings did not alter that fundamental interpretation of the War and Reconstruction to which the liberal press had originally objected, and they did not prevent some damning reviews. The Chicago *Defender*, 6 January 1940, described it as a more vicious film than *Birth of a Nation*, a 'weapon of terror against black America'; the Los Angeles *Sentinel* printed a front-page editorial headlined 'Hollywood Goes Hitler One Better'; the Pittsburgh *Courier* dubbed the black characters 'happy house servants and unthinking, hapless clods'. The Communist

Daily Worker fired its movie critic for refusing to pan the film when the Party was trying to boycott it. (Pickets outside the movie theatres held banners saying 'You'd Be Sweet Too Under a Whip.')[24] In 'An Open Letter to Mr. Selznick', 9 January 1940, black dramatist Carlton Moss attacked the film's historical verisimilitude, arguing that its 'falsification of a progressive era in American life' promoted two major lies:[25]

1. That the Negro didn't care about or want his freedom.
2. That he had neither the qualities nor the 'innate' ability to take care of, let alone govern, himself.

Moss was also appalled by all the Negro characters, describing the line-up as 'shiftless and dull-witted Pork, Young Prissy, indolent and thoroughly irresponsible, "Big" Sam with his radiant acceptance of slavery and Mammy with her constant haranguing and doting on every wish of Scarlett.'[26] But ironically, it was Selznick's casting of black characters which subdued the storm of criticism – especially that of Hattie McDaniel. While *Birth of a Nation* and other Southern films had used white actors in blackface, or marginalised the black players, in *GWTW* the black characters were distinctive and distinguishable. Though there are fewer than in the book, and in the case of Pork and Uncle Peter the characterisation is weak, nevertheless the two female slaves – Mammy and Prissy – are memorable and are given some scope to demonstrate acting skills. And McDaniel's Academy Award delighted the liberal press, for the first time drawing attention to the considerable amount of underrated black work in Hollywood and helping to shift a rather stale agenda. Thomas Cripps is not alone in believing that 'as an incident in American cinema history it did more to signal the

changing racial arrangements than any other movie', and
he argues that it ended that 1930s genre of regressive
Southern films, leading eventually to a widening of black
roles.[27]

But in order to assess Margaret Mitchell's and David
Selznick's treatment of black characters and issues,
we need to take a sideways look at the history of
white representation of the South in fiction and film.
I would summarise this in terms of four M's: moonlight,
magnolias, Mammy and miscegenation. From the earli-
est plantation novels, through the anti-slavery best-seller
Uncle Tom's Cabin (and all its many film versions in
the first decades of this century), the postbellum novel
idealising the Old South, the 'Southern film' from *Birth
of a Nation* to *Beulah Land*, and the post-1960s sex-and-
slavery school of writing and movie, the South's history
is overwhelmingly remembered in terms of its slave
economy and the great War which it lost in 1865. This
history repeatedly defines the South in pastoral terms, as
a rural agrarian community of courtly squires and happy
piccaninnies, 'a culture of economic and social units of at
least a hundred blacks, an overseer, grand surroundings,
and a life of ease'.[28] This 'Never-Never Land of Dixie'[29]
– created despite, and indeed within, the New South –
is one of pastoral sensuousness (the dogwoods heavy
with blossom, the heady magnolias shading nocturnal
pleasures) and titillating racial and sexual congress. It is
a popular myth which, from Dixie Belle gin in the 1930s
to Southern Comfort in the 1980s, has been the stuff of
liquor advertisements.

Little Southern fiction by Whites focuses on the slave
system and Civil War in purely economic and political
terms – this is left to the historians and political scientists
. . . Novelists show Whites' greatest fear after the War as
the besmirching of white women's sexual purity through
black rape; the Ku Klux Klan's formation is justified as
a defender of white femininity. Obsessively, Southern

white writers return to the miscegenation theme, using the mulatto who is born of mixed sexual union as a symbol of the South's tragic racial-sexual history. And by the 1960s, this history has become steamily sexy. It is epitomised by the multi-volumed 'Falconhurst' saga written by Kyle Onstott and Lance Horner; the books' blurbs promise 'a fiery novel of slavery, lust and depravity', 'candid scenes of love and lust [which] depict the stark reality of a by-gone age when to be white was to inherit the earth and to be black was to know fear'. The taster quotations for these describe horrific beatings of naked black backs and buttocks. Violence – titillating in many recent works – is done to and by Blacks; the patient Uncle Tom figure gives way to the revolutionary and dangerous Nat Turner character (in Onstott's *Drum*, as in the 1969 film *Slaves*, slaves turn vengefully on masters). Blacks are virtually always on or fleeing from plantations. It is rare to see them depicted as sharecroppers, small farmers, and indeed migrants to the cities, urban workers and citizens. Slavery and racial problems are always defined as *Southern* issues; the North's role in black oppression and racism is rarely depicted.

With some notable exceptions (William Faulkner is the most celebrated example) the popular representation of Blacks in fiction and film has been – in William Van Deburg's words – 'as feeble-willed noble savages, comically musical minstrel figures, and dehumanized brutes'.[30] In film, until the 1960s, Blacks were characterised through figures such as the dandy Zip Coon and the shiftless drunken Jim Crow – straight out of the minstrel tradition; blackface white actors rolled their eyes and grinned inanely in *Birth of a Nation* and silent versions of *Uncle Tom's Cabin*; and the successful black actor Stepin Fetchit (as his insulting name suggests) played a series of lethargic, subservient figures, while Hattie McDaniel was offered dozens of Identikit mammy roles. In 1946 the New Orleans *Times-Picayune* described Walt

Disney's *The Song of the South* as 'the Old South in sticky pastels'. Three years earlier, actress Lena Horne had bravely complained of her treatment in Hollywood: 'All we ask is that the Negro be portrayed as a normal person. Let's see the Negro as a worker at union meetings, as a voter at the polls, as a civil service worker or elected official.'[31] (This, ironically, at a time when few Blacks were able to join unions, vote or become officials.)

Exasperation has been expressed in recent years by black critics and liberal white historians of fiction and film. In 1965 black novelist John Oliver Killens accused Hollywood of keeping Afro-Americans in 'economic, social, sentimental, psychological slavery', and in 1979 Jim Brown said: 'Hollywood is the way it is in Mississippi. We've retreated to a new plantation.'[32] Although since the 1960s there have been many exceptions to this, and many novels and films by Whites as well as Blacks which counter the myth of Southern Blacks as rural, simple-minded, bojangling happy darkies, none the less the plantation story and characters (as Jim Brown's words suggest) remain supreme. And it is significant that contemporary writers and film-makers are still reinterpreting this powerful mythic subject – from the white John Jakes, who in his *North and South* trilogy is producing an extensive white liberal version of the Civil War and its effects on black and white, to black writer Toni Morrison, in her first novel to tackle the slavery theme, Pulitzer Prize-winning *Beloved* (1987). But while for Jakes the subject was approached through a fascination with the Civil War period, for Toni Morrison, this was hardly an easy choice. The granddaughter of a slave and daughter of sharecropper parents burned out of their apartment by a white landlord, she found this novel – her fifth – the most painful to write. 'It rocked me in a way nothing else has done', and it forced her into what she calls 'rememories'. Most Afro-Americans have 'not remembered' slavery because, she asks, how else could they get up and go to work each day?[33] So it took her five novels and almost two decades of writing before she could tackle the subject.

Black Responses to *Gone With the Wind*

Toni Morrison's *Beloved* is the latest, and without doubt the most haunting and brilliant interpretation of the slave experience from a black perspective. But she is not the first. Many other black writers have chosen the large plantation, and slave experiences leading up to and sometimes beyond the Civil War, as theme and setting for their work – Frank Yerby: *The Foxes of Harrow* (1946), Ernest J. Gaines: *The Autobiography of Miss Jane Pittman* (1971), Alex Haley: *Roots* (1976), Ishmael Reed: *Flight to Canada* (1976), David Bradley: *The Chaneysville Incident* (1981) and Sherley Anne Williams: *Dessa Rose* (1986). Of course these writers are working within a long and honourable tradition of Afro-American fiction, which draws on slave narratives and oral history. But they are also writing primarily for an American readership which has established Margaret Mitchell's version of slaves' lives and the causes and effects of the Civil War as received wisdom, and which reveres 'Mammy' as the ideal black cultural icon.

Their version of those events and figures casts a very different light on the political and social disruptions and upheavals which, to middle-class Southern Whites, brought their 'civilisation' to an end. Just how 'civilised', ask these black writers' novels, were the auction block, the branding and hanging of runaway slaves, the rape of women slaves and selling away of their babies, overseer cruelty, enforced illiteracy, long hours of hard labour in fields and kitchens with inadequate food, warmth, shelter and rest? Through all these texts reverberate the questions usually implied or voiced by a militant slave: how could a 'civilised' race enslave another, and by what code of morality could slavery be justified? Finally, how can a civil war which led to Emancipation, and eventually to the legal recognition of Blacks as American citizens, be regarded as a terrible and tragic event?

Reader-Viewers on Race

Despite the fact that most of my reader-viewers had read little or no black fiction about the War and Reconstruction (Frank Yerby, commonly assumed to be white, was the only black writer mentioned with any frequency), some of my correspondents have asked those rhetorical questions in relation to *Gone With the Wind*, and for a few the work itself had led them to appreciate the situation of Blacks in slavery and the years following Emancipation. Many of them differentiated between and commented in some detail on the black characters, and since their first readings and viewings have shifted perspective on the representation of Blacks and black history.

A number of respondents who read the book or saw the film in the early 1940s admitted to racial myopia; one acknowledged that she had never seen a black person at that time, and thus accepted without question the way black characters were portrayed. Mavis Findlay voiced the feelings of many who had changed their minds, and believed the author would have to today:

> If Margaret Mitchell was writing this book now it couldn't possibly be the same. It was a pre-Civil Rights book before everyone was aware of the deep rifts between Blacks and Whites in America. It was rather a romanticised version of the relationships between black and white.

Diana Churchill commented on the obviously white perspective from which Mitchell was writing, creating black characters who were 'childlike, dependent, rather stupid, not human really though at the same time to be protected'. She observed that on her most recent rereading she was shocked by the way Blacks were described as smelling, looking like apes and so on, and she concluded: 'It must be horrible to read if you are a black person.'

As I said in chapter 1, I received only a handful of responses from women who described themselves as black, and in fact most of those are black Americans. They were all highly critical of the black characters, using terms such as 'one-sided and patronising', 'almost parodies of stereotypes', Prissy an 'ignorant buffoon'. G. Michelle Collins felt that in the film, the black characters had 'a kind of slapstick quality to them, rather like what I associate with The Three Stooges or Abbott and Costello'. Sandi Russell felt that the black characters were either dutiful and loyal to the point of absurdity, or shiftless and stupid:

> I would imagine that it is comforting for some
> white Americans (I cannot speak for Britons) to see
> Blacks in grinning, grovelling, subservient roles.
> My first-hand knowledge of some Whites in
> America attests to the fact that they would like
> such portrayals of Blacks to be a reality.

But you do not need to be black to see the limited way in which race relations are presented in *Gone With the Wind*. Questions of racial difference and racial attitude have been placed high on our national and international agenda since the 1960s, and have therefore heightened women's critical awareness of *GWTW*'s racial myopia. Muriel Ryder's words are representative of a general suspicion about the harmonious plantation society:

The book depicts only the good side of slavery;
no doubt there were many slave-owners whose
paternalistic care for their slaves was exemplary,
like the O'Haras and the Wilkeses, but there
were much darker and unhappier aspects of the
institution which the book ignores.

Darlene M. Hantzis, picking up this theme of the
'darker and unhappier aspects', asked:

Where are the abolitionists? Where are the other
Northerners? Where are the angry slaves, thrilled to
be free? Where are the average Southerners? Too
much romanticisation equals trivialisation.

The book and film's patronising character was well
summarised by those correspondents who described
the black characters as 'like children with learning
disabilities' or – worse – like 'articulate pets'. Teresa
Wilkins provided a sardonic analogy: 'They reminded
me very much of faithful black labradors – trusting and
loyal when kept to a normal routine but bewildered
and protesting when something different is required of
them.' And this excessive dependence, like that of slow
children or dumb animals, has annoyed some women
who otherwise took no overtly political perspective
on the work. Dorothy Fraser admitted that 'The film
brought home to me what a terrible thing the American
Civil War was . . . It also opened my eyes to the terrible
treatment of the slaves which hadn't really hit me
before.' And Edith Hope observed wittily: 'I felt sorry
for the Negro slaves working all hours while the white
pampered Southern Belles rested (from what?) in the
afternoon before an evening of pleasure.'

There is a clear generational and political difference
in the responses to my questions about race. More than
any other issue, they reveal a reader-viewer's age and

political attitudes. Although some older women found the race questions baffling or irritating, and sometimes did not reply, most of my correspondents were aware of the difficulty in the 1980s of celebrating too uncritically the clear divisions between the two races which never meet as equals. And younger women, who have more experience of living in a multiracial society, frequently criticised the book and film's racial bias and treatment of black characters.

My feelings about the black characters have shifted over the years. In early readings and viewings, I am sure I hardly noticed them; registering them as marginal members of the O'Hara family, I laughed at their comic lines and mistakes. Like a few other women who wrote to me, I skipped many of Mammy's dialect lines because I found deciphering them too tedious. In recent years, influenced by debates and readings about race, I have focused more closely on them, and now feel uncomfortable about the way they are used to argue in favour of the values of the white plantocracy. All the slaves, especially Mammy, seem inflexible and absurdly unable to get things in proportion in changing times. Mammy's rigid determination to maintain social and racial codes begins to seem sinister; in the midst of a terrible war, her horror at Scarlett's unladylike blistered hands and sunburned face, and outrage at being expected to pick cotton like a field hand, suggest that it was black slaves rather than white owners who insisted on preserving the status quo and thus precipitated a civil war.

While Hattie McDaniel's interpretation is superb (within the narrow limits she is allowed) I find the scenes between her and Scarlett painful to watch. Since Mammy lavishes on Scarlett such enormous maternal care (oh yes, she is Scarlett's only true mother) and is always there, ready to support, cajole, persuade and warn her surrogate daughter on all possible matters, why is Scarlett so careless of her, so dismissive of her needs and rights? The last time I saw the film, I was struck by the rather subdued Mammy of the second half. As Victor Fleming's direction leads us away from the Civil War epic into intimate melodrama, Mammy's querulousness is presumably out of place, so she becomes rather lugubrious. This is half explained as a back complaint, in one reference when Mammy comes to Scarlett's room the morning after the 'Row and Rape'. When asked by a jubilant Scarlett how she is, she answers: 'Well . . . my back ain' what it useter be with this ol' miz'ry', and that is all we ever know about that. Mammy's health and welfare are usually seen as completely contingent on those of 'her' white folks, so her back trouble seems an intrusive detail. It made me realise how much we accept her subservient maternal functions as *natural* and *given*, and how little this woman with no name of her own is allowed any autonomy – enslaved or free.

Mothering Women

I have described the very positive, warm feelings many of my correspondents have for Mammy, and their recognition of her special dignity and power. Certainly, it is she and the other women slaves who stay in our memories; among the stereotyped male figures, only Uncle Peter is recalled for his cameo role in the book. In order to explain this appeal of black women characters to (predominantly white) women reader-viewers, I return to my description of Mammy as icon of black Earth Motherhood. For it is the very motherly, caring quality in the black women which is so appealing – especially in a book and film which are so much concerned with mothers, mothering and nurture of all kinds.

Each woman fan of *Gone With the Wind* is someone's daughter; many of us are also mothers, grandmothers

and – in some cases – great-grandmothers. Whether
biological or adoptive parents, or mother-figures in
our family and work lives, we all know what it feels
like to be mothered and to mother in turn. Margaret
Mitchell, close to her maternal grandmother and other
female relatives, lost her mother at a crucial age and was
haunted by her memory and the powerful feminist role-
model Maybelle had become. It seems to me that one
of the most compelling aspects of *GWTW* for women
is its obsessive concern with mothers and daughters –
real and surrogate, good and bad, dutiful and rebellious,
black and white. Both book and (to a lesser extent)
film celebrate and demonstrate the problematic nature
of motherhood, mothering, mother–daughter relationships, lost and substitute mothers, and the power of
mothers – even after death – to dominate and constrain
women's lives.

Covering the full spectrum of mother–daughter
themes, there is the short-lived relationship of Scarlett
and her sisters to the patient Ellen O'Hara; the
reluctant motherhood of Scarlett and Melanie's joy
in difficult – finally fatal – childbearing; the fraught
childbirth in burning Atlanta; Scarlett's miscarriage;
the devoted mothering of both Scarlett and Bonnie
Blue by Rhett, followed by the girl's tragic death; and
the effect of a daughter's death on a shaky marriage.
GWTW abounds with good, bad and indifferent mothers, mother-figures and surrogate mothers and daughters
– especially Melanie and Scarlett, who care for each
other, each other's children, Ashley, Aunt Pittypat and
the slaves/servants in a variety of maternal roles.

Unorthodox figures are introduced to complete this
array of mother types. Arriving early at the Wilkes
barbecue is the formidable mother-of-eight Beatrice
Tarleton, who takes the reins of her own carriage,
handles horses better than any man in the County,
and – to Scarlett's envious astonishment – romps with

her daughters, who treat her like an equal. Scarlett tells Rhett of her Grandma Robillard (a role-model Ellen clearly did not follow) who, though cold and strict about manners, married three times and wore rouge, low-cut dresses and scarcely any undies. Ellen is recalled with awe, but Scarlett's imagination seems to have been captured by these more bohemian mother-figures.

GWTW does not entirely shirk the darker sides of motherhood. Belle Watling, thanked by Melanie for saving Ashley after the Klan raid, confides that she too has a son, whom she has not seen since he was little; the book hints that he is her illegitimate son by Rhett, a suggestion of yet another form of unconventional motherhood. And Grandma Fontaine reminds the shocked women of her family of the 'mulatto babies' of slave days, and predicts more to come with Emancipation; the threat of black rape with resulting mixed-race offspring remains an unspoken but powerful threat throughout the Reconstruction scenes.

GWTW's central absent mother-figure is of course Ellen O'Hara, who dies early while performing the classic feminine role of tending the sick and poor; her selflessness and courage have made her the 'great lady' Scarlett says she would like to emulate. As we know, Scarlett protests too much. While expressing many a pang of regret and remorse at falling short of her mother's example, she rarely follows Ellen's lead, instead modelling her behaviour on the *male* survivors around her – not for her a virtuous, self-denying, feminine death . . . But Ellen is a frequent point of reference and inspiration, and her spirit pervades the story.

However, as a live mother Ellen is curiously insignificant. Though we are told she has been a major figure to her growing daughters, in book and film she maintains a considerable physical and emotional distance from them. The day-to-day detailed vigilance, discipline and concern are demonstrated not by the biological mother but by her slave, then employee, the woman who has no name but that of her function: Mammy. The best mother any girl could possibly have, Mammy is intimately, constantly and self-abnegatingly concerned with her charges, never asks anything for herself, refuses to leave after Emancipation, never gets ill and does not die. From beginning to end, without any complaint or question, she is – quite simply – there. No wonder women reader-viewers adore her, and sweep aside the racially divisive assumptions underlying her role in favour of acclaim for this Earth Mother Goddess in whose bosom we would all like to take refuge.

A Different Kind of Mammy

However, it is worth looking briefly at two novels which transform that stereotyped figure of white imagination into a living, suffering woman. When read together with GWTW, Margaret Walker's Jubilee (1966) and Sherley Anne Williams's Dessa Rose (1986) reinterpret the 'Mammy' figure immortalised in GWTW, and bring her alive in new ways.[34] Both these novels draw on real incidents and characters – Walker on her great-grandmother's life, Williams on black historians' accounts. Leaving behind the white plantation house dwellers in favour of the slaves in kitchen and quarters, they challenge Margaret Mitchell's sanitised version of race relations with the heavily documented brutal and unsavoury aspects. They describe vividly the white master's sexual exploitation of slave girls and women; the problems of a mixed-race girl; the treatment of slaves as valuable chattels to be sold away, beaten and branded if they try to escape; and the separation of slave women from their new babies.

While *Dessa Rose* ends before the Civil War, *Jubilee* charts the confusion and isolation of slaves and newly freed blacks after Emancipation. During Reconstruction the main character, Vyry, endures the problems of a freed Black who must settle on land that floods, share-crop for a corrupt farmer, and have her home burned out by Ku Klux Klan members who resent her mod-est prosperity. Vyry's story concludes with her family finding peace and safety in a white community where she will be 'granny' midwife, and 'best true example of the motherhood of her race' (p. 407). In *Dessa Rose*, an extraordinary friendship – albeit reserved and ultimately impossible to sustain – grows between a white planta-tion mistress, Rufel, and a black slave 'mammy', Dessa Rose. Dessa, a heavily pregnant runaway slave who seeks refuge at Rufel's farm, helps the white woman to recognise how little she has understood the humanity of the Blacks she and her husband have owned. Painfully, Rufel comes to realise that she cannot easily recall her dead Mammy's real name, and that she never asked or knew whether her Mammy, Dorcas, had any children. Like *Jubilee*, the novel concludes joyfully, with Dessa *acting* as Rufel's Mammy in order to escape – with the white woman's collusion – to the free West, where she settles with her husband and children, to whom she tells her story.

Both novels, in different ways, demonstrate how cheaply the lives of black women, their lovers and children were held, and how casually slave women's babies were sold away from them to free those women to be good mammies to their white charges, and to keep breeding. Both see the worst crime of slavery as the ignorance it imposed on black men and women, and the impossibility for Blacks of sustaining any emotional bonds beyond those of 'their' white 'family'. And both celebrate the revolutionary potential of women's abil-ity to understand and identify with one another across boundaries of race and class in order to create a just and equal society. Most significantly, the two novels reject the idealised notion of an eternal Mammy figure awaiting her white charge behind the white curtains of a white-owned plantation house. These mammies are real, autonomous women with their own needs, and they offer an ironic response to the one-dimensional self-effacing nurturance of Margaret Mitchell's figure, the Mammy of Them All.

Margaret Walker and Sherley Anne Williams use oral history to demonstrate different perspectives from Mitchell on the issues of class, gender and race raised by the Civil War period. *Jubilee*'s Vyry and Dessa Rose – and all other alternative black female fictional characters – help us to remember that Mammy, the 'Great Black Mother of us all', that selfless anonymous figure 'without a history or a future', exists only in fiction, film, pancake boxes, maple-syrup bottles, and in a café on a Mississippi highway.

8

Looking Back and Forward:
Gone With the Wind, History and Heritage

The whole film was such a relief from all the grey days, bombs and so many horrific casualties. (Gladys Millman)

I adored the detailed accounts of Scarlett's dresses, and sitting in my drab grey school uniform I'd imagine myself tightly laced in frills and flounces, scented with Mother's lemon verbena, rustling like Mammy's petticoat. (Jacqueline Wilson)

We have seen that *Gone With the Wind*'s interpretation of Southern history has been emulated and challenged in a variety of different fictional works, both novels and films. Black writers have drawn on their family oral histories to produce dramatically different versions of the American Civil War and Emancipation in the South. Nevertheless, considering that the War has been the subject of well over 30,000 books, of which roughly 2,000 are novels, as well as dozens of Hollywood film and television series, *GWTW* remains easily the best-known work. As one critic said, it has 'probably done more to shape the popular view of the Civil War and Reconstruction than all of the scholarly works in that notably sophisticated and well-developed field'.[1]

But whether it is 'true' to historical fact remains a debating point. Though most of my correspondents admire Margaret Mitchell's command of historical context and detail, critics and historians are divided. Mitchell has been extravagantly praised for historical verisimilitude, and also bitterly blamed for historical distortion and blatant propaganda. How you view *GWTW*'s relationship to historical complexities seems to depend (like so much else in the work) on your sex, race, age, regional identity, political beliefs and knowledge of American history. Yet wherever you stand you cannot escape the impact made by this century's most internationally fêted historical fiction. *GWTW* appeals profoundly to a nostalgia for the past, for Golden Ages and Paradises Lost, and its historical themes and biases are often blurred in a general celebration of this unique phenomenon – by critics and publicists, and also through those heritage industry markers of tourist sites, fiftieth anniversary celebrations, special issue postage stamps and items of memorabilia.

Women Interpreting History

First, it is useful to remember that the way in which human beings make sense of the past, and their own and others' histories, is complex. Historians have enough trouble interpreting and agreeing among themselves; though they are regarded as different from historical novelists, their investigative methods and interpretative strategies have much in common with those of the fiction-writer. As Julian Barnes wrote in his novel *Flaubert's Parrot*, 'Every so often we are tempted to throw up our hands and declare that history is merely another literary genre: the past is autobiographical fiction pretending to be a parliamentary report.'[2] In other words, 'history' is a record of subjective readings of the past; it exists only in the perspective of the lens through which it is viewed.

Furthermore, history is not simply a study of the *past* by official historians. We are all historians of the *present*; 'popular memory' is produced socially and collectively as a précis of the past, and everyone is a kind of historian. We can all examine the relationship of present to past through our own reminiscences, memories, diaries, letters, photos, family anecdotes, friends' jokes, as well as 'public' sources such as history textbooks, national record offices, museums, the media – and, of course, historical fiction and film.[3]

Since women have always been avid consumers of historical fiction and costume-drama films and television series, for us this is clearly a major source of historical knowledge and pleasurable understanding – and for many, a more accessible means of approaching the past than war diaries, accounts, novels and films which are popular with a male market. Some of my correspondents, while denying regular reading of romances and conventional history books, acknowledged a wide reading of historical novels and gave as a reason for delight in *GWTW* the fascination of its period setting, and their interest in that episode in American history. In Britain during and immediately after the Second World War, historical romance-reading was popular with (especially middle-class) women who completed diaries and questionnaires for the 'Mass-Observation' survey of people's lives; Mass-Observation's male readers preferred 'real history', Hemingway and detective fiction. Women explained their pleasure in terms of 'a sense of proportion, escapism, access to a historically vivid past'.[4]

However, they often expressed shame at their pleasure because they were aware of the low status of such fiction. As with romances, critics have long scorned those historical novels popular with women and little serious attention has been paid to writers who have been staples of women's reading, such as Georgette Heyer, Norah Lofts and Jean Plaidy. In recent years, however, feminist critics have turned their attention to historical novels and films in order to understand their power over women. They have shown that the roles female characters play in such historical romances – such as mistresses, wives, mothers or daughters of famous men, confined to

the margins of major affairs of state, wars and kingships –
assure readers that 'the personal *matters*', and 'nothing is
personal which is not also *social*'.[5] Intimate relationships,
family structures and women's influence (albeit at various
removes from the centre of power) have significance for
historical events and transformations.

Moreover, for female reader-viewers of historical
romance there are specific pleasures related to women's
particular interest in fashion, fabric and decor. The costume drama – in print, but especially on celluloid –
affords us great imaginative and visual satisfaction; we
lap up details of texture, setting, dress and spectacle.
Gainsborough Studio costume film melodramas of the
1940s (*The Man in Grey*, 1943; *The Wicked Lady*, 1945;
Jassy, 1947) – which, like the novels on which they were
based, were aimed primarily at women – present the past
as a place of sensual pleasure, with costume one of the
film audience's main delights. And probably more than
in any subsequent decade, for a 1940s British female
film-goer this enjoyment was exceptionally collective.
In 1941 clothes rationing was introduced to release
workers from the clothing industry into munitions,
and 'utility' clothes comprised every woman's wardrobe. Compared with the widespread drab uniform
of plain underwear, low-heeled shoes, limited fabrics,
practical trousers and no embroidery, the flamboyant
Gainsborough costumes must have afforded for mothers and daughters, sisters and friends attending cinema
together a special visual pleasure: all those tight bod-
ices, heavy layers of material, elaborate embroidery,
diamanté studs. As one sixteen-year-old hairdresser said,
she imagined herself as 'the lovely heroine in a beautiful blue crinoline with a feather in her hair'.[6]

Since some of the female characters also dressed in
male costumes and the men were as gorgeously attired
as the women, there was many an androgynous delight
to be had in the 1940s cinema. In these films, women's

erotic power was much emphasised through the flamboyant display of female breasts bursting provocatively from tight corsetry; just as, in 1939, *GWTW* director Victor Fleming had irritated Vivien Leigh by demanding more display of her breasts in key scenes. So extravagant costume made of generous lengths of colourful, rich fabrics, and erotic, tempting displays of cleavage and male genitals outlined clearly by tight leggings, together with luxuriant wigs and exaggerated make-up, have all offered women varieties of sensual pleasure which have undoubtedly made the past seem a more friendly and human 'place'. That enjoyment which we as a sex have long derived from dressing up, the adornment of ourselves and others, has been well catered for by the minutely detailed descriptions by historical novelists and the sumptuous costumes of historical film and television series. And whether or not this helps women relate differently from men to historical event and figure, there is no doubt that the potential of such fiction and film to influence and inspire women has been considerable. *Gone With the Wind*, with its spectacular settings, elaborate dresses and glamorous characters, has proved a supremely successful prototype for subsequent historical dramas, and still remains one of women's favourite historical romances.

Gone With the Wind: 'Authentic' or 'False' History?

Of course, the way in which a woman understands a historical novel or film depends on her perspective on or knowledge of any given period, and on the number of alternative versions of the period already known to her. How, for instance, does a woman reader or filmgoer interpret the steamy *Forever Amber* in the light of other recalled associations with the Restoration in British history – school history lessons, laughing cavaliers,

myths about Nell Gwyn, the Restoration play and poem?
And how much more baffling is a British reader-viewer's
response to a book and film about the American Civil
War, a period of history taught in British schools only
recently and with little immediate or familiar meaning to her? Scarcely any American woman (especially
a Southerner) could read or watch *GWTW* without
hearing and seeing a myriad voices and sights of school
and college, battle sites and war memorials, paintings,
photos, family anecdotes, novels, the Lincoln Memorial, resonant names like Gettysburg, Sherman, and so
on. Compare this with one of my British respondents
who read the book in 1939 and who, I believe, speaks
for many more readers:

> I never thought of *Gone With the Wind* as a 'his-
> torical novel'. I don't think, when I read it, that
> I had ever heard of the Civil War – I'm quite sure
> it was never mentioned in school history lessons.
> I was brought up when the British Empire was all!
> I think I thought the 'history' was fictional too.

Not all my correspondents spelled out so clearly this
reading of the novel as fictionalised history, though
on the questionnaire in response to my query, 'Do
you think *GWTW* gives a true picture of the South
before and after the Civil War?', the replies betrayed
considerable nervousness and confusion. While one-
third of respondents wrote 'Yes', most answered
'Don't know' or 'In some ways'. Only one in ten
said unequivocally 'No' – a judgement requiring a
certainty about historical 'truth'. My impression is that
most people felt they were experiencing a work with a
firm grasp of historical fact, which in most cases they
were ill equipped to judge. Few women said that *GWTW*
was Southern propaganda, though a significant minority
pointed to its 'inaccuracies' or 'bias' in terms of *racial*

issues. A number of letters said that *GWTW* taught them a great deal, and a few claimed to have been converted to the Confederate cause (including one woman who had studied American history at college and read widely in Civil War historiography). Most *GWTW* enthusiasts repeatedly used words such as 'authentic', 'accurate' and 'realistic' to describe its relationship to Southern history.

These terms of approval echo words chosen by *GWTW* publicists and early critics; indeed, the first reviews almost all spoke of the book's 'authenticity', 'convincing ring of folk-lore', 'its definitiveness, its truthfulness and its completeness'. In all publicity, the author's personal authority over her material is seen to stem from intimate knowledge of her subject. In blurb, critical and advertising material, Mitchell's credentials as objective reporter of the Civil War period are recounted, so that readers may feel they are participating in a formidable historian's account rather than the emotionally charged, partisan version which its minority critics believe it to be. For example, the 1974 Pan paperback edition gives Mitchell's biographical sketch a ring of authority:

> Margaret Mitchell was born in Atlanta, Georgia,
> the daughter of an attorney who was president of
> the Atlanta Historical Society. All the family were
> interested in American history and she grew up
> in an atmosphere of stories about the Civil War.

Thus we are lulled into a sense of security that the writer speaks with the ring of historical 'truth'.

Many of the adverse critical discussions of *GWTW* attack it on the grounds of detail, leaving the question of Mitchell's overall interpretation and structuring of historical material relatively unchallenged. Floyd Watkins, in his much-quoted article '*Gone With the Wind* as Vulgar Literature', goes for the jugular on general grounds, but weakens his case by an increasingly obsessive documentation of minor historical inaccuracies – everything from the number of acres farmed by the poor white Slatterys to Scarlett's 'improbable' seventeen-inch waist and Gerald O'Hara's wearing a cravat on a weekday.[7]

So how far do we get by asking how accurate *GWTW* was in its every detail of the Old South, Civil War and Reconstruction periods? If we prove that Margaret Mitchell had done her homework thoroughly, and that the days on which her cravats are worn and the size and shape of her plantation houses are scrupulously correct, would we have proved her to be a great historical novelist? I think not, and I feel this leads nowhere. For whether Scarlett could really have had a seventeen-inch waist involves us in irrelevant debates about a spurious notion of historical accuracy. As historian Raphael Samuel has said, 'The past can never be transcribed, but has always to be re-invented.'[8]

In most critics' and readers' eyes, Mitchell has certainly reinvented the past satisfactorily. Southern critic Louis Rubin, Jr, despite describing in detail the author's many historical distortions and errors, concluded that 'in an ultimate sense her presentation is both remarkably accurate and deeply moving' because of the 'glimpse into the times' afforded us by the figure of Scarlett O'Hara and her career as entrepreneur and opportunist.[9] Another critic, Darden Asbury Pyron, demonstrates that it takes a hard look at the 'dissonances of Southern society itself'. In seeing history as 'defeat, loss, and the inevitability of death', Margaret Mitchell has created a Southern epic.[10] So the 'truths' which the work has successfully documented are not necessarily those of detail, or indeed of historical objectivity (whatever that may be), but more of a mythic, epic and indeed tragic nature.

But myths are not apolitical, and their meanings are rarely universal. In a few liberal and black voices raised against *GWTW*, we are reminded of how the work's 'mythic' power is not for all time and all people but

excludes certain perspectives and groups. Liberal critic
Floyd Watkins (the same who nit-picks over Gerald's
cravat) described *GWTW*'s 'myth' as one which

> seems to ease the hunger of all extravagantly
> Southern and little romantic souls, but it propa-
> gandizes history, fails to grasp the depths and
> complexities of human evil and the significances
> of those who prevail.

Dramatist Carlton Moss described it from the perspective of 'the Negro people':

> Sugar-smeared and blurred by a boresome Holly-
> wood love story and under the guise of presenting
> the South as it is in the 'eyes of the Southerners',
> the message of *GWTW* emerges in its final entity
> as a nostalgic plea for sympathy for a still living
> cause of Southern reaction.[11]

In the context of Southerners' frequent claims that
the Civil War is still continuing, and the semi-humorous
bumper-stickers and T-shirts that proclaim that slogan
many a conservative Southerner welcomes, 'The South
Shall Rise Again', *GWTW* plays an important ideological
role. It continues to serve up ladles of delicious nostalgia
and images of endurance, survival and fighting for kith
and kin which stoke jingoistic fires. It also inspires in
many a non-Southern reader-viewer who lives in a
troubled world a generalised nostalgia for a soft-focus,
mythic Golden Age of harmony based on an ordered
hierarchical social structure and family life in which
both sexes, all races and generations, know and accept
their place.

War and Peace

But the nostalgia which is evoked by *GWTW* is not merely
for an idealised Golden Age or Paradise Lost. For as well

as being part of the genre of general historical novel and film, *GWTW* is also a work about war, and like many epic novel-films it treats vividly the impact on people's lives of those terrible disruptions caused by civil strife. However, unlike those nineteenth-century epics often compared with *GWTW*, *War and Peace* and *Vanity Fair*, this was a war novel and film with a difference – no sustained battle scenes. Though Mitchell conscientiously described military strategies and major events in the course of the Civil War, she did not dwell on blood and gore but confined herself mainly to the War as experienced on the home front.

The heroics of this version of the Civil War all take place not at Gettysburg and Shiloh but in Atlanta and at Tara; occupying centre stage in book and film is the courage not of soldiers but of *women* – sewing and planting for the Confederacy, nursing the wounded, shooting the Yankee deserter-pillager. Always, though, the absent soldiers and battles are present, in the words of letters and lists of the dead, the shortages suffered and sacrifices made, as well as the resonant absence of fighter-prisoner Ashley Wilkes and the outrageous presence of blockade-runner Rhett Butler. The heightened intensity of life – death, suffering, dangerous childbirth, fear of the next dispatch, the relaxation of social codes and the breakdown of class (if not race) distinctions – all contrast with the abundance and excess of the moonlight-and-magnolia life which is so rudely interrupted early in the story.

Unashamedly, then, *GWTW* focuses on the War from the perspective of those left behind: women, children, the old and sick, the wounded and feckless. The romantic image of women in wartime passively waiting is, of course, debunked. The home front, far from being a place of passive endurance and anticipation, is a centre of activity, ingenuity and creativity. For many women reader-viewers, this must have the attraction of offering a metaphorical picture of our lives – excluded from the central, significant and glorious battlegrounds and confined to the relatively invisible but indispensable margins where we are expected to mend men's uniforms, to keep the home fires burning and morale high. The fact that women are forced suddenly and dramatically to take control of their very survival, not to mention all forms of social and economic life, must be one of the most appealing fictional fantasies for women who feel that their own daily lives are controlled by men and male-dominated structures.

Moreover, as a book and film about war, *GWTW* has a very particular set of meanings for those British women who read the book or saw the film during the Second World War, when their own menfolk and homes were in continual danger and their daily lives in total disruption. I have found it fascinating to discuss *GWTW* with women in both the American South and Britain. For anyone from the South 'The War' always signifies the American Civil War, the last significant war to be fought on their own soil and with huge impact on their families; while for any Briton 'The War' means either the 1914–18 or, more usually, the 1939–45 World War. (I imagine that for American Northerners there would be a variety of associations, perhaps depending on age, race and politics.) So for reader-viewers of our two nations, the resonances of 'war' itself have different historical inflections. Certainly, among women who lived through either World War and whose lives were turned upside down, *GWTW* is remembered as capturing well that mingled fear, intensity of feeling, stoicism and euphoria experienced by those who were left behind.

The 'sense of proportion, escapism, access to a historically vivid past' which 1940s Mass-Observation women gave as pleasures of reading historical novels all feature in terms of the particular needs women wanted fiction and film to satisfy during a long and terrible war in which

many lost their loved ones and homes but others gained
new jobs, confidence – and indeed, joys. Patrick Wright,
describing the 'quickening' effect of war, summarises
the special feeling which it can induce:[12]

> In war – *and surely not just for men* – personal
> actions can count in a different way, routine can
> have a greater sense of meaning and necessity, and
> there can be some experience not just of extremity
> . . . but also of purpose.   (my emphasis)

GWTW captures this sense of meaning and purpose
(demonstrating the 'surely not just for men' very well)
and many of my correspondents echo this. For several, it
stands as a reminder of a particularly poignant period in
their own histories; as Vera Bancroft put it, ' "something
special" because I associate it with that lovely long hot
summer before the war – the last wholly young and
carefree time in our lives'.

Many described first reading this book about a bloody
civil war in an air-raid shelter, waiting for bombs to fall
in the midst of a world war. In 1940, Hylda Fletcher's
family were crowded into a small larder under the stairs
while Manchester received its worst bombing. She felt
no fear, since

> [I was] completely immersed in my book, oblivious
> to the noise of falling bombs and anti-aircraft guns,
> and only glad of the opportunity to read all night
> without parental criticism.

Thirteen-year-old Paddy Ferris also found the book
peculiarly relevant and moving. Having stayed behind
at home with *GWTW* while the rest of her family had
gone to the shelter, she was found by a family friend who
misinterpreted her weeping. He thought it was for fear
of the bombing; it was, she records, because the book
was so sad. Similarly, the act of watching the film took on
a special meaning for the women who watched Atlanta

in flames while fearing that the cinema over their heads might explode. Mrs E.M. Bloomfield recalls that the Rex Cinema, Coventry 'was itself "Gone With the Wind" ' on the Saturday night in 1940 before *GWTW* was due to be shown on the Monday, when a bomb destroyed the cinema, and a few women describe diving beneath their seats when a Doodlebug (flying bomb) was heard. Elsie Kingdom, struck by the film's burning of Atlanta scenes, emerged from the cinema to see the City of London and docks on fire; the Blitz had begun. Poor Doris Marston was watching Rhett say his final farewell to Scarlett when the sirens went. She spent the night in the cinema's cellar and had to wait twenty years to find out what happened at the end. In chapter 6 I described Margery Owen's experience of people fleeing the cinema in anticipation of air-raids, in the misplaced certainty of a happy ending.

So the 'quickening' effect of war on people's everyday lives, intensifying many experiences and relationships, led to particularly strong identification with the situations described in *GWTW*, and with the book and film themselves. Of all my correspondents, the women who had first read and seen it during the war wrote of their memories at greatest length and with special emotional force. They spelled out the powerful effect of reading about women who were in their own position, facing similar troubles. Grace F. Ince wrote: 'We knew, from our own experience, the heartbreak and suffering when loved ones went to war', and Gila Wilding explained:

> In times fraught with danger and suffering with
> the shortage of all but the bare necessities it was
> easy to feel a kinship with the families in the South
> and it was not difficult to understand Scarlett's
> determination 'never to go hungry again'.

For many women who endured those war years, the figure of Scarlett stands as a model of resilience and stoicism. For instance, Gwenith Llewellyn:

> You could admire [Scarlett's] iron will and resolve
> in the face of the severe adversity she suffered, but
> self-preservation ruled her life completely . . . Her
> attitude did act as a spur to myself, when doubt
> and fears of our unknown future as a family and
> nation were sometimes overwhelming.

June M. Woodford read the novel in 1942, when she
was sixteen – the same age as Scarlett at the beginning
– and identified with her situation because she was living
'under very similar circumstances such as war, privations
in food, dress, even shortage of hairpins, not to mention
love affairs going awry!' Several women commented on
the fact that *GWTW* showed women's *active* role in a
war, something they shared and so well understood.

For some, however, the identification was too close
and painful, and *GWTW* is recalled sorrowfully. Jessica
Alborough recalls the reaction of her stepbrother's wife:
her husband was in the army in Burma, where he later
lost his life, and the war scenes disturbed her badly.
Margaret Bosworth saw the film in 1942 with her fiancé
on 'embarkation leave' (he was shortly to leave for a battle zone) and found it intensely depressing: 'The part I
remember the most was the return of the soldiers from
the fighting, all wounded, defeated and dishevelled.' She
has never wanted to read the book or see the film since
that time.

By contrast, for many women *Gone With the Wind*
remains a highlight of escapist pleasure in dark days – as
Doreen Howells put it, 'a wonderful treat at a time when
treats were few and far between'. Like the Gainsborough
films, *GWTW* offered a spectacle which compensated
women for their own drab lives; Mrs G. Hobbs loved
it because it 'epitomised everything that was lacking in
our own lives then – glamour, and colour and romance'.
For many, of course, film-going was one of the great

treats of the war and *GWTW*, with its extraordinary length, Technicolor, costumes and fine casting, remains a profoundly happy cinematic memory. Mrs Phyllis Bush evokes beautifully the euphoric associations *GWTW* had at the time:

> On June 8th when the war ended I had stayed
> up in the West End to celebrate and shout for
> an appearance of Winston Churchill, and my friend
> and I had missed all the transport so had to walk
> home and on that long trek to north London we
> followed a girl and her fellow who was playing
> [the theme tune] 'Tara', on an accordion. I've never
> forgotten it. Marvellous.

In small, unexpected ways *GWTW* gave pleasure to those suffering wartime privations. Letter after letter from women of that generation described as a most memorable scene the transformation of Tara's green velvet curtains into an outfit for Scarlett to seduce Rhett Butler into paying Tara's taxes. This scene, almost unmentioned by younger correspondents, had special resonance at that time. Edith Taylor is one of many:

> Being wartime, all clothes and dress materials
> were only obtainable by clothing coupons. These
> were very limited. However, curtain material was
> coupon-free. Observing how Scarlett used her own
> velvet curtains to make herself a gown, I bought
> curtain material for a rather glamorous housecoat,
> greatly admired by my colleagues, and lasting
> for many years.

War, Peace, and the Post-nuclear *Gone With the Wind*

Joyous and liberating, nostalgic and poignant, or both,

the war elements in *GWTW* spoke vividly to women reader-viewers between 1939 and 1945. For some, *GWTW* argued a powerful case against wars of all kinds. Mrs E.M. Bloomfield speaks for others when she recalls the impact of the film on viewers in 1941 Coventry, a heavily bombed city:

> We also were lulled into a sense of false security
> by the glamour of men leaving home in smart
> new uniforms to fight for their beliefs, completely
> oblivious of the holocaust about to overtake us
> and our city. [Similar to] the Civil War in America
> it was like one big picnic, one great party until
> it was too late.

By contrast, very few women under fifty commented on *GWTW* as a war book and film. For British reader-viewers who have no memories of war on their own soil, and little or no memories of fathers or uncles killed in conflict, *GWTW* is interpreted primarily as a historical romance. It would be interesting to review American women's associations of *GWTW* with the Korean and Vietnam Wars. The perspective which *GWTW* takes on war and women's sufferings is perhaps too remote and mannered to speak emotionally to a British generation which has lived through the Falklands War – though the themes of strong nationalism and the heroism of dying for a lost cause may well speak in new ways to families directly affected by that war, and 1980s readers and audiences who recall its national impact.

Almost thirty years after the film of *Gone With the Wind*, an independent film-maker from the American South, Ross McElwee, decided to make a documentary about the route of General Sherman's scorched-earth march across Southern states from Atlanta to the sea (*Sherman's March*, 1986). However, because of his troubled love life and recurrent dreams of nuclear war, he became diverted into making a film which is – as its subtitle indicates – 'A Meditation on the Possibility of Romantic Love in the South During an Era of Nuclear Weapons Proliferation'. In a brilliant series of vignettes of Southern life McElwee traverses the route Sherman took, filming war memorials, burned plantations, Atlanta's Confederate monuments, as well as modern nuclear-waste processing plants, disused military centres, and a Mormon isolationist centre in the woods with its own bunker and tennis courts ready for nuclear war. Along the route he meets and has relationships with women of all kinds: one who welcomes the nuclear war as forerunner to the Old Testament's vision of Apocalypse; another who is protesting at the dumping of nuclear waste; a friend who urges him to marry because passion is the only thing of meaning in contemporary life; and an older woman he encounters at a Fort Sumter monument who mutters, 'Nothing glamorous about war – death and destruction.'

The preoccupations of McElwee's film are significantly similar to those of *GWTW*: war, holocaust, women's experience of and feelings about conflicts on the battlefield and in bed, the problematic nature of masculinity. His awareness of the fragility of peace and love, his evocation of a rich and luxuriant land which is vulnerable to total destruction, and the often comic demonstration he gives of the intensity and difficulty of permanent relationships in a nuclear age, all recall the earlier themes and motifs of *GWTW* and perhaps help us to see it in similarly contemporary terms. For there is no doubt that *GWTW* can also be read as a powerful anti-war text of the kind Mrs Bloomfield describes, one which has relevance to many contemporary women's involvement in the peace movement and ecological issues. Many letters described the powerful impact of Selznick's wonderful overview of the wounded lying in rows outside the Atlanta makeshift hospital, while

Scarlett picks her way through looking for a doctor to deliver Melanie's baby. The devastating effects of the Civil War on both those fighting and the civilian population, described on the page and in the film's gruesome colour shots, may act to remind us of the far more terrible effect any future war will have on both our armed forces and, especially, everyone on the home front who will need more than guts and cotton-picking skills to put the earth back together. *GWTW* has been extremely popular in Japan since the Second World War, and considering the devastation caused by nuclear bombs on Hiroshima and Nagasaki, followed by a resolute postwar will to survive defeat and rebuild a nation, *Gone With the Wind* may serve to remind the Japanese what a tragic waste is all war, and how urgent is the need for peaceful international coexistence.

The Nostalgia Industry

So in terms of historical resonances, *Gone With the Wind* offers women a rich source of nostalgia. Evoking as it does a past which is both real and mythic, as well as a sense of the tragic poignancy of war's impact on the home front, it has also become a treasured part of many women's personal histories and family memories. I have described the many ways in which my correspondents enshrined their enthusiasm for *GWTW* into daily life: through naming their houses Tara, their dogs and cats Rhett and Scarlett; by collecting posters, plates, books and dolls. Perhaps more than any other work *GWTW* has a life beyond the page and screen, carefully cultivated by manufacturers of memorabilia to the enthusiasm of fans who, it seems, can never get enough. Now, rather belatedly, the heritage and tourism industries have jumped on to the *GWTW* bandwagon – exactly as Margaret Mitchell had feared they would.

In the last stages of preparing this book I decided to pay a return visit to Atlanta, Georgia, home of Margaret Mitchell and setting for much of the novel. My purpose was to find out the extent to which that city's most famous writer and work were commemorated there. I knew that the States, like Britain, was increasingly aware of the advantages to the booming tourism business of opening writers' birthplaces and homes: just as England has used Shakespeare's birthplace in Stratford and Thomas Hardy's cottage in Dorset as key centres for regional tourism, so the USA offers visitors the homes of such writers as Louisa M. Alcott, William Faulkner, and – in Atlanta itself – Joel Chandler Harris (of 'Brer Rabbit' fame).

Many people are drawn to places associated with writers in an attempt to understand, or in some ways to relive the fiction. Indeed, a visit to the Yorkshire moors may well enhance an American's reading of *Wuthering Heights* (after all, as Maya Angelou once wrote, most Americans have no idea what a 'moor' is), and a tour of Faulkner's Mississippi home may help a non-Southern reader to understand the gothic atmosphere of his novels and their film adaptations. Reader-viewers find endlessly fascinating the relationship between writer and his or her region, between real and fictional place. They often want to feel that writers – and film adapters – have drawn on *actual* regions, towns, houses and people. The idea that fiction creates imaginary composite places or characters, taken from a number of sources – one of the qualities which distinguishes a poem or novel from a guide-book – is something we strongly resist. Many of us walk the streets of Bath and Lyme Regis, wanting to make new associations with Jane Austen's *Persuasion*; visitors look in vain for 'Charles Dickens's London'. We can recall *GWTW* sequel-writer Alexandra Ripley's confusing childhood direction of tourists to 'Rhett Butler's grave' in Charleston.

When I visited Atlanta, I was told repeatedly that visitors galore arrive asking where 'Tara' is, disappointed to be told it never existed. Accustomed as they are to seeing Dallas's 'Southfork Ranch' and Universal Studios' *Psycho* motel, they assume, with that wonderful confusion of fantasy and fact, that Tara must be standing in or around Atlanta. So, in this modern glass and steel city, which has apparently turned its back on the Old South and defined the New, the home of vast corporation headquarters for Coca-Cola, Days Inn of America and Cable News Network, tourists by the coachload are frustrated to find meagre commemoration of *GWTW* and its Atlanta-born creator.

There are a few Mitchell markers scattered around. Her grave stands in Oakland Cemetery; there is a Mitchell Street and a Margaret Mitchell Square (actually a small triangle of land which a Chinese woman sculptor has designed); and collections of artefacts and memorabilia at the Atlanta Historical Society, the public library and newspaper offices. The Gray Line Tour of the city points out the site of the long-destroyed Mitchell family home, the point on Peachtree Street where the writer was knocked down and killed by a drunken taxi-driver, and the apartment block in which *GWTW* was written. There are Mitchell biographies and *GWTW* glossy books in the stores, and 'Miss Prissy Brittle' candy at the airport. You may eat plantation country barbecue and blackened shrimp vidalia at the restaurant 'Pittypat's Porch', then go on to the headquarters of Cable News Network (empire of Ted Turner, owner of the *GWTW* film) to catch one of the twice-daily, seven-days-a-week viewings of the movie.

However, everyone in Atlanta and surrounding areas with whom I discussed *GWTW* recognises its considerable, as yet untapped potential in terms of the museum and memorial business. This recognition of *GWTW*'s capacity to pull the crowds and revenues into the city is not new. For many years ventures have been proposed, funds raised and sites confirmed, but with little lasting success. Margaret Mitchell herself asked that no memorial in Atlanta be constructed to her book or herself, and it was only with Atlanta's rise as a convention and tourist centre that people began to think again. On the other hand, in Jonesboro, Clayton County, a few miles from Atlanta, where the fictional Tara and Twelve Oaks are said to have stood, there is a long tradition of capitalising on their literary fame. As well as a Tara Boulevard, Auto Sales, Mobile Home Park and many more, the town's Warren House boasts bullet-holes on an inside wall, which local legend has claimed were made by a Confederate woman who shot and killed a Yankee soldier on the stairwell – supposedly the origin of Scarlett O'Hara's brave deed at Tara. Another house, the L-shaped, clapboard farmhouse with sagging front porch which belonged to Margaret Mitchell's ancestors, the Fitzgeralds, has long been regarded locally as the model for Tara, much closer to Mitchell's description than the smart white-columned mansion Selznick created on a studio lot. It was purchased by Atlanta businesswoman Betty Talmadge, who had it moved brick by brick from Jonesboro to her own land. I was told that the land on which it stood has been designated the site of a non-profit-making Margaret Mitchell museum and centre.

On a more commercial basis, Dunaway Gardens Inc. is planning a *GWTW* theme and amusement park near Roscoe (which has *no* connection with book or film) and intends to raise two million dollars. Central to this project is the Fitzgerald home and the original façade of Selznick's Tara, which Betty Talmadge bought for $5,000 and has stored in boxes, awaiting a permanent site. There is local scepticism about the ambitious Dunaway project getting off the ground (and even more about the durability of a flimsy movie façade, built for a Hollywood set, in the heavy Georgia rains), but the competition between this and the Clayton County scheme has become fierce. Both recognise that if they could attract enough funds to establish an impressive park or centre, tourists would flood in.

Mindful of this gap in the market is the redoubtable Betty Talmadge. She claims, along with some local historians, that her large, white-columned plantation house, Lovejoy, was Mitchell's model for Twelve Oaks, the Wilkes's home: 'People, when they go West, look for cowboys. When they come to Atlanta, they look for Tara, Scarlett and Rhett. I've got the nearest thing to Tara right here.'[13] Betty Talmadge Enterprises holds barbecues or 'Magnolia Suppers' with the *GWTW* soundtrack flooding Lovejoy's lawns through loudspeakers. For one hundred guests, an eleven-item menu will cost you $5,000. Large companies from within the States and other countries (especially the Japanese) have enjoyed Betty's sumptuous hospitality, as did many visitors to the Democratic Convention in July 1988. Her *Lovejoy Plantation Cookbook* has sold over 20,000 copies.[14]

During my visit to Atlanta, I was taken to see a derelict building which has become the centre of a major dispute. This large apartment block, built in 1913 at 927 Crescent Avenue, in which Margaret Mitchell lived and wrote her novel (and which she hated, calling it 'The Dump'), could become the greatest *GWTW* tourist attraction of all. The building, the last remaining on a vacant lot due for development into a landscaped park, is the subject of dispute between the city of Atlanta, Mitchell House Inc. and the Trammell Crow development company. Trammell Crow has tried to obtain a demolition permit from the city, and although this seemed likely to go ahead, at the eleventh hour Atlanta's mayor Andrew Young refused to sign, offering the restoration group some time to raise money to save it.

Mitchell House Inc. was set up on a commercial basis after the failure of the low-funded 'Margaret Mitchell

Museum' group which had raised local awareness of the apartment's historical significance. While the Museum group argued that it should be saved because 'It's all we have' as a material marker of Mitchell's life, and some of them claim to feel her spirit strongly by the window in the apartment where the book was written, MHI takes a more pragmatic line. Its president, John Taylor, quoted a university study of the house which surveyed such sources as tourism businesses and the Convention and Visitors Bureau, concluding that large numbers of people who come to Atlanta want to see something pertaining to *GWTW*. The Bureau estimated that a restored Mitchell house would draw between 300,000 and 400,000 tourists annually. As I left Atlanta, Trammell Crow was threatening to sue the city for non-signing of the demolition order. By Christmas 1988, however, meetings to discuss possible compromises were being planned between various property companies and MHI.

But whether the restoration campaign succeeds or not, it will be seen as a significant conservation battle in Atlanta. For too long, many argue, old and historically interesting buildings have been demolished to make way for the fast-growing concrete and steel office blocks, hotels and sports facilities of a boom town which sells itself as a major convention and leisure centre. The mayor was quoted as describing Atlanta's oldest buildings as 'hunks of junk', but his willingness to delay the Mitchell house demolition may be a sign of relenting – if only because he has a shrewd eye to tourist possibilities. For this project, supported as it is by the Mitchell heirs, is receiving backing from bodies as diverse as the Metropolitan Foundation of Atlanta, Jack Daniels Distilleries, The National Homebuilders Assocation and a Japanese businessman, as a showcase for conservation and heritage preservation.[15]

Saying 'No' to the *Gone With the Wind* Museum

There are detractors of the whole scheme, even among Mitchell friends and *GWTW* supporters. Richard Harwell, the influential Mitchell scholar who died in 1988 after many years of publishing articles and books about *GWTW*, felt that 'The Dump' should not be saved because Mitchell herself hated it; *Atlanta Constitution* journalist Celestine Sibley, who (like Harwell) knew Mitchell, argued against the museum because Mitchell did not want a memorial, and it is churlish to go against her wishes. Of the belief that the author's spirit remains in the apartment, Sibley simply told me, 'People are sappy'. She is sceptical of the whole business of literary heritage:

> When the Mitchell family house was torn down,
> the builders – who were no fools – dumped
> rubbish there and sold it off as souvenirs.
> A whole bunch of people all over the state of
> Georgia have told me they own Margaret Mitchell's
> toilet, bathtub and so on.

There are also some who suggest that the failure of any group to establish a successful museum to the writer is a result of the jinx which her disapproving spirit casts from the grave over any memorial enterprise . . .

But there are other objections, to which some journalists and Mitchell enthusiasts will admit. These are of a more politically sensitive nature, related to the city's racial heritage and present. I have indicated that Atlanta markets itself as – and certainly looks at first sight like – a city which has turned its back on its racially divided past. The Old South of large plantation houses boasting of white wealth and privilege, segregated districts, schools, hospitals and buses seems to have been erased. The majority of Atlanta's citizens are black (as is their world-famous major) and there is a large black bourgeoisie. The citizens of this city 'too busy to hate' claim that Atlanta is integrated, democratic and forward-looking. For Blacks it is now a pilgrimage centre, as it houses the Martin Luther King, Jr Historic Site, home of Nobel Peace Prize-winner King's tomb, restored birthplace, and Center for Nonviolent Social Change. It seemed fitting that the Reverend Jesse Jackson, the first black contender for the Democratic Presidential nomination, should arrive triumphantly in the city for the Convention at the climax of his 1980s 'freedom ride' from Chicago to Atlanta's State Capitol.

Of course, Jesse Jackson did not win the nomination because 'the time wasn't right' for a black President, and Atlanta has by no means become the cosmopolitan, post-modern multiracial city it claims. For as Jackson (victim of hundreds of death threats throughout his campaign) rode into town for the Convention, there was a demonstration by the Ku Klux Klan against homosexuals, Blacks and those Democrats (of whom Jackson had been the most vocal) who oppose apartheid in South Africa. One banner, attacking the mayor, ran 'Andrew Young, Head Atlanta House Nigger'. In a review of the recent history of the Klan, white journalist W.J. Weatherby observed:

> When you talk to some Georgian whites about the way some of the power in Atlanta has passed into black hands, they sound the way Mafia leaders do when they angrily discuss how much of their drug trade has been taken over by Asian groups.[16]

Moreover, although the Klan's centre and headquarters have moved out of Atlanta in recent years, its influence (and sometimes actual presence) remains to haunt the city. Many suspect that the murders of the black children between 1979 and 1981, though by implication attributed to Wayne Williams, were a highly successful Klan plot to terrorise the black community. In 1985 there were suggestions of retrial in the case, something James Baldwin referred to in an essay on Atlanta:

> Inevitably, and especially considering the bloody record of the heirs of Manifest Destiny, Atlanta's first reaction to the murders was to assume that this was an action of the Ku Klux Klan – alive, my friends, and well, and living in the USA.[17]

The power which the Klan exerted in Margaret Mitchell's youth, and during the bitter civil rights struggles of the 1950s and 60s, has mercifully declined; its latest manifestations have had limited success. But in terms of the city's projection of itself and its history, that past of slavery, white supremacy, racial segregation and Klan violence is in some ways represented in a glorious and dignified light. The Cyclorama, a major tourist attraction, is an impressive painting-in-the-round of the Battle of Atlanta, and reminds us of the tragic defeat of Confederate troops (with its final caption, 'So perishes a Cause'). Its bookshop boasts a large number of books describing Confederate battles, heroism and privations. One of the sites of crucial engagement in this battle, Kennesaw Mountain, has been made into a 'battlefield park' with a museum, picnic sites and hiking trails; one may 'step into yesteryear' by visiting the antebellum homes and antique shops at Allenbrook Historical Society. Near Atlanta you may begin a one-hundred-mile 'Antebellum Trail', a reminder that – according to the Atlanta Visitors' Guide – Georgia is 'a part of the Deep South, where memories are still vivid of the plantation era that marked its way of life before the 1861–65 War Between the States'.

Most significant and best known of all landmarks, however, is the vast 3,200-acre Stone Mountain Park. The mountain itself boasts the world's largest bas-relief sculpture on granite; the Confederate Memorial Carving featuring Civil War heroes Stonewall Jackson, Jefferson

Davis and Robert E. Lee is a blatant tribute to the
Lost Cause. In the park's recreational extravaganza,
overshadowed by the granite heroes, you may explore
a reconstructed antebellum plantation, paddlewheel
riverboat, Civil War exhibits, and buy original and
reproduction guns, swords and buckles at Stone Mountain Relics, Inc. The Ku Klux Klan rededicated itself
there in 1915, and − with provocative timing − at
the beginning of the 1988 Democratic Convention
its owners named a park in honour of James R.
Venable, former Imperial Wizard of the Klan.[18]

Besides providing leisure opportunities for Atlanta's
citizens and visitors, Stone Mountain is clearly of enormous symbolic importance to those 'who still hear the
guns' and believe in the resurgence of the Old South. For
instance, in a 1983 edition of *Blue and Gray Magazine*,
one of many pro-Confederate publications in the USA
and UK, there is a poem by Carl Freeman, paying tribute to the Mountain's carving. Its last stanza goes thus:

> So, friend, when you come to the mountain
> Look up at these mighty men
> And reflect how a Time has gone now
> But remember, the Dream never ends.[19]

This never-ending dream which Freeman celebrates is
one shared by many pro-Confederate individuals and
groups in all the Southern states, as well as an unknown
number of sympathisers in other countries. The British
organisation The Confederate High Command is
devoted to research to correct what it sees as the
falsifications of liberal historians, while Dixie Rebels
re-enact Civil War battles and camp conditions (with
women going along dressed in homespun and cooking
with typical 1860s rations); polemical magazines such
as *The International Confederate Johnny Reb* disseminate
information and keep the Confederate spirit alive.
There is considerable international correspondence and

co-operation; the hot debate which took place in recent years in Atlanta's newspapers and television stations over whether the Confederate flag that is woven into the Georgia state flag should be removed is the kind of issue in which British Confederate groups take a keen interest.

The fundamental belief of all these groups, a belief immortalised in granite, is that the wrong side and cause won the Civil War, that the economy and social life of antebellum days was preferable to the unified economic and (eventually) racial relations which followed a Union victory. And though the rhetoric of Confederate High Command and most publications is reasonably restrained, the logic of this position is vividly demonstrated every time the Klan makes its presence felt in Southern cities and towns, and exerts influence across the Atlantic.

The writer Robert Lumley, describing the explosion of museum-building in the late twentieth century, sees the museum as 'a potent social metaphor and . . . a means whereby societies represent their relationship to their own history and to that of other cultures'. He goes on to say that history is thus drawn on as a 'political resource whereby national identities are constructed and forms of power and privilege justified and celebrated'.[20] In the case of Atlanta, I see an uneasy relationship between the downtown face of booming progressive daily city life, and the other faces celebrating a past time of upper-class white power and privilege, black slavery and oppression. The Martin Luther King, Jr Center is modest in size, classically simple in design and profoundly moving in its exhibits, peace centre, and King's tomb reflected in a luminous pool. But this does not offer the colour, spectacle, razzmatazz and splendour of the more heavily funded Cyclorama, Stone Mountain and antebellum-style mansions of the wealthy in the suburb of Buckhead. And there is no doubt that the appeal to the popular imagination of the region's controversial past which is packaged so seductively is unlikely to fade as long as people take a skylift past the Confederate carving and marvel at antebellum architecture and antiques.

In view of this uneasy coexistence of the reactionary and enlightened, the nostalgic and forward-looking, it is perhaps understandable that Mayor Andrew Young was tempted to allow Trammell Crow to dynamite Margaret Mitchell's house, to erase the memory of a book which has brought his city more fame and attention than anything else. For, mindful of his own heritage and history, he cannot have failed to notice that *Gone With the Wind* – with its pro-Confederate polemic, energy and emotional power – is used in the South and elsewhere to vindicate and celebrate the militaristic Stone Mountain carvings far more than that assassinated black hero's body lying in a white tomb by a peaceful pool.

Afterword

I feel very strongly about *Gone With the Wind*, and it must be because I found out about love and sex and violence and childbirth and war and racism – all those important things – *through* reading this book. (Leslie Dick)

Much of the joy of preparing this book has come from my growing sense of being part of a community of women reader-viewers. These days, when I settle down with the book or in front of the film or video, I hear the voices not just of Margaret Mitchell's characters but of all the women who shared their *Gone With the Wind* memories with me. I think of those women in the 1940s taking sandwiches to eat in the Intermission, or diving beneath seats in bombing raids; and I recall Gillian Darward and friends, snuffling their way through their afternoon's video watching, food, sherry and handkerchiefs in the middle of the floor. As the swelling notes of the 'Tara' theme begin, I am reminded of Phyllis Bush's wartime trek to north London behind a man playing the tune on his accordion. I cannot read the scene in which Scarlett pulls down the green velvet curtains without remembering those women for whom dress-material rationing made this such a wonderful gesture. The temptation to label Scarlett glibly as a 'survivor' has acquired new resonance since I read Anne Karpf's association of the story with her parents' survival of the Holocaust. And I find it hard to laugh any more at Mammy and Prissy when I recall the words of Leslie Dick's teacher on the Klan, and imagine Hosea Williams's unsmiling Jemima raising her fist.

What my researches have revealed is the extent to

231

which women use reading and viewing to comfort and help us to explain and work through real problems and dilemmas. The intense feeling which my correspondents and interviewees have for *GWTW* is special, but not unique. Most of us turn to fiction, in book, film, television series and soap opera, in order to experience vicariously the daily conflicts we endure, which must usually be muddled through alone, or with a little help from our friends. The fact that so many of my correspondents described *GWTW* as 'a friend', and have found it a bond between them and their flesh-and-blood friends, mothers, daughters and workmates, indicates that *GWTW* has a vibrant life and function beyond the bookshelf, library, cinema and publicity machine.

In the preceding pages, women's voices have spoken of the varied and contradictory ways this one work has accumulated significance in their lives, making the notion of a *single GWTW* impossible. For those hundreds of women who wrote and talked to me, *GWTW* has a personal and often collective association, and each has brought to and taken from it elements appropriate to her at the time of reading and viewing, and at the particular period of her life and experience when she became hooked. Of course, as I have argued, the ways in which Margaret Mitchell wrote the book and David Selznick produced and publicised the film, as well as the manner in which its historical, political, racial and feminist themes have evolved over the last fifty years, all influence the reading-viewing experience of every woman fan. But through dogs, cats and children called Rhett, Ashley and Bonnie, houses named Tara, lavatory walls covered with posters, rereadings which produce new interpretations, and arguments about the ending with other enthusiasts, women show considerable resourcefulness. Even if loved ones laugh, they will not be dictated to about the worth of *GWTW*: regarded as one of the family, it has been incorporated by many into daily imaginative life.

I have argued strongly against *GWTW*'s presentation of black characters and racial issues, and I have suggested that the myth it offers of a Southern Paradise Lost is a difficult one to sustain and celebrate in the closing years of the twentieth century. But as I have found amply demonstrated in all my correspondence and interviews, this work has offered a profoundly evocative experience which has sustained and enriched people's lives in a multitude of ways, which it would be churlish to condemn. Condemnation would also ignore the fact that many women have responded against the apparent grain of the work, seeing it as an argument for peace, not war, and for equal rights for all people, rather than white domination. It is hard to know whether the book would have remained a world best-seller had it not been made into one of Hollywood's greatest movies; or whether the film would have become a box-office record-breaker without Selznick's production flair, as well as the coincidence of the film's première with the outbreak of the Second World War. If we then throw in the Pulitzer Prize, eight Academy Awards, and the early deaths of author, male and female stars . . . we can see there are good reasons for book and film to have become the legend they are today. This cannot explain the phenomenon away, but it does suggest that *GWTW* captured people's imagination at the right time, and with the help of biographers, critics, the memorabilia and tourism industries, television companies, sequel writers and so on, it has been kept at the forefront of many imaginations in many countries.

Speaking personally, my perceptions of *Gone With the Wind* have changed a great deal in the quarter-century since I first read it in early adolescence. It now seems less sexy and daring than it did then, and Scarlett, who delighted me as a timid teenager with her wickedness, shocks me – in crustier middle age –

with her carelessness of the community, other women and her children. I still admire her daring and stylish resilience, but (since I am now old enough to be her mother) I share older correspondents' impatience with her selfishness. Furthermore, I have had enough disastrous fantasies about Rhett-style men in my life to know that you pay dearly for bonnets from Paris and a spoiled daughter like Bonnie Blue. Rhett's humour and insouciance still charm me, but I would never trust a man who boasted of his own kissing. And I am now more interested in reading and viewing novels and films which challenge and reinterpret *GWTW* than in knowing how Margaret Mitchell or another sequel-writer would bring Scarlett and Rhett together again.

But in case all that sounds too pious for words, I freely admit to an enduring pleasure in all those gorgeous costumes, lavish Southern social gatherings, and spectacular events and effects. And like many other women, I still sigh weakly at Clark Gable's first appearance at the staircase, and sob bitterly as he slams the front door for the last time.

Appendix:
Questionnaire on *Gone With the Wind*

I am writing a book on *Gone With the Wind*, the book and film, and am very interested in memories and experiences of readers and cinema-goers. I would be very pleased if you would complete this as fully as you can, and if possible add any additional ideas or points in the blank space at the end. If you would like your name acknowledged in my book, or would be prepared to be interviewed, please complete the final section; if not, I will of course treat this information in confidence. I regret that I cannot pay any respondents or interviewees.

Helen Taylor

PLEASE ANSWER THE FOLLOWING QUESTIONS BY
TICKING APPROPRIATE BOXES. PLEASE TICK ANYTHING
WHICH APPLIES TO YOU – MORE THAN ONE TICK IN
SOME CASES.

1 Have you read the book *Gone With the Wind* by Margaret Mitchell?

yes ☐ no ☐

2 When did you first read the book? (approximate year or your approximate age) ☐

3 Did you enjoy it?

yes ☐ no ☐ some of it ☐

4 Have you reread it? Many times? ☐

5 Why did you enjoy it? Tick as many boxes as apply:

☐ A gripping story
☐ Strong heroine (Scarlett O'Hara)
☐ Strong hero (Rhett Butler)
☐ I like romantic novels
☐ I like historical novels
☐ I like a long novel which I can read over a long period
☐ Other reasons (please specify)

6 Have you read any other novels about the American South?

yes ☐   no ☐   can't remember ☐

7 Can you name any?

[ ]

8 Have you seen the 1939 film *Gone With the Wind*, starring Clark Gable and Vivien Leigh?

yes ☐   no ☐

9 When did you first see the film? (approximate year or your approximate age)   [ ]

10 Did you enjoy it?

yes ☐   no ☐   some parts ☐

11 Have you been to see the film again?
How many times?   [ ]

12 What did you most like about the film?

☐ good acting
☐ the spectacular war scenes
☐ the plantation scenes before the war
☐ the romance between Scarlett and Rhett
☐ strong story
☐ stirring epic qualities
☐ other (please say)

13 There are some differences of plot and emphasis
    between the novel and film. Have you noticed any?
    If so, what are they?

14 Does *Gone With the Wind*, book or film, have any
    pleasant/unpleasant/romantic/distasteful
    associations or memories for you? Please say what
    these are.

15 Who is your favourite main character in the book/
    film?

    ☐   Scarlett O'Hara
    ☐   Rhett Butler
    ☐   Ashley Wilkes
    ☐   Melanie Wilkes
    ☐   Mammy

16 Why?

17 Who is your least favourite?

18 Why?

19 For you, which were the most memorable scenes of
    the book or film?

- [ ] early plantation scenes before the War
- [ ] War scenes, including the burning of Atlanta
- [ ] Tara Plantation after the War – Scarlett in charge
- [ ] Scarlett's marriage to Rhett Butler and the house in
    Atlanta, with Bonnie Blue
- [ ] Death of Melanie, Scarlett's losing Rhett and return
    to Tara
- [ ] other

20 Which is your single most vivid memory of book or
    film?

21 What did you think of the presentation of Negro
    characters in the book and/or film?

- [ ] respectful
- [ ] rather patronising
- [ ] insulting
- [ ] other (please specify)

22 How do you think Mammy and Prissy (Negro slaves)
    come across?

- [ ] humorous
- [ ] foolish
- [ ] dignified
- [ ] loyal
- [ ] other (please specify)

23 Do you think *Gone With the Wind* gives a true picture of the South before and after the Civil War?

yes ☐   no ☐
don't know ☐   in some ways ☐

24 At the end of the book, it's not clear whether Scarlett gets Rhett back.
Do you:

☐ think she does?
☐ think she doesn't?
☐ not care?
☐ feel cheated of a happy ending?
☐ other – please say

25 Why do you think as you do about the ending?

26 Have you seen any other 1930s films about the American South (e.g. *Jezebel*, *Showboat*, *So Red The Rose*, *The Littlest Rebel*)? How would you compare those with *Gone With the Wind*?

27 Do you have any other thoughts or ideas about *Gone With the Wind*? Please give details below – and on an extra piece of paper if you wish.

DETAILS ABOUT YOU

NAME (if you wish to be acknowledged in my book)

ADDRESS (if you'd be prepared to be interviewed)

Phone number:

Are you prepared to be quoted in my book,
with your name given?   yes ☐   no ☐

Are you   Male ☐   Female ☐

What age are you?
(not necessary but very helpful
for my research)   ☐

What race are you?
(not necessary but very helpful)   ☐

What is your occupation?   ☐

THANK YOU VERY MUCH FOR COMPLETING THIS
QUESTIONNAIRE

Helen Taylor

Notes

1 The Phenomenal *Gone With the Wind*

1 Richard Nalley, *United Airlines Magazine*, June 1986, p. 100.
2 J. Taylor (ed.), *Ways to Reading*, London, Macmillan, 1986.
3 Joan Collins, *Past Imperfect*, London, Coronet, 1979.
4 Some of the most influential and interesting books on the subject are: Herb Bridges and Leonard J. Leff, *The Filming of Gone With the Wind*, Macon, Ga., Mercer University Press, 1984; Roland Flamini, *Scarlett, Rhett, and a Cast of Thousands*, London, André Deutsch, 1976; Gerald Gardner and Harriet Modell Gardner, *The Tara Treasury: A Pictorial History of Gone With the Wind*, Westport, Conn., Arlington House, 1980; Richard Harwell (ed.), *Margaret Mitchell's 'Gone With the Wind' Letters 1936–1949*, New York, Macmillan, 1976 (London, Sidgwick & Jackson, 1987); Susan Myrick (ed. Richard Harwell), *White Columns in Hollywood: Reports from the Gone With the Wind Sets*, Macon, Ga., Mercer University Press, 1982; Richard Harwell (ed.), *Gone With the Wind as Book and Film*, Columbia, SC, University of South Carolina Press, 1983; Sidney Howard, *Gone With the Wind: The Illustrated Screenplay*, ed. Andrew Sinclair, London, Lorrimer, 1986; Jack Temple Kirby, *Media-Made Dixie: The South in the American Imagination*, Baton Rouge, Louisiana State University Press, 1978; William Pratt, *Scarlett Fever: The Ultimate Pictorial Treasury of Gone With the Wind*, New York, Collier Macmillian, 1977.
5 There have been lively debates about issues of reading, reader response and popular culture reception. The best and most influential study to date on fiction is Janice

241

A. Radway, *Reading the Romance: Women, Patriarchy, and Popular Literature*, Chapel Hill, University of North Carolina Press, 1984. See also Janet Batsleer *et al.*, *Rewriting English: Cultural Politics of Gender and Class*, London, Methuen, 1985 (especially 'Some Women Reading', pp. 140–55) and Dave Morley, 'Texts, readers, subjects', in Stuart Hall *et al.* (eds), *Culture, Media, Language*, London, Hutchinson, 1980. For studies of television and film, see especially: Dorothy Hobson, *Crossroads: The Drama of a Soap Opera*, London, Methuen, 1982; Ien Ang, *Watching Dallas: Soap Opera and the Melodramatic Imagination*, London, Methuen, 1985; and Tony Bennett and Janet Woollacott, *Bond and Beyond: The Political Career of a Popular Hero*, London, Macmillan, 1987.

6 The letter read:

Dear –, I have been commissioned to write a book about *Gone With the Wind*, book and film, and would like to hear from fans of either or both. I would like to know when and where you first read the book or saw the film; whether you've reread it or re-viewed the film; what you most like about it; which is the single most memorable incident for you; and whether you have any special associations or memories related to the book or film. I'd also like to hear from anyone who dislikes or is strongly critical of *Gone With the Wind*. Would you also please indicate whether you'd be prepared to complete a detailed questionnaire (postage paid) and/or be interviewed on the subject. Unfortunately I can't pay respondents or interviewees, but in the published book will acknowledge all who allow their names to be used.

I received most letters from readers of 'Home and Country' (around 110 altogether), followed by readers of *Options*, 'Townswoman' or an unspecified journal or magazine (thus they could have been from any of these)

– roughly sixty-five each. There were a couple of dozen from the feminist journal *Women's Review* and my local West Country newspaper *The Western Daily Press*. A handful came from the other papers, or – by word of mouth – from women who had heard of my request. I am still receiving occasional letters from women who pick up old magazines in dentists' waiting-rooms or hair salons! Most questionnaires were from the south-east and south of England, including London, while a large number were from the south-west and north of England, with a surprisingly small sample from the Midlands, Scotland, Ireland and Wales. Thirty-eight came from the United States, mostly from students and teachers in Whitewater, Wisconsin and Baton Rouge, Louisiana. A few arrived from other countries, usually from British women whose husbands were working abroad. (For the questionnaire, see Appendix.)

2 Scarlett's Women

1 See Herb Bridges, *'Frankly, My Dear . . .' Gone With the Wind Memorabilia*, Macon, Ga., Mercer University Press, 1986.
2 William Pratt, *Scarlett Fever: The Ultimate Pictorial Treasury of Gone With the Wind*, New York, Collier Macmillan, 1977, p. 233.

3 The Woman Who Started it All

1 The two full-length biographies of Margaret Mitchell are Finis Farr, *Margaret Mitchell of Atlanta: The Author of 'Gone With the Wind'*, New York, William Morrow, 1965; and Anne Edwards, *The Road to Tara: The Life of Margaret Mitchell*, London, Hodder & Stoughton, 1983. A third, by the Mitchell scholar Darden Asbury Pyron, promises to be the most thorough and the most germane to my work; it will be published, alas, after I have completed this book. Also see Margaret Mitchell, *A Dynamo Going*

to Waste: Letters to Allen Edee 1919–1921, ed. Jane Bonner Peacock, Atlanta, Peachtree Publishers, 1985.

2 Finis Farr, op. cit., p. 154.

3 ibid., p. 30.

4 ibid., p. 88.

5 Margaret Mitchell, *Gone With the Wind*, London, Pan, 1974, p. 772. Richard Harwell (ed.), *Margaret Mitchell's 'Gone With the Wind' Letters 1936–1949*, London, Sidgwick & Jackson, 1987, p. 38.

6 For a good summary of this position, see the excellent Wyn Craig Wade, *The Fiery Cross: The Ku Klux Klan in America*, New York, Simon & Schuster, 1987, pp. 115–16.

7 Letter to Miss Ruth Tallman, July 30, 1937, in Richard Harwell (ed.), op. cit., p. 162.

8 Letter to Mr Stanley F. Horn, March 20, 1939, in Richard Harwell (ed.), op. cit., p. 263.

9 See David C. Roller and Robert W. Twyman (eds), *The Encyclopedia of Southern History*, Baton Rouge, Louisiana State University Press, 1979, pp. 86–89.

10 Kenneth T. Jackson, *The Ku Klux Klan in the City 1915–1930*, New York, Oxford University Press, 1967, p. 29.

11 Linda M. Lovell, 'Perceptions of the Ku Klux Klan Activities in the 1920s with Particular Reference to the Congressional Hearing of 1921', Special Study, BA Humanities, Bristol Polytechnic, 1982.

12 See C. Vann Woodward, *Origins of the New South 1877–1913*, Baton Rouge, Louisiana State University Press, 1951, pp. 350–56.

13 Finis Farr, op. cit., pp. 31–32.

14 Anne Edwards, op. cit., p. 78.

15 Kenneth T. Jackson, op. cit.; Wyn Craig Wade, op. cit.

16 Kenneth T. Jackson, op. cit., p. 22.

17 Wyn Craig Wade, op. cit., p. 180.

18 Kenneth T. Jackson, op. cit., p. 249.

19 Quoted in Margaret Mitchell, *A Dynamo Going to Waste*, p. 113.

20 Richard Harwell (ed.), op. cit., p. 72.

21 Letter to Miss Susan Myrick, February 10, 1939, in Richard Harwell (ed.), op. cit., p. 252.

22 See Anne Goodwyn Jones, *Tomorrow is Another Day: The Woman Writer in the South, 1859–1936*, Baton Rouge, Louisiana State University Press, 1981; and Helen Taylor, *Gender, Race, and Region in the Writings of Grace King, Ruth McEnery Stuart, and Kate Chopin*, Baton Rouge, Louisiana State University Press, 1989.

23 Marian Elder Jones, 'Me and My Book', *Georgia Review*, 16 (Summer 1962), p. 186. The Louisiana writer Grace King quotes a similar remark made to her by the editor Richard Watson Gilder, who challenged Southerners to write their version of the truth (in response to the critical Louisiana writer George Washington Cable, whose version of the South's racial history was attracting considerable notice in the North).

24 Letter to Mr Stark Young, September 29, 1936, in Richard Harwell (ed.), op. cit., p. 66.

25 William Styron, 'Author's Note', *The Confessions of Nat Turner*, New York, Signet, 1968.

26 Letter to Mrs Julia Collier Harris, July 8, 1936, in Richard Harwell (ed.), op. cit., p. 26. There is a woman living currently in Atlanta who believes that she is a reincarnation of Mitchell, whose first life was so frustrated that she wishes her unfinished business to be accomplished. There are uncanny connections between the two lives; a forthcoming publication will reveal all.

27 Letter to Mr Donald Adams, July 9, 1936, in Richard Harwell (ed.), op. cit., p. 33.

28 Kathryn Lee Seidel, *The Southern Belle in the American Novel*, Tampa, University of South Florida Press, 1985, pp. 3, 53–57.

29 Eliza Frances Andrews, *The War-Time Journal of a Georgia Girl, 1864–1865*, New York, D. Appleton and Co., 1908. See Richard Harwell (ed.), op. cit., p. 36 for other examples. For an interesting discussion of early experiments

with feminist themes, see Darden Asbury Pyron, *Towards a Feminist Apprenticeship: Margaret Mitchell's Juvenile Fiction*, Women's Studies Center, Florida International University, 1985.

30 Letter to Mr Alexander L. May, July 22, 1938, in Richard Harwell (ed.), op. cit., p. 217.

31 Letter to Mr Henry Steele Commager, July 10, 1936, in Richard Harwell (ed.), op. cit., pp. 39–40.

32 Letter to Mrs Julia Collier Harris, April 28, 1936, in Richard Harwell (ed.), op. cit., p. 5. In *Towards a Feminist Apprenticeship*, Darden Asbury Pyron reports that Mitchell told Elinor Hillyer von Hoffman, an independent-minded woman who took her job at the *Atlanta Journal*, that she intended to write a novel which would redeem woman's place in regional history; this suggests more purposefulness than she usually acknowledged.

33 Richard Harwell (ed.), op. cit., Letter to Mrs Julia Collier Harris, pp. 5–6, and Letter to Mr Harry Stillwell Edwards, June 18, 1936, p. 15.

34 Letter to Honourable Robert W. Bingham, February 23, 1937, in Richard Harwell (ed.), op. cit., pp. 123–24.

35 Letter to Miss Astride K. Hansen, January 27, 1937, in Richard Harwell (ed.), op. cit., p. 112.

36 Anne Edwards, op. cit., pp. 100–01.

37 Letter to Very Reverend Monsignor Jas. H. Murphy, March 4, 1937, in Richard Harwell (ed.), op. cit., p. 126.

4 Scarlett Woman

1 Margaret Mitchell, Letter to Mr Harry Stillwell Edwards, June 18, 1936, in Richard Harwell (ed.), *Margaret Mitchell's 'Gone With the Wind' Letters 1936–1949*, London, Sidgwick & Jackson, 1987, p. 15.

2 Margaret Mitchell, *Gone With the Wind* (1936), London, Pan, 1974, p. 412. All subsequent quotations from the novel will refer to this edition.

3 James Baldwin, 'Nobody Knows My Name: a letter from the South', in *Nobody Knows My Name: More Notes of a Native Son*, New York, Dell, 1961, p. 87.

4 Alexander Walker, *Vivien: The Life of Vivien Leigh*, London, Weidenfeld & Nicolson, 1987, p. 84; Gavin Lambert, *GWTW: The Making of Gone With the Wind*, New York, Bantam, 1973.

5 Richard Dyer, *Stars*, London, British Film Institute, 1979, p. 11; John Ellis, *Visible Fictions: Cinema: Television: Video*, London, Routledge & Kegan Paul, 1982, p. 108.

6 Peter Conrad, 'In Praise of Profligacy', *Times Literary Supplement*, 10 September 1976, p. 1094; Roland Flamini, *Scarlett, Rhett, and a Cast of Thousands*, London, André Deutsch, 1975, p. 73. Clare Boothe, *Kiss the Boys Goodbye*, New York, Random House, 1939. Interestingly, her Introduction says: 'This play was meant to be a political allegory about Fascism in America. But everywhere it has been taken for a parody of Hollywood's search for Scarlett O'Hara' (p. vii).

7 Roland Flamini, op. cit., p. 154.

8 Gerald Gardner and Harriet Modell Gardner, *The Tara Treasury: A Pictorial History of Gone With the Wind*, Westport, Conn., Arlington House, 1980.

9 William Pratt, *Scarlett Fever: The Ultimate Pictorial Treasury of Gone With the Wind*, New York, Collier Macmillan, 1977.

10 Margaret Mitchell, Letter to David Selznick, January 30, 1939, quoted in Richard Harwell (ed.), op. cit., p. 243.

11 Anne Edwards, *Vivien Leigh*, London, Coronet, 1978, pp. 96, 118.

12 ibid., pp. 11, 44; 146, 147. Alexander Walker, op. cit., p. 207.

13 Anne Edwards, op. cit., p. 122.

14 Victoria O'Donnell, 'The Southern Woman as Time-Binder in Film', *Southern Quarterly*, 19, 3–4 (1981), pp. 156–63.

15 Roland Flamini, op. cit., p. 52.

16 See Annette Kuhn, *Women's Pictures: Feminism and Cinema*, London, Routledge & Kegan Paul, 1982, pp. 34–5.

17 Angela Carter, 'The Belle as Businessperson', in *Nothing Sacred*, London, Virago, 1982, p. 140.

18 See an excellent study: Kathryn Lee Seidel, *The Southern Belle in the American Novel*, Tampa, University of South Florida Press, 1985.

19 Molly Haskell, *From Reverence to Rape: The Treatment of Women in the Movies*, London, New England Library, 1975, p. viii.

20 Louis Rubin, Jr, 'Scarlett O'Hara and the Two Quentin Compsons', in Darden Asbury Pyron, *Recasting: Gone With the Wind in American Culture*, Miami, University Presses of Florida, 1983, p. 90.

21 Michael Joseph, London, 1983.

22 Elizabeth Fox-Genovese, 'Scarlett O'Hara: The Southern Lady as New Woman', *American Quarterly*, 33, 4 (1981), p. 407. Also, for another interesting analysis of *GWTW* in terms of maternal loss, see Madonne M. Miner, '*Gone With the Wind:* "And the Cupboard Was Bare" ', in *Insatiable Appetites: Twentieth Century American Women's Bestsellers*, Westport, Conn., Greenwood Press, 1984, pp. 14–34.

5 The King and the Wimp

1 Richard Harwell (ed.), *Margaret Mitchell's 'Gone With the Wind' Letters 1936–1949*, London, Sidgwick & Jackson, 1987, p. 290.

2 Richard Harwell (ed.), *Gone With the Wind as Book and Film*, Columbia, SC, University of South Carolina Press, 1983, p. 170.

3 Gerald Gardner and Harriet Modell Gardner, *Pictorial History of Gone With the Wind*, New York, Bonanza Books, 1980, p. 43.

4 Other feminist critics have noted the focus on men's sensuous bodies and tight clothing in romantic fiction. See,

for instance, Ann Barr Snitow, 'Mass Market Romance: Pornography for Women is Different', *Radical History Review*, 20 (Spring/Summer 1979), p. 144.

5 See also Kathryn Lee Seidel, *The Southern Belle in the American Novel*, Tampa, University of South Florida Press, 1985, p. 56. She reads Rhett's darkness in terms of Southern black men (see my discussion, pp. 129–37).

6 The buggy-pushing is a detail in the film only. Although no respondent mentioned this, for a 1930s–1950s audience the sight of a man pushing a baby in buggy must have been most disconcerting, in terms of gender roles.

7 Lesley Garner, 'The greatest love story yet to be told', *Daily Telegraph*, 16 February 1987, p. 14.

8 For further discussion of this male type, see Ann Barr Snitow, op. cit.; Alison Light, ' "Returning to Manderley" – Romantic Fiction, Female Sexuality and Class', *Feminist Review*, 16 (Summer 1984), pp. 7–25; and Janice A. Radway, *Reading the Romance: Women, Patriarchy, and Popular Literature*, London, Verso, 1987.

9 Floyd C. Watkins, '*Gone With the Wind* as Vulgar Literature', in Richard Harwell (ed.), *Gone With the Wind as Book and Film*, p. 207.

10 Anne Jones, ' "The Bad Little Girl of the Good Old Days": Gender, Sex, and the Southern Social Order', in Darden Asbury Pyron, *Recasting: Gone With the Wind in American Culture*, Miami, University Presses of Florida, 1983, p. 115.

11 *The Woman Who Married Clark Gable*, Brook Films, 1985, directed by Thaddeus O'Sullivan, based on a short story by Sean O'Faolain.

12 Joan Mellon, *Big Bad Wolves: Masculinity in the American Film*, London, Elm Tree Books, 1977, p. 116.

13 Jane Ellen Wayne, *Gable's Women*, London, Simon & Schuster, 1987, p. 73.

14 ibid.

15 A film of their marriage was made in 1976: *Gable and Lombard*, directed by Sidney J. Furie, with James Brolin and Jill Clayburgh.

250   Scarlett's Women

16 Joan Mellon, op. cit., notes the Eastwood mannerism.

17 Jane Ellen Wayne, op. cit., p. 10.

18 Roland Flamini, *Scarlett, Rhett, and a Cast of Thousands*, London, André Deutsch, 1975, p. 110.

19 ibid.

20 Susan Myrick, *White Columns in Hollywood: Reports from the GWTW Sets*, ed. Richard Harwell, Macon, Ga., Mercer University Press, 1982, p. 87.

21 Jane Ellen Wayne, op. cit., pp. 16, 73, 10, 18.

22 Margaret Mitchell, Letters to Mr George A. Cornwall and to Miss Katharine Brown, in Richard Harwell (ed.), *Letters*, pp. 46, 71.

23 Gerald Gardner and Harriet Modell Gardner, op. cit., p. 38.

24 Susan Myrick, op. cit., p. 44.

25 New York, Berkley Windhover Books, 1977.

26 For examples of posters and illustrations from different countries, as well as book covers, lobby cards, etc., see Herb Bridges, *'Frankly, My Dear . . .' Gone With the Wind Memorabilia*, Macon, Ga., Mercer University Press, 1986, pp. 59–150, 165.

27 See Roland Flamini, op. cit., for a fuller account.

28 Joan Mellon, op. cit., p. 117.

29 Joan Didion, 'John Wayne: A Love Song', in *Slouching Towards Bethlehem*, Harmondsworth, Penguin, 1974, p. 39.

30 Leslie A. Fiedler sees it as one of three 'attempted rapes' (the other two are the Union Soldier at Tara and the black man in Shantytown) in 'The Anti-Tom Novel and the Great Depression: Margaret Mitchell's *Gone With the Wind*', in Richard Harwell (ed.), *Gone With the Wind as Book and Film*, p. 248; Kathryn Lee Seidel, op. cit., pp. 56–57; and Angela Carter, 'The Belle as Businessperson', in *Nothing Sacred*, London, Virago, 1982, pp. 142–43.

31 Susan Brownmiller, *Against Our Will: Men, Women and Rape*, Harmondsworth, Penguin, 1976, p. 15.

32 Angela Carter, op. cit., pp. 142–43.

33 Kathryn Lee Seidel, op. cit., pp. 56, 148.
34 Frances Newman, *The Hard-Boiled Virgin*, New York, Boni & Liveright, 1926, p. 29; quoted in Seidel, op. cit., p. 42.
35 Ann Barr Snitow, op. cit., p. 144.
36 Lynne Segal, *Is the Future Female? Troubled Thoughts on Contemporary Feminism*, London, Virago, 1987, pp. 99–100. (For an excellent discussion of male and female sexuality and violence, rape and so on, see pp. 117–61.)
37 Quoted in Anne Edwards, *The Road to Tara: The Life of Margaret Mitchell*, London, Hodder & Stoughton, 1983, p. 272.
38 Joanna Russ, 'Somebody's Trying to Kill Me and I Think it's My Husband: The Modern Gothic', *Journal of Popular Culture*, 6 (1973), p. 668.

6 Tomorrow is Another Day

1 Margaret Mitchell, Letter to Mrs E.L. Sullivan, August 18, 1936, in Richard Harwell (ed.), *Margaret Mitchell's 'Gone With the Wind' Letters 1936–1949*, London, Sidgwick & Jackson, 1987, p. 54.
2 Anne Edwards, *The Road to Tara: The Life of Margaret Mitchell*, London, Hodder & Stoughton, 1983, p. 294.
3 Cora Kaplan, *Sea Changes: Essays on Culture and Feminism*, London, Verso, 1986, p. 118.
4 ibid., p. 119.
5 See Charles Bremner, 'Going for Scarlett and gold', *The Times*, 26 April 1988, p. 14.
6 Alexandra Ripley, *Charleston*, New York, Avon, 1981.
7 See James Baldwin, 'Everybody's Protest Novel', in *Notes of a Native Son*, London, Michael Joseph, 1964, pp. 9–17.
8 See Resa Lynn Dudovitz, 'The Myth of Superwoman: A Comparative Study of Women's Bestsellers in France and the United States', D.Phil. thesis, University of Illinois at Urbana-Champaign, 1987.

9 The references to Susann and Krantz are taken from Madonne M. Miner, *Insatiable Appetites: Twentieth Century Women's Bestsellers*, Westport, Conn., Greenwood Press, 1984.

10 John Sutherland, *Bestsellers: Popular Fiction of the 1970s*, London, Routledge & Kegan Paul, 1981, p. 77. Sutherland notes how irritated McCullough was with the comparison with *GWTW*. His (most unfair) comment in support is that 'her own authorial professionalism is in stark contrast to Mitchell's small-town amateurism' (ibid.).

11 For instance, Jennifer Blake, *Southern Rapture*, New York, Fawcett Columbine, 1987, a steamy story of a Boston pro-abolitionist woman who comes to Reconstruction Louisiana to find the cause of her brother's murder. She is seduced, both sexually and politically, to support the South's cause. Her brother's murderer (also her would-be rapist) is lynched by the Louisiana equivalent of the Ku Klux Klan, Knights of the White Camelia. The author's note, claiming objectivity because of family ties with both North and South, also refers ostentatiously to the scholarly research that has gone into this 'ripper'.

12 Madonne M. Miner, op. cit., p. 8.

13 ibid., p. 141.

14 Leslie Halliwell, *Halliwell's Film Guide* (5th edn), London, Grafton, 1986, p. 66.

15 Examples are taken from Edward D.C. Campbell, Jr, *The Celluloid South: Hollywood and the Southern Myth*, Knoxville, The University of Tennessee Press, 1981, and William Pratt, *Scarlett Fever: The Ultimate Pictorial Treasury of Gone With the Wind*, New York, Collier Macmillan, 1977. I am very grateful to Hazel V. Carby for the Spielberg observation.

7 The Mammy of Them All

1 Diane Roberts, 'Faulkner's Women', D.Phil. thesis, Oxford University, 1987, p. 99.

2 'Mammy, a Home Picture of 1860', in *The Land We Love*, 6 (March 1869), quoted in William L. Van Deburg, *Slavery and Race in American Popular Culture*, Madison, The University of Wisconsin Press, 1984, p. 93.

3 Leslie Fiedler, 'The Anti-Tom Novel and the Great Depression: Margaret Mitchell's *Gone With the Wind*', in Richard Harwell (ed.), *Gone With the Wind as Book and Film*, Columbia, SC, University of South Carolina Press, 1983, p. 246.

4 bell hooks, *Ain't I a Woman: Black Women and Feminism*, London, Pluto Press, 1981, p. 84.

5 Frederick Douglass, *Narrative of the Life of Frederick Douglass: An American Slave*, New York, Signet, 1968, pp. 61–62.

6 Gloria Naylor, 'The Myth of the Matriarch', *Life* (Spring 1988), Special Issue, 'The Dream of Then and Now', p. 65.

7 V.S. Naipaul, 'The Mahatma of Forsyth County', *The Independent Magazine*, 17 September 1988, pp. 46–47.

8 Susan Myrick, *White Columns in Hollywood: Reports from the GWTW Sets*, ed. Richard Harwell, Macon, Ga., Mercer University Press, 1982, p. 293.

9 ibid., p. 49.

10 Quoted in Leonard J. Leff, 'David Selznick's *Gone With the Wind*: "The Negro Problem"', *Georgia Review*, 38, 1 (1984), p. 156.

11 Quoted in Jacqui Roach and Petal Felix, 'Black Looks', in Lorraine Gamman and Margaret Marshment (eds), *The Female Gaze: Women as Viewers of Popular Culture*, The Women's Press, 1988, pp. 137–38.

12 *Time* quoted in William Pratt, *Scarlett Fever: The Ultimate Pictorial Treasury of Gone With the Wind*, New York, Macmillan, 1977, p. 261; Jim Pines, *Blacks in Films: A*

Survey of Racial Themes and Images in the American Film, London, Studio Vista, 1975, p. 48.

13 Quoted by Stephen Bourne, 'Pride and Prejudice', *The Voice*, 1 September 1984, p. 16.

14 Malcolm X, *The Autobiography of Malcolm X*, London, Penguin, 1965, p. 113; Alice Walker, 'A Letter of the Times, or Should This Sado-Masochism Be Saved?', in *You Can't Keep a Good Woman Down*, London, The Women's Press, 1982, p. 118.

15 Richard Harwell (ed.), *Margaret Mitchell's 'Gone With the Wind' Letters 1936–1949*, London, Sidgwick & Jackson, 1987, p. 85.

16 Wyn Craig Wade, *The Fiery Cross: The Ku Klux Klan in America*, New York, Simon & Schuster, 1987, pp. 402–03.

17 Simon Hoggart, 'President for Slumberland', *Observer*, 6 November 1988, p. 15.

18 Sallyann Jacobson, ' "When I put on that gown, people get out of my way" ', *Woman*, 9 August 1986, p. 52.

19 Wyn Craig Wade, op. cit., p. 331.

20 V.S. Naipaul, op. cit., pp. 46, 48.

21 For further discussion of Mitchell, Atlanta and the Klan, see my article '*Gone With the Wind*: The Mammy of Them All', in Jean Radford (ed.), *The Progress of Romance: The Politics of Popular Fiction*, London, Routledge & Kegan Paul, 1986, pp. 113–38.

22 Malcolm Cowley, 'Going With the Wind', *New Republic*, 16 September 1936, quoted in Darden Asbury Pyron, *Recasting: Gone With the Wind in American Culture*, Miami, University Presses of Florida, 1983, p. 19.

23 Leonard J. Leff, op. cit., pp. 147, 151; Rudy Behlmer (ed.), *Memo From David O. Selznick*, New York, Viking Press, 1972, p. 152.

24 John D. Stevens, 'The Black Reaction to *Gone With the Wind*', *Journal of Popular Fiction*, 2, 4 (1973), p. 367; Leonard J. Leff, op. cit., p. 159.

25 Carlton Moss, 'An Open Letter to Mr. Selznick', *Daily Worker*, New York, 9 January 1940, in Richard Harwell

(ed.), *Gone With the Wind as Book and Film*, p. 158.

26 ibid., p. 159.

27 Thomas Cripps, *Slow Fade to Black: The Negro in American Film, 1900–1942*, London, Oxford University Press, 1977, p. 356.

28 Edward D.C. Campbell, Jr, *The Celluloid South: Hollywood and the Southern Myth*, Knoxville, The University of Tennessee Press, 1981, p. 28.

29 This is a term coined by Jack Temple Kirby.

30 William L. Van Deburg, op. cit., p. xi.

31 *Times-Picayune*, quoted in Edward D.C. Campbell, Jr, op. cit.; Lena Horne quoted in Mary Ellison, 'Blacks in American Film', in Philip Davies and Brian Neve (eds), *Cinema, Politics and Society in America*, Manchester, Manchester University Press, 1981, p. 181.

32 William L. Van Deburg, op. cit., p. 128; Jim Brown, 'On the record', *Time*, 11 June 1979, p. 45, quoted in Mary Ellison, op. cit., p. 190.

33 Toni Morrison, Interview by Melvyn Bragg, *The South Bank Show* (London Weekend Television), 11 October 1987; Reggie Nadelson, 'Joy Writer', *Elle* (January 1988), p. 23.

34 Margaret Walker, *Jubilee*, London, W.H. Allen, 1978; Sherley Anne Williams, *Dessa Rose*, London, Futura, 1988. It is interesting that on the cover of its New York Bantam edition, *Jubilee*'s Vyry is described as 'a heroine to rival Scarlett O'Hara', despite the fact that she is clearly a reworking of the Mammy character. I am indebted to Hazel V. Carby for this reference.

8 Looking Back and Forward

1 Barbara Melosh, 'Historical Memory in Fiction: The Civil Rights Movement in Three Novels', *Radical History Review*, 40 (Winter 1988), p. 65.

2 Julian Barnes, *Flaubert's Parrot*, London, Picador, 1985, p. 90.

3 Richard Johnson *et al.* (eds), *Making Histories: Studies in History-Writing and Politics*, London, Hutchinson, 1982. 'Popular memory' is a term used by Michel Foucault; Antonio Gramsci speaks of 'précis of the past'.

4 Sue Harper, 'Historical Pleasures: Gainsborough Costume Melodrama', in Christine Gledhill (ed.), *Home is Where the Heart Is: Studies in Melodrama and the Woman's Film*, London, British Film Institute, 1987, p. 172.

5 Lillian S. Robinson, 'On Reading Trash', in *Sex, Class, and Culture*, New York and London, Methuen, 1986, p. 221; Alison Light, 'Towards a Feminist Cultural Studies: Middleclass Femininity and Fiction in Post Second World War Britain', *Englisch Amerikanische Studien*, 1 (1987) pp. 58–72.

6 Quoted by Sue Harper, op. cit., p. 189.

7 Floyd C. Watkins, '*Gone With the Wind* as Vulgar Literature', in Richard Harwell (ed.), *Gone With the Wind as Book and Film*, Columbia, SC, University of South Carolina Press, 1983, pp. 204–06.

8 Raphael Samuel, 'Little Dickens', *Guardian*, 19 February 1988, p. 23.

9 Louis Rubin, Jr, 'Scarlett O'Hara and the Two Quentin Compsons', in Darden Asbury Pyron, *Recasting: Gone With the Wind in American Culture*, Miami, University Presses of Florida, 1983, p. 95.

10 Darden Asbury Pyron, 'The Inner War of Southern History', *Southern Studies*, 20, 1 (1981), p. 17.

11 Quoted in Richard Harwell (ed.), op. cit., pp. 200; 157.

12 Patrick Wright, *On Living in an Old Country: The National Past in Contemporary Britain*, London, Verso, 1985, p. 23.

13 David J. Morrow, 'Betty', *Business Atlanta*, December 1987, p. 38.

14 Betty Talmadge, *Lovejoy Plantation Cookbook*, Atlanta, Peachtree Publishers, 1983. I am indebted to Betty Talmadge and her secretary for sparing time to talk to

me and send articles about Talmadge Enterprises.

15 Information taken from *The Atlanta Constitution*, 31 December 1987, p. 12 and 12 February 1988, 2C. I am grateful to Debra James for these and other items of information.
16 W.J. Weatherby, *Guardian*, 31 July 1987, p. 11.
17 James Baldwin, *The Evidence of Things Not Seen*, New York, Holt, Rinehart & Winston, 1985, p. 79.
18 Alex Brummer, 'Democrats strain for new image', *Guardian*, 16 July 1988, p. 6.
19 Carl Freeman, 'Stone Mountain's Reflecting Pool', *Blue and Gray Magazine*, 1, 2 (October–November 1983), p. 53.
20 Robert Lumley (ed.), *The Museum Time-Machine: Putting Cultures on Display*, London, Comedia/Routledge, 1988, p. 2.

Bibliography

Andrews, Eliza Frances, *The War-Time Journal of a Georgia Girl, 1864–1865*, New York, D. Appleton & Co., 1908

Ang, Ien, *Watching Dallas: Soap Opera and the Melodramatic Imagination*, London, Methuen, 1985

Baldwin, James, 'Nobody Knows My Name: A Letter from the South', in *Nobody Knows My Name*, New York, Dell, 1961

—— 'Everybody's Protest Novel', in *Notes of a Native Son*, London, Michael Joseph, 1964

—— *The Evidence of Things Not Seen*, New York, Holt, Rinehart & Winston, 1985

Barnes, Julian, *Flaubert's Parrot*, London, Picador, 1985

Batsleer, Janet *et al.*, 'Some women reading', in Batsleer *et al.* (eds), *Rewriting English: Cultural Politics of Gender and Class*, London, Methuen, 1985

Behlmer, Rudy (ed.), *Memo from David O. Selznick*, New York, Viking, 1972

Bennett, Tony and Woollacott, Janet, *Bond and Beyond: The Political Career of a Popular Hero*, London, Macmillan, 1987

Boothe, Clare, *Kiss the Boys Good-bye*, New York, Random House, 1939

Bourne, Stephen, 'Pride and Prejudice', *The Voice*, 1 September 1984, p. 16

Bridges, Herb, '*Frankly, My Dear . . .*' *Gone With the Wind Memorabilia*, Macon, Ga., Mercer University Press, 1986

Bridges, Herb and Leff, Leonard J., *The Filming of Gone With the Wind*, Macon, Ga., Mercer University Press, 1984

Brownmiller, Susan, *Against Our Will: Men, Women and Rape*, Harmondsworth, Penguin, 1976

Campbell, Edward D.C., Jr, *The Celluloid South: Hollywood and the Southern Myth*, Knoxville, The University of Tennessee Press, 1981

Carter, Angela, 'The Belle as Businessperson', in *Nothing Sacred*, London, Virago, 1982

Collins, Joan, *Past Imperfect*, London, Coronet, 1979

Conrad, Peter, 'In Praise of Profligacy', *Times Literary Supplement*, 10 September 1976, p. 1094

Cripps, Thomas, *Slow Fade to Black: The Negro in American Film, 1900–1942*, London, Oxford University Press, 1977

Didion, Joan, 'John Wayne: A Love Song', in *Slouching Towards Bethlehem*, Harmondsworth, Penguin, 1974

Douglass, Frederick, *Narrative of the Life of Frederick Douglass: An American Slave*, New York, Signet, 1968

Dudovitz, Resa Lynn, 'The Myth of Superwoman: A Comparative Study of Women's Bestsellers in France and the United States', D.Phil. thesis, University of Illinois at Urbana-Champaign, 1987

Dyer, Richard, *Stars*, London, British Film Institute, 1979

Edwards, Anne, *Vivien Leigh, A Biography*, London, Coronet, 1978

___ *The Road to Tara: The Life of Margaret Mitchell*, London, Hodder & Stoughton, 1983

Ellis, John, *Visible Fictions: Cinema: Television: Video*, London, Routledge & Kegan Paul, 1982

Ellison, Mary, 'Blacks in American Film', in Davies, Philip and Neve, Brian (eds), *Cinema, Politics and Society in America*, Manchester, Manchester University Press, 1981

Farr, Finis, *Margaret Mitchell of Atlanta: The Author of 'Gone With the Wind'*, New York, William Morrow, 1965

Flamini, Roland, *Scarlett, Rhett, and a Cast of Thousands: The Filming of Gone With the Wind*, London, André Deutsch, 1976

Fox-Genovese, Elizabeth, 'Scarlett O'Hara: The Southern

Lady as New Woman', *American Quarterly*, 33, 4 (1981) pp. 391–411

Freeman, Carl, 'Stone Mountain's Reflecting Pool', in *Blue and Gray Magazine*, 1, 2 (October–November 1983), p. 53

Gardner, Gerald and Gardner, Harriet Modell, *The Tara Treasury: A Pictorial History of Gone With the Wind*, Westport, Conn., Arlington House, 1980

Garner, Lesley, 'The greatest love story yet to be told', *The Daily Telegraph*, 16 February 1987, p. 14

Halliwell, Leslie, *Halliwell's Film Guide* (5th edn), London, Grafton, 1986

Harper, Sue, 'Historical Pleasures: Gainsborough Costume Melodrama', in Gledhill, Christine (ed.), *Home is Where the Heart Is: Studies in Melodrama and the Woman's Film*, London, British Film Institute, 1987

Harwell, Richard (ed.), *Gone With the Wind as Book and Film*, Columbia, SC, University of South Carolina Press, 1983

——— (ed.), *Margaret Mitchell's 'Gone With the Wind' Letters 1936–1949* (1976), London, Sidgwick & Jackson, 1987

Haskell, Molly, *From Reverence to Rape: The Treatment of Women in the Movies*, London, New English Library, 1975

Hobson, Dorothy, *Crossroads: The Drama of a Soap Opera*, London, Methuen, 1982

Hoggart, Simon, 'President for Slumberland', *Observer*, 6 November 1988, p. 15

hooks, bell, *Ain't I a Woman: Black Women and Feminism*, London, Pluto Press, 1981

Howard, Sidney, *Gone With the Wind: The Illustrated Screenplay*, ed. Andrew Sinclair, London, Lorrimer, 1986

Jackson, Kenneth T., *The Ku Klux Klan in the City 1915–1930*, New York, Oxford University Press, 1967

Jacobson, Sallyann, ' "When I put on that gown, people get out of my way" ', *Woman*, 9 August 1986, p. 52

Johnson, Richard *et al.* (eds), *Making Histories: Studies in History-Writing and Politics*, London, Hutchinson, 1982

Jones, Anne Goodwyn, *Tomorrow is Another Day: The Woman*

Writer in the South, 1859–1936, Baton Rouge, Louisiana State University Press, 1981

Jones, Marian Elder, 'Me and My Book', *Georgia Review*, 16 (Summer 1962), p. 186

Kaplan, Cora, '*The Thorn Birds*: Fiction, Fantasy, Femininity', in *Sea Changes: Essays on Culture and Feminism*, London, Verso, 1986

Kirby, Jack Temple, *Media-Made Dixie: The South in the American Imagination*, Baton Rouge, Louisiana State University Press, 1978

Kuhn, Annette, *Women's Pictures: Feminism and Cinema*, London, Routledge & Kegan Paul, 1982

Lambert, Gavin, *GWTW: The Making of Gone With the Wind*, New York, Bantam, 1973

Leff, Leonard J., 'David Selznick's *Gone With the Wind*: "The Negro Problem" ', *Georgia Review*, 38, 1 (1984), pp. 146–64

Light, Alison, ' "Returning to Manderley" – Romantic Fiction, Female Sexuality and Class', *Feminist Review*, 16 (Summer 1984), pp. 7–25

_____ 'Towards a Feminist Cultural Studies: Middleclass Femininity and Fiction in Post Second World War Britain', *Englisch Amerikanische Studien*, 1 (1987), pp. 58–72

Lovell, Linda M., 'Perceptions of the Ku Klux Klan Activities in the 1920s with particular reference to the Congressional Hearing of 1921', Special Study, BA Humanities, Bristol Polytechnic, 1982

Lumley, Robert (ed.), *The Museum Time-Machine: Putting Cultures on Display*, London, Comedia/Routledge, 1988

Mellon, Joan, *Big Bad Wolves: Masculinity in the American Film*, London, Elm Tree Books, 1977

Melosh, Barbara, 'Historical Memory in Fiction: The Civil Rights Movement in Three Novels', *Radical History Review*, 40 (Winter 1988), pp. 64–76

Miner, Madonne M., *Insatiable Appetites: Twentieth Century American Women's Bestsellers*, Westport, Conn.,

Greenwood Press, 1984

Mitchell, Margaret, *Gone With the Wind* (1936), London, Pan, 1974

—— *A Dynamo Going to Waste: Letters to Allen Edee 1919–1921*, ed. Jane Bonner Peacock, Atlanta, Ga., Peachtree Publishers, 1985

Morley, Dave, 'Texts, readers, subjects', in Hall, Stuart *et al.* (eds), *Culture, Media, Language*, London, Hutchinson, 1980

Morrow, David J., 'Betty', *Business Atlanta*, December 1987

Myrick, Susan, *White Columns in Hollywood: Reports from the GWTW Sets*, ed. Richard Harwell, Macon, Ga., Mercer University Press, 1982

Nadelson, Reggie, 'Joy Writer', *Elle*, January 1988, p. 23

Naipaul, V.S., 'The Mahatma of Forsyth County', *The Independent Magazine*, 17 September 1988, pp. 44–48

Naylor, Gloria, 'The Myth of the Matriarch', *Life*, Spring 1988 (Special Issue, 'The Dream Then and Now')

O'Donnell, Victoria, 'The Southern Woman as Time-Binder in Film', *Southern Quarterly*, 19, 3–4 (1981), pp. 156–63

Pines, Jim, *Blacks in Films: A Survey of Racial Themes and Images in the American Film*, London, Studio Vista, 1975

Pratt, William, *Scarlett Fever: The Ultimate Pictorial Treasury of Gone With the Wind*, New York, Macmillian, 1977

Pyron, Darden Asbury, 'The Inner War of Southern History', *Southern Studies*, 20, 1 (1981), pp. 5–19

—— *Recasting: Gone With the Wind in American Culture*, Miami, University Presses of Florida, 1983

—— *Towards a Feminist Apprenticeship: Margaret Mitchell's Juvenile Fiction* (Occasional Papers in Women's Studies), Women's Studies Center, Miami, Florida International University, 1985

Radway, Janice A., *Reading the Romance: Women, Patriarchy, and Popular Literature*, Chapel Hill, University of North Carolina Press, 1984

Ripley, Alexandra, *Charleston*, New York, Avon, 1981

Roach, Jacqui and Felix, Petal, 'Black Looks', in Gamman,

Lorraine and Marshment, Margaret (eds), *The Female Gaze: Women as Viewers of Popular Culture*, London, The Women's Press, 1988

Roberts, Diane, 'Faulkner's Women', D.Phil, thesis, Oxford University, 1987

Robinson, Lillian S., 'On Reading Trash', in *Sex, Class, and Culture*, New York and London, Methuen, 1986

Roller, David C. and Twyman, Robert W. (eds), *The Encyclopedia of Southern History*, Baton Rouge, Louisiana State University Press, 1979

Russ, Joanna, 'Somebody's Trying to Kill Me and I Think it's My Husband: The Modern Gothic', *Journal of Popular Culture*, 6 (1973), pp. 666–91

Samuel, Raphael, 'Little Dickens', *Guardian*, 19 February 1988, p. 23

Segal, Lynne, *Is the Future Female? Troubled Thoughts on Contemporary Feminism*, London, Virago, 1987

Seidel, Kathryn Lee, *The Southern Belle in the American Novel*, Tampa, University of South Florida Press, 1985

Snitow, Ann Barr, 'Mass Market Romance: Pornography for Women is Different', *Radical History Review*, 20 (Spring–Summer 1979), pp. 141–61

Stevens, John D., 'The Black Reaction to *Gone With the Wind*', *Journal of Popular Fiction*, 2, 4 (1973), pp. 366–72

Styron, William, 'Author's Note', *The Confessions of Nat Turner*, New York, Signet, 1968

Talmadge, Betty, *Lovejoy Plantation Cookbook*, Atlanta, Peachtree Publishers, 1983

Taylor, Helen, '*Gone With the Wind*: The Mammy of Them All', in Radford, Jean (ed.), *The Progress of Romance: The Politics of Popular Fiction*, London, Routledge & Kegan Paul, 1986

—— *Gender, Race, and Region in the Writings of Grace King, Ruth McEnery Stuart, and Kate Chopin*, Baton Rouge, Louisiana State University Press, 1989

Van Deburg, William L., *Slavery and Race in American*

Popular Culture, Madison, The University of Wisconsin Press, 1984

Van Woodward, C., *Origins of the New South 1877–1913*, Baton Rouge, Louisiana State University Press, 1951

Wade, Wyn Craig, *The Fiery Cross: The Ku Klux Klan in America*, New York, Simon & Schuster, 1987

Walker, Alexander, *Vivien: The Life of Vivien Leigh*, London, Weidenfeld & Nicolson, 1987

Walker, Alice, 'A Letter of the Times, or Should This Sado-Masochism Be Saved?' in *You Can't Keep a Good Woman Down*, London, The Women's Press, 1982

Walker, Margaret, *Jubilee*, London, W.H. Allen, 1978

Wayne, Jane Ellen, *Gable's Women*, London, Simon & Schuster, 1987

Weatherby, W.J., 'Pale Fire', *Guardian*, 31 July 1987, p. 12

Williams, Sherley Anne, *Dessa Rose*, London, Futura, 1988

Wright, Patrick, *On Living in an Old Country: The National Past in Contemporary Britain*, London, Verso, 1985

X, Malcolm, *The Autobiography of Malcolm X*, London, Penguin, 1965

Index